LIFE ON
PLANET
ROCK

LIFE ON
PLANET ROCK

FROM GUNS N' ROSES TO NIRVANA,
A BACKSTAGE JOURNEY THROUGH ROCK'S
MOST DEBAUCHED DECADE

LONN FRIEND

MORGAN ROAD BOOKS

NEW YORK

Published by Morgan Road Books, an imprint of The Doubleday Broadway Publishing Group, a division of Random House, Inc.

PRINTED IN THE UNITED STATES OF AMERICA

Morgan Road Books and the M colophon are trademarks of Random House, Inc.

Visit our Web site at www.morganroadbooks.com

Book design by Ellen Cipriano

Library of Congress Cataloging-in-Publication Data
Friend, Lonn.
    Life on planet Rock / by Lonn Friend.
        p.   cm.
    1. Friend, Lonn. 2. Periodical editors—United States—Biography. 3. Rock music—History and criticism.
ML429.F84A3 2006
781.66092—dc22
[B]
                                            2005058441

ISBN-13: 978-0-7679-2208-1
ISBN-10: 0-7679-2208-5

1 3 5 7 9 10 8 6 4 2

For Megan Rose, star pupil in the school of rock
and eternally first in my heart

"From the earliest times man seems to have been endowed with a conscience. When we penetrate the wisdom of the truth-sayers we discover that conscience was not meant to be a burden; that it was to be used instinctively and intuitively. It is only in periods of decadence that truth becomes complicated and conscience a heavy sack of guilt."

—*Henry Miller*

Contents

Foreword

My older son's favorite band is Skid Row. He's infatuated with Sebastian Bach.

Every morning on the way to school we get there a little faster courtesy of "Slave to the Grind." It's really fuckin' *TRIPPY* driving around in the quirky semi-suburbs north of San Francisco sharing Skid Row (with the odd AC/DC, Megadeth, or Ramones song thrown in) with my six-year-old offspring.

Now let's stay with the word *trippy* for a second . . .

When I say trippy, I mean it in the most positive sense of the word (it's all good in the hood, real fuckin' cool, all that shit, etc.), BUT it is a trip. A real fuckin' trip. A mindfuck-and-a-half. Because the trip part of trippy takes me on a journey back a good fifteen years to the turn of a new decade, where the excesses of the '80s not so quietly rolled over into the further excesses of the '90s.

When I think of that state of mind called 1990, Sebastian Bach in some way becomes the gateway, the gatekeeper to a real motherfucker-of-a-time period in rock music, a real crossroads, a time of blink-and-you'll-miss-it excitement, fireballs, meteor showers, and likewise outpourings and effusions of feelings, thoughts, and vibes called Rock 'n' Roll.

And lurking in the shadows with pen and paper was the man who built the Gatehouse . . . that moment's Lester Bangs, that moment's Cameron Crowe, that moment's Geoff Barton, one Lonn Michael Friend (aka: Dude).

"Do you smell that? The smell of rock 'n' roll" as the object of my five-minute hunt in the attic has been retrieved. Out of an old, cobwebbed Evian box marked, with a black Sharpie, *WHITE AXL JACKET*, comes, well, my . . . uh . . . white leather jacket (!!) Primed on by my friend Steve and sportin' white leather, black gloves, and mirrored shades, I am now fully inspired to write the definitive story of Lonn M. Friend. Oh wait! The definitive story of Lonn M. Friend is actually what comes on the following hundreds of pages, because who the fuck else is gonna write the definitive story of Lonn other than the man himself? I'm merely here to remind you (and actually me and him, too) that his memories, stories, and experiences are obviously not only the definitive story of Lonn M. Friend (duh!) but probably THE definitive look into this bygone era of excessive rock 'n' roll that ran parallel to Lonn's tenure at *RIP* magazine, the Gatehouse, from 1987 to its demise in 1994.

Use 1990 as your springboard . . .

If it was going on three years either side of 1990, if it was goin' on in harder rock 'n' roll, and if it was going on in America, it was in *RIP*. And if it was in *RIP*, it was Lonn. Because Lonn was *RIP* and *RIP* was Lonn. The two words are really one and the same. Like *Rolling Stone* decades earlier, like *Creem*, *New Musical Express*, *Sounds*, and even *Kerrang!*, *RIP* magazine became synonymous with a movement, an era. It was (and remains) a time capsule . . . IT became the hard-rock scene in the late '80s.

A gateway . . . the way in for the fans, the kids, the followers . . .

A mirror . . . for the musicians, the band members, the hangers-on . . .

RIP was as vital to that scene—to that moment—as any of the above-mentioned mags were to their classic times.

It was the only time in my career that there was a magazine in America that actually meant something. Sure we all read X, Y & Z on airplanes, buses, etc. We all got hard-ons when we saw ourselves in X, Y & Z and sure, some of us have fond memories of the moments and spreads in X, Y & Z over the years, but *RIP* was different. I cared about *RIP*. I wanted to be in *RIP*. I wanted to be on the cover of *RIP*. I wanted *RIP* to care about me. I wanted *RIP* to care about my band. The funny thing was that for a good six to seven years, I know that every other fuckin' band member in any of the bands on the hard-rock scene in America felt the same way. We all wanted to be in. We all wanted to be on the cover . . . and most of all, we all wanted Lonn's attention.

Ahhh . . . Lonn's attention.

How good that made me feel.

How important that made me feel.

Elsewhere in this book, you'll probably get to places where Lonn talks about "the scene," stories, and so on, and he'll most likely use the phrase "fly on the wall" to describe his place in that scenario. I appreciate that phrase and I appreciate his humility, but when Lonn was around, he was no fuckin' fly on the fuckin' wall. When Lonn was there, we gave him attention. We were right there . . . around him, clamoring for his recognition. Each one of us tried to one-up the other with the funny quote, the printable sound bite, the outrageous story, the best one-liner about the previous evening's excessiveness to get his attention, to be quoted, to be included.

Actually, come to think of it, Lonn was the least "fly on the wall" guy/journalist who ever hung around, because of what he represented, what he stood for. The sheer force and magnetism of his personality, perfectly balanced with the right dose of humility and enough innocence left in his eyes, made it impossible for him to be invisible, made it impossible for him to be just another face. Doesn't matter where we were: on the road, where Lonn would fly out to get some "road dirt"; down in the studio, he'd report on the progress of the recording of the "Black Album," showing up with boxes full of everything from *Barely Legal* to *Women Over 50* hot off Larry Flynt's presses; or he'd hang around at my house to get a little staged insight into the private life of . . . I/we/whoever he was around would always clamor around him, because it made us feel important, vying for his attention, ready to devour and chomp on whatever he was the bringer of, whether it was news and tall tales of our friends and peers, dirt and gossip on our enemies, or another box of fresh porn to lend its inspiration to yet another dreadful day in the studio.

Fly on the wall? Nahhh. More like fly in your face! Fly in his face! Flies on shit! Flies on the SAME shit! Pigs in shit! A bunch of content, aloof, self-obsessed pigs rolling around, having the time of their lives, living it up gloriously IN THE SHIT OF ROCK 'N' ROLL . . . (and I do mean that in the most positive way).

The swelling of Metallica . . . Munich, August 1991 . . .

The "Black Album" has just entered the charts at number one in 209 countries, more or less, and one diminutive Danish drummer was feeling pretty fuckin' good about it. On tour in Europe with AC/DC, Motley Krellmonster, etc., the boys were out livin' it up, throwin' it down, high on their own supply, and feeling pretty good about the state of the world.

At midnight, one Lonn M. Friend walks into the Munchen Rock Star Hangout (??!!) nightclub, finds the debauched gathering of assorted hard-rock characters, who are busy celebrating another day of possibilities, spots the Danish drummer, plops himself down right next to him with a huge shit-eating grin on his face, and says, "Congratulations on the number ones!" A pause follows as the drummer travels to the far reaches of his alcohol-soaked brain and number-one bruised ego, contemplates the presence of a mere mortal, and utters something along the lines of, "Oh, it's Mr. *RIP*, the journalist who likes to hang out with rock stars. Why don't you go sit with somebody else— I'm too fuckin' busy!!!"

That moment of severe swelling ended up being immortalized by a VERY LIMITED EDITION run of Lonn M. Friend–produced T-shirts—most of which, thankfully, are safely stored upstairs in my attic next to that Evian box with that white leather—depicting your humble intro deliverer with a small body and an enormous, grossly oversized head!

But much more important, that moment was the beginning of the unswelling of the Metallica Ego, because by bringing the moment to its much needed sarcastic extreme, Lonn M. Friend stopped being "journalist," stopped being "fly on the wall," stopped being *RIP* magazine, and started becoming a FRIEND (no pun intended), the Friend, the Brother, the Confidant, the Kindred Spirit . . . Dude . . . the Muse that he's truly been to me ever since that moment passed and thankfully faded to black.

Tear down the rat racial slime / Can't be king of the world if you're slave to the grind.

It's 8:22 A.M. and the next generation are singing along, bliss-fully unaware, as we run late for school as usual. The Mindfuck. The Trip. The journey my mind has just been on—the flash-backs, the excesses, the debauchery, the time capsule I've just visited—thankfully stays up front in the driver's seat.

But hey, man, guess what? You can visit too. It's all here, in the next coupla hundred-whatever pages, courtesy of the Gatehouse-builder, the Fly-on-the wall, in-the-face, in-the-shit . . . the Muse . . . Dude.

There's still hope for the next generation as long as the kids in the backseat are lucky enough to find another Lonn M. Friend . . . just as I did. Enjoy.

Lars (M.) Ulrich
San Francisco

Introduction

"CAN YOU SEE THE REAL ME,
CAN YA? CAN YA?"

—*Pete Townshend*

I was standing alone in front of Blue Man Group's theater in the bowels of the bustling glass pyramid that is the Luxor Resort and Casino. It was a balmy spring night in 2004 and I was on assignment for *Las Vegas Life* magazine, doing research for a feature about the much heralded and wildly successful avant-garde performance phenomenon. This was not a road story. The previous October, I had left my hometown of Los Angeles and relocated to the desert with the goal of searching my soul and, perhaps, writing a book.

As I prepared to enter the venue, a thirty-something brunette approached me. She appeared tentative, even a little giddy. "Excuse me," she said with a smile. "But you look a lot like Lonn M. Friend." It had been a while since anyone had recognized me in public, much less mentioned the middle initial with which I used to identify myself at the top of the masthead. "Do you know who I'm talking about?" she asked. "He ran *RIP* magazine. Man, he had the dream job."

This is where the look on my older, wiser, and less metallic face must have given me away. "Wait a minute!" she cried. "You're Lonn! Oh my God!" My close-cropped 'do and Amish goatee could no longer hide my identity. I was fully exposed.

"What's your name?" I asked.

"This is so cool," she gushed. "It's Hope. Lonn M. Friend! No way!"

"So you were a rocker, huh?" I mused rhetorically.

"Are you kidding!" she said. "I'm from Baltimore. Those were the days, GN'R, Metallica, Def Leppard, the Crüe, Scorpions, Bon Jovi, Judas Priest, Whitesnake. That was the best time ever. I used to listen to you on WIYY on Saturday nights, too."

I thought about the life, family, house, and career I'd left behind, flashed on the fifty cents a word I was being paid as the exiled freelance music journalist and the nine-hundred-dollars-a-month apartment I was living alone in, and felt about as far from a hero as you could possibly imagine. I dropped the *M.* in my byline years ago. Contrary to popular belief, it never stood for *metal*. "You're making me blush," I said. "Please stop. That's ancient history."

In the past, I often felt like a cartoon character, an animated idiot with long hair and a beard, walking around the backstage areas of clubs, theaters, arenas, or stadiums with a laminate hanging around my neck. My badge of courage, sword of power, ticket to ride any amusement I cared to in the rock-'n'-roll circus. And there were some pretty crazy attractions. The Guns N' Roses Jack n' Coke Jungle Cruise was alone worth the price of admission.

One minute I was commanding the big bucks in a notorious

Beverly Hills–based publishing company with a nice expense account, getting paid to rock the planet and report what I saw. The next, I was unemployed, emotionally, professionally, and spiritually decomposing, taking trips to see rock concerts in foreign lands on frequent flier miles so I wouldn't lose touch with the Source.

Music, in its myriad manifestations, whether heavy metal, slightly mental, soft and supple, crass and crippled, jazzy, sassy, mainstream, upstream, off stream, dynamic, dependent or independent—wherever it comes from and whomever it is passing through at its moment of creation, *that* is the essence of who I am. I can't play a lick or keep a beat, but I can feel every note whether it's a soul-bending solo off Jimmy Page's Les Paul or the velvet growl of an Eddie Vedder "yeahhhh!"

This book is a collection of moments where I was the fly on the wall, the buzzin' insect with the microscopic notepad. If I hit the mark, you were there with me. It's also a memoir and, in places, deeply personal. I made mistakes, stepped in shit, enjoyed rockin' success and exasperating failure. When I cut myself open to find the truth, I discovered that I was both a friend and a chameleon who shape-shifted his way through life to make the right connections for the sake of the experience and the story.

To be perfectly honest, I was never rich or famous, but I came about as close to being almost famous as anyone. Cameron Crowe had Led Zeppelin and the Allman Brothers in the '70s; I had GN'R and Metallica in the '80s and '90s. But even though I wore the headbanging media hat with passion and conviction during metal's heyday, *RIP* and hard rock represented but one dimension of my own musical persona. Everyone was "dude," everything "rocked," and when I gazed at my hairy mug in the mirror, I wasn't sure whether I was seeing the real me or a media manifested facsimile thereof. Back then, it didn't matter either way. I was too caught up in the hoopla to care.

Life on Planet Rock is my gift back to the universe for landing me in this body in 1956—the year Elvis broke, or to put it more succinctly, the year rock 'n' roll was born—and later putting an all-access pass around my neck so I could witness the miracle up close and personal.

The adventures are, to the best of my recollection, the way things happened. I've got a pretty sharp memory, but I've had to exercise some literary license when quoting artists and individuals when there was no tape rolling. It's a he said/he and she said situation. Whether you perceive me as Chauncey Gardiner or Chance the Gardener is out of my hands. I was there.

Portions of this final read have come from hither and yon over the past several years. My journal could anchor a cruise liner. Ninety-five percent of the narrative was constructed from scratch. There are a hundred wild and wonderful bands with whom I crossed paths that are not represented here (you know who you are). Whether or not you were mentioned by name, trust me: this book belongs to you, too.

Next to my divorce, excavating *Planet Rock* was the most challenging endeavor of my life. During the composition process, the Earth was rattled by an unjust war and a pair of apocalyptic natural disasters, the December 2004 tsunami and August 2005's Hurricane Katrina. In addition, two authors whom I've long admired—Spalding Gray and Hunter S. Thompson—committed suicide. As the world whirled out of balance, I often asked myself how a rock 'n' roll memoir served humanity, especially one focused on such a decadent and *inhuman* time.

In my darkest moments, I wasn't sure whether I'd survive to

see the end product of my labors. Letting go of the past while documenting it was no easy feat. Neither was losing my sense of humor for extended periods of time. Chameleon, fly on the wall, friend—I guess I should add drama queen to the list. I also fell in love with the resident director of the Blue Man Group show while researching that assignment. Without the angel Carrie Ann Hanson, *Life on Planet Rock* would have died on the sand.

If my story touches one person by reminding them how blessed they are to be alive and in love with rock 'n' roll, then it was worth every drop of blood, sweat, and tears. If I fail in that regard, I'll stop pretending I'm a writer and get a job emptying slot machines at the Luxor. Rock's melancholy poet Morrissey once crooned, "If you have five seconds to spare, then I'll tell you the story of my life." This might take a bit longer, but I pray it's worth the ride.

Peace, love, and infinite riffs,
Lonn Michael *Friend*
Las Vegas
November 2005

LIFE ON
PLANET
ROCK

1
Welcome to My Jungle

"THERE IS NOTHING STABLE IN THE WORLD;
UPROAR'S YOUR ONLY MUSIC."

—*John Keats*

I've never had trouble making friends. Probably has something to do with the name I was born with. The moniker has been both a curse and blessing. When I was growing up, kids would tease me. "What's up, Lonn Enemy?" Preschool sticks and stones, but I was born sensitive so it hurt nonetheless. When my professional train started rollin', however, that's when my name started to take on deeper significance.

Running a rock magazine, I was everybody's friend. Friend to artist. Friend to executive. Friend to whoever shook my hand or dialed my number in need of connection, acceptance, favors, ink, respect, or whatever goods and services I could provide. But the simple fact is, I like people and my intention when meeting someone new has always been to extend my hand and make a connection. Bricklayer to rock star, everyone seeks contact. If authentic, that union can take you to the craziest places. It sure as hell took me.

I was in the Guns N' Roses dressing room while opening act Skid Row heated up the L.A. Forum. The only thing flowing harder and faster than the love was the Jack Daniel's. It was July 29, 1991, my thirty-fifth birthday. Band manager Doug Goldstein handed me a brand-new Yonex 200 driver (this golf club was the shit back in the early '90s). The media was out in force: there was no other show in town but this one, and pity another band trying to get attention.

"Hey, Lonn, you wanna bring us onstage tonight?" asked Slash, the group's mop-top lead guitarist.

"What, dude? Bring you onstage?" I replied, thinking I may have heard the wily rocker wrong. It took a nanosecond for me to grasp the magnitude of the situation.

"Let's rock!" I cried.

Slash smiled that perfect, disarming, drunken smile, sipped his Jack 'n' Coke and fired back, "Yeah, man! But listen, there's one catch. You have to do it in your underwear! And wear my hat and boots!"

Duff McKagan and Izzy Stradlin were on the sofa smoking cigarettes. "Do it, dude," they encouraged.

Stage manager Tom Mayhue grabbed me by the collar and planted me on a spot in the dark area off the stairs that led to the stage from the arena floor. All I heard besides the thumping in my chest was the roar of twenty thousand maniacal GN'R fans howling like hungry hyenas. Next thing I knew, the lights were still up and there I was, standing in front of the mike at the foot of the stage, staring down a sea of hair, boobs, tattoos, mascara, blood, sweat, and beers.

I think the audience was too shocked or too stoned to fully realize that a long-haired, bearded, overgrown child was standing in front of them in boxer shorts, black leather boots, and Slash's top hat. "I'm Lonn Friend from *RIP* magazine," I roared, the veins in my neck commencing to protrude, "and I'd do anything for this fucking band! Tonight, they're going to do everything for you. Coming out in a minute, the heaviest fucking band in the world, Gun N' Roses!"

As I cut through the curtain, lead singer Axl Rose flashed me a grin and said softly, "That was cool." The strawberry blond thunder from Lafayette, Indiana, proceeded to lay absolute waste to Angel City by conducting his band through a monstrous three-hour-plus set that delivered just about every track from the GN'R catalog and then some. This was rock's new jungle, and if you were a friend, you were welcomed in.

How did I get on an arena stage in my boxers introducing the most successful and disreputable rock group of the day? Professionally speaking, it started with a guy in a gold-plated wheelchair and his notorious wife. My introduction to the publishing kingdom of Larry and Althea Flynt resulted from the efforts of a college pal named Nancy Gottesman, who was an editor with the UCLA *Daily Bruin*, my alma mater's paper.

In the spring of 1982, I paid the rent by working as a publisher's assistant at *Gambling Times* magazine. Nancy called me up and said that her boyfriend, Ed Dwyer, executive editor of *Gentlemen's Companion*, had an opening for an associate editor. "*Gentlemen's Companion*? Never heard of it," I said.

"It's a Flynt publication," she replied. "You know, *Hustler*! Well, do you want an interview?"

I thought about it for ten seconds and said, "Yeah! Set me

up!" I had no clue what a magazine editor did, but I was twenty-five years old, single, a pathological flirt, and not offended by pornography.

On April 19, 1982, I exited the elevator on the thirty-eighth floor of 2029 Century Park East (the towers featured on the cover of Yes's *Going for the One* LP). As fate would have it, the associate editor of *Hustler* had just been fired, so when Dwyer and I had concluded our interview, he sent me over to the other side of the building to meet the "big boys," *Hustler* managing editor Kelly Garrett, executive editor Don Evans, and Flynt editorial director Bruce David.

Garrett was superintelligent and loved music. We connected instantly. Evans was a laid-back, old-school vet of the publishing wars who lived for happy hour. We hit it off, too. David was the toughest. Loud and confident, he intimidated me, but I cracked a couple jokes and acted like I knew what the fuck I was talking about. Whatever I said or did worked because after two hours, both magazines wanted to hire me. I accepted the *Hustler* offer, of course. Why fly coach when there's an open seat in first class?

My debut year in the company, I never saw Larry. He rarely made an appearance in the building. Instead, his wife, Althea, would pop in, usually unannounced, and make David's life as miserable as possible by ordering him to push the content envelope as far as the law would allow. Althea wanted the photo spreads to be more anatomically revealing than *Penthouse* (*Hustler*'s motto was "Think Pink") and insisted on unexpurgated feature stories with psychopaths, murderers, political activists, and four-letter stand-up comics—in other words, fascinating people.

I was given the "Mail Order Feedback" column to edit, where it was my job to assess the quality of X-rated 8-mm films (known as "loops") and other sexually oriented products available for purchase through advertisements in the back of the magazine. Larry refused to take ad dollars from tobacco and alcohol companies, opting instead to turn the last thirty pages of each issue into an erotic catalog. Fly-by-night companies that sold everything from dildos to penis enlargers were now under my scrutiny. If one of our readers got ripped off, I'd get the product, evaluate it (never mind), and expose the sleazy outfit in print.

I was also tasked to do brief but penetrating (sorry) Q&A's for *Hustler*'s sister publication *Chic* as editor of the "Close Up" section. I interviewed two convicted killers, a child molester (thankfully, these were done by mail), the first phone-sex proprietor in America, the infamous Atlanta madam Dolores French, and a fledgling filthy stand-up comic named Robert Schimmel, whose jokes tore my colon apart. I was making about $400 a week and having a great time. Life on planet *cock* was not half bad.

Then one summer afternoon in '83 the mysterious Mrs. Flynt emerged from her red-velvet executive enclave to pay a visit to the grunts in the editorial department. I just happened to have Mötley Crüe's new record, *Shout at the Devil*, blaring from my boom box, not for my own listening pleasure but because it was being reviewed for a new monthly column I was writing for *Chic* called "Music Notes."

"I love the Crüe!" shouted Althea, marching into my workspace like Nefretiri visiting Moses in the mud pits. She was decked out in full glam regalia—red leather skirt, black fishnets, crimson pumps, and a nose ring dangling from her right nostril that quivered when she spoke. "Nikki Sixx and Tommy Lee are so sexy! Do you like W.A.S.P.?" We talked for an hour while the execs at the end of the hall muttered beneath their breath,

"What's Althea doing in there with that punk Lonn Friend?" That afternoon I'd met my first true metal maven, and a bizarre friendship ensued.

Althea gave me the feature assignment that would fore-shadow my future high-volume tenure at *RIP*. In April 1985, *Hustler* published "Rock's Outer Limits: The Loud and 'Lude World of Heavy Metal," my baptismal blast of metallic reporting. For the article, I interviewed Blackie Lawless from W.A.S.P.—an early graduate of Alice Cooper's shock-rock school of theatrics—who'd cultivated a nice following around Hollywood by humili-ating and torturing sexy women onstage while his band cranked out the speed-metal background music. I spent an entire evening at the Rainbow Bar and Grill on Sunset culling the most heinous tales of sex, drugs, and rock 'n' roll abuse I'd ever heard.

Researching that story proved that I was either entering Hell myself—falling deeper into the pit of prurient reportage and the debauched culture that nurtured it—or I was in divine route to my true, journalistic calling. Either way, the winds blowing me forward (or downward) were getting warmer.

Like her notorious significant other, Althea lived to fuck with the system. She once posed a naked woman on the cover of *Hustler* in an arched-over position so her ass would resemble the head of a penis. Another time, she got it in her craw to give Billy Idol—soaring high on the charts with "White Wedding"—her gold-trimmed '59 Cadillac once owned by Elvis Presley. She thought Billy was a postmodern rock reincarnation of the King and would be blown away by the gift.

Of course, it was I who received the assignment to deliver the car. But the day I was scheduled to drive the block-long beast to the Sunset Marquis Hotel, where Billy and his manager, Bill Aucoin, were staying, the damn thing wouldn't start! I ended up spending the entire afternoon having the Caddie towed out of the office-building basement to the dealership five miles away.

The Ohio stripper turned millionaire Mrs. had talked Larry into starting a rock magazine the previous fall, but the company's CEO, Jim Kohls, Larry's tightfisted right hand in all things concerning the business of Flynt Publications, didn't peg me to take the reins out of the box.

I'd been promoted several times in the previous five years and was near the top of the *Hustler/Chic* editorial food chain. I'd gotten to know Larry since he returned to the editorial saddle after radical surgery at Duke University. He dug my weird sense of humor and involved me in all manner of content decisions. He even invited me up to the Bel Air mansion one night to be a shill at a poker game he was hosting for Peter Fonda and Dennis Hopper, handing me a thousand dollars to fill the seat and help keep the banter lively.

Joyce Combs was a graphic artist for *Hustler* who had graduated from Chico State (voted *Playboy's* Number One Party School in America numerous times) and had relocated to Los Angeles in 1984 with hopes of working for a magazine. She was tall and sexy. I flirted with all the girls on the floor, but one day, I up and asked Joyce out. "Sure!" she said. I told her to meet me at my apartment in West Hollywood that evening. She was late so my friend Lee and I left without her. I put a note on the mailbox telling her that I was at the Palace in Hollywood and, if she still wanted to rock, to meet me there. I had tickets to see the festive salsa rock ensemble Kid Creole and the Coconuts. She showed up two hours later with a girlfriend from work. Lee hooked up with her and Joyce came home with me. We dated for a year before she moved in with me, and we got married on June 8, 1986, at the Wayfarers Chapel in Palos Verdes.

Joyce wasn't bothered by porn or designing layout badges like "Mandy: Cum Fly Me." She wasn't into watching the films with me, but some of the subculture's more animated characters amused her. Joyce met Ron Jeremy—the pudgy New York porn actor with the homely face and ten-inch penis nicknamed the Hedgehog—during a party we attended at the 1985 Consumer Electronics Show in Las Vegas. "You know, your gal is pretty hot, Lonn," he said with a chuckle. "Mind if I take her for a spin?" She rolled her eyes and responded, "No thanks—Hedgehog!"

At heart, Joyce was a homebody, a gardener, and would someday be the perfect devoted mother. She was raised on the Stones, Rod Stewart, the New York Dolls, and Tom Waits. When rumblings about a possible new gig for me with a rock magazine began, she was supportive and excited. I wasn't really thinking about changing positions at this time, but I was obviously curious about the new publication in the building.

Illustrating both a lack of early commitment to Althea's vision and typical corporate conservatism, Kohls (whom Joyce privately referred to as "His Cheapness") opted instead to promote a low-salaried copy editor named Michael Levine to man the *RIP* helm. While his intentions were noble and his knowledge of hardcore and punk laudable, he had virtually no personality and even less leadership ability. The magazine struggled the first few months to find its voice and niche as Levine championed fringe acts like the Mentors and Black Flag. There was something huge happening right underneath everyone's nose called the Sunset Strip, but Levine and *RIP* were deaf to the strains flying off Mick Mars's motley guitar.

Althea died of AIDS-related complications on June 27, 1987. She was thirty-three, same age Jesus was when he was crucified, but that's where the similarities end. Her profligate lifestyle and bathtub demise were brilliantly captured in Milos Forman's 1996 biopic, *The People vs. Larry Flynt*. I saw her two weeks before she passed away. She weighed less than a hundred pounds but remained feisty till the end, calling in her opinions on magazine content when she could barely muster enough volume in her voice for the editors gathered around the speaker phone to hear her.

Althea's funeral took place on July 25 at the Church of the Hills in the Hollywood Hills Forest Lawn Memorial-Park. I was nervous and sad. Few people in the company connected with or understood Larry's peculiar other half as well as I did. She once took me and a mailroom clerk named Michael DiGregorio (who resembled Pacino's Michael Corleone from *The Godfather)* out clubbing. I was living in a $375-a-month one-bedroom shack on Robertson Boulevard. The limo that picked me up was longer than my entire building. When the chariot door swung open, there was Althea, smiling, ready to rock.

"Hey, Lonn, you want a quaalude?" she asked before we'd pulled away from the curb.

"Sure," I said. "Are you going to have one?" I asked.

"I never have *one* of anything," she giggled and tossed three of the '80s grooviest little helpers down the gullet.

At the funeral, Larry rolled up the aisle past Joyce and me and stopped. "Lonn, would you say a few words about Althea?" he asked. "She really liked you." I was both honored and terrified. I spoke right after avant-garde rocker Mark Mothersbaugh, leader of the demented new-wave band Devo. Althea respected Mark, even though he was constantly berating her for using drugs. Mark once tossed an ounce of Althea's cocaine into the fireplace.

Among all the anecdotes I could have related while standing

up on that podium in front of an iconoclastic crowd of mourners, my eulogy for Althea was short, sweet, and without scandal. I told the audience about the time she tried to talk Larry into getting his ear pierced. She wanted him to be hipper. I looked down into the first row when I'd finished and noticed a gentle, affirming smile on the face of the world's most notorious pornographer. The knot in my stomach disappeared, and a wave of despair overcame me as I marched back to my place in the pew. Althea Flynt was more than my boss. She was my friend and saying good-bye was painful.

Joyce had heard rumors around the art department that Flynt was contemplating a quick demise of their fledgling rock magazine and suggested this time that I make a play. "You love music," she said. "This is your chance to get out of porn and into something you really love." I took the cue and went to see the company's CEO the week after the funeral. Fifteen minutes into the meeting, Kohls had offered me the editorial helm of *RIP*.

I was intrigued but didn't take the bait immediately. I told him I'd have to have total editorial autonomy and that the magazine needed better color and heavier paper stock. The bands selling the most records were the big-arena rock acts like Def Leppard, Mötley Crüe, Scorpions, and Bon Jovi. We needed to cover them and the heavier acts, like Metallica and Slayer. "*RIP* can be the hard-rock *Rolling Stone*," I said. "Editorially credible but still a fan's magazine, loud and fun."

My instinct told me that my personality and ability to bond with people regardless of their trade or title would be key to the success of the magazine. Becoming friends with the bands while producing the slickest, most honest, well-intentioned, journalistically superior rock magazine seemed to me the right path. The test was how to remain plausible while catering to the artists and their heroic, egotistic agendas.

In the late '80s, the best metal mag in the world was being published six thousand miles away in England. It was called *Kerrang!* America had nothing like it. *Metal Edge* was a teenybopper rag, fun to read but possessing little editorial grit.

Circus was an established name with a strong fan base run by an upstanding music fan named Ben Liemer. It took few risks and ran mostly live-concert photos. *Hit Parader* was the low-budget benchmark of metal reportage, bent on covering anything and everything that rocked whether they were given access to the artist or not. It wasn't unusual to find a rewritten press release pawned off as a new feature.

This unholy magazine trinity competently covered the scene, but they all lacked one key ingredient: soul. To set itself apart from the field, *RIP* needed to access that elusive element and infuse it into every page.

The memo went out from Kohls' office on July 15, 1987. It read, "Lonn Friend has been elected executive editor of *RIP* magazine. I think Lonn's enthusiasm and expertise can help to improve the look and sales potential of *RIP*." I had my mandate. All I needed was a set of earplugs and faith the size of a Marshall Stack.

Within days of my appointment, I was invited to a showcase in Memphis for a Van Halen–clone metal group that had no major record deal but, instead, a band member whose father was rich and wanted his kid to have a shot playing for the rock press. This was where I first heard the words, "You have to hear the Guns N' Roses record," from not one but several of the scribes who had flown in for the gig.

When I returned to L.A., I summoned my brand-spanking-new editorial staff and sent them out to get to know Axl, Slash, Izzy, Duff, and Steven, up close and personal. Half the bunch had already partied with the guys and gotten home phone numbers. Most of the bonding came from serendipitous meetings at local clubs or bars. To their credit, nothing about GN'R was ever scripted.

During the latter months of 1987, *RIP* ran several raw and wild stories of the group, accompanied by equally raw and wild photos. During this period, I also took on the raw-and-wild image by sprouting a beard and letting my hair grow to shoulder length. The shape-shifting had begun.

Then in early spring 1988, my staff and I were contemplating which badass buzzing band of the land should dis-grace the next *RIP* cover. I'd been listening to the advance of the new Poison record, *Open Up and Say . . . Ahhh!*, and thought that they were ready to break big. It was my assumption that a cover story featuring the glam rockers would be a hit. That was until one of my editors bitch-slapped her boss—me—to wake up and smell the chaos.

She had been hanging out with Slash, GN'R's affable and often intoxicated lead guitarist. "Lonn, you're making a mistake," she said, shutting my office door behind her. "Poison is cool but they're not hard enough. Our readers are heavier. You should put Guns N' Roses on the cover. No one's given them a full cover yet. *Hit Parader* won't give a band a full cover until they've sold platinum [one million units]. We'll be the first!" GN'R was still months from that at this stage, but the word of mouth on them was deafening. And frankly, I didn't feel that commercial-unit-sales criteria were a proper gauge for who should make the cover of *RIP*. But I was still reticent. I told her I'd think about it.

"Hello, Lonn," came the voice over the phone the next day. It was clear, coherent, not a hint of afternoon-bottle-tipping slur. "This is Slash from Guns N' Roses. We think *RIP* is awesome and we want to be on the cover. Lonn, Guns is going to be bigger than Poison, dude. Give us a shot."

I hung up, called the editor into my office, told her about the conversation. "I know," she said. "I told him to call you." That afternoon, I made the decision. The June 1988 cover story with the banner "Metal's New Supergroup," featuring a supercool, sleazy, sensational shot of Axl and Slash taken in a five-minute photo session backstage at the Celebrity Theater in Anaheim, was the defining moment when *RIP* soared in the blink of a newsstand-sweeping eye from underground metal fanzine to the most talked about rock publication in the industry. Poison's record went on to sell five million copies—a huge success—but it would pale in comparison to *Appetite*'s gargantuan accomplishment.

Hard rock music was approaching a crossroads, and the signpost read Sunset Boulevard. Freaky bands and freakier fans choked the infamous Strip every night from sundown till after 2 A.M., when the parking lot of the Rainbow Bar and Grill took on the look of a Fellini swap meet. The clubs now closed, metalheads of various persuasions would network on the sidewalk to determine where the drug-and-groupie-drenched afterparties were taking shape.

The local glam-metal movement was ignited by Mötley Crüe in '82 with their lecherous landmark debut, *Too Fast for Love*, and taken to further cacophonous extremes in '83 by Quiet Riot's *Metal Health* and Dokken's *Breaking the Chains*. The following year brought Mötley running mates Ratt into the fray with their *Out of the Cellar* LP—a blistering out-of-the-box smash. By the time the cat dragged in four disparate cartoonish characters collectively known as Poison in 1986, the Sunset Strip had become the vortex of volume and decadence for not just Los Angeles, but the entire rockin' planet.

Into this fray stumbled Guns N' Roses, catering to the deranged desires of both the hard core and hair farmer. They weren't really "metal" in the archetypal Iron Maiden/Judas Priest sense of the word, nor were they KISS/Crüe lipstick glam. If anything, Guns N' Roses evoked the beautifully bad image and riffage of early Stones and Aerosmith, intoxicating to the eye and ear, gloriously untamed, and absolutely authentic. Consult your front-man scripture: "Jagger begot Tyler begot Axl."

"Welcome to the Jungle" launched *Appetite for Destruction*'s fifty-eight-minute assault on the senses that seduced fans, critics, musical peers, and an entire nation of rock-loving misfits waiting patiently for something to wake America out of its pathetic, disco-pop ego-driven me-generation stupor. In its own demented way, Guns N' Roses was the antidote for a civilization on the brink of collective narcolepsy.

Appetite unfolded like a prurient postcard depicting the zeitgeist of Hollywood near the end of the millennium's most dubious decade. "It's So Easy," "Nightrain," "Out ta Get Me, "Mr. Brownstone," "Paradise City," "My Michelle," "Think about You," "Sweet Child o' Mine," "You're Crazy," "Anything Goes," and "Rocket Queen"—the LP is a seamless glorification of excess where every recorded moment burns with ball-busting truth.

Producer Mike Clink—who would prove to be the George Martin of GN'R, manipulating the dials to every release the band would create—told me that the female groans of ecstasy during "Rocket Queen" were authentic. "The guys were taking turns fucking this girl in the studio," recalled Clink. "Those are actual sounds of sex, captured live on tape." But above all, *Appetite* signaled the breech birth of the most charismatic, morally corrupted, possessed, and passionate front man since the mike-stand-wielding, loose-lipped junkie Steven Tyler stepped off the Cambridge streets fourteen years before.

Growing up William Bailey in the heartland town of Lafayette, Indiana, W. Axl Rose sang, stalked, swam, and smelled like no other fish in the big-hair, heavy-eyeliner, poseur-polluted L.A. hard rock sea. While he borrowed bits in vocal technique and body language from his heroes Iggy Pop, Elton John, Freddie Mercury, Thin Lizzy's Phil Lynott, and, of course, Jagger and Tyler, Axl was a complete and inexplicable original, prone to personal misbehavior and public misunderstanding.

With their record-breaking debut LP, *Appetite for Destruction*, the controversial EP, *GN'R Lies*, and the historic double release of *Use Your Illusion I* and *II*, the Gunners won the hearts, minds, souls, and ears of rock fans across the globe. Of course, along with the success came the scrutiny of a voracious, tabloid-driven media.

The press, both metal and mainstream, exploited the GN'R phenomenon, zeroing in on the snake-walking, sandpaper-voiced lead singer. When the band finally put its foot down and refused to play the game any longer, ignoring requests for interviews and photo sessions, the backlash of negative opinion from the legitimate and metal media was astounding. I began to realize then, purely and simply, that these newshounds and gossip-mongers just didn't get it. No one got it, except the ones who usually get it: the fans.

Many nights on tour, the adored front man tested the patience of the good folks who put him on the pedestal. But it wasn't out of malice or a sociopathic need to fuck with people's heads. Axl was a pathological perfectionist when it came to getting on stage and delivering. He pushed his vocal ability to excruciating limits because he was emotionally and ethically unable to give a half-assed performance. Hence, if his throat or voice was not ready when showtime came, the show didn't go on. Some nights when I was out on the road with GN'R, Axl was at the gig, raring to go onstage at 7:00 in the evening. Other nights, it was well past midnight.

Axl could hypnotize a sold-out stadium or an empty room. I witnessed the latter miracle in June 1989 when *RIP* senior editor (and friend of Axl's) Del James informed me that Axl and Slash were in Chicago working on material for the next LP. "You up for a road trip?" I asked Del. A rhetorical question to a rising scribe in the early years of his rockin' journalistic journey. "Dude, let's go!" and off to Chicago we flew for a glimpse of the creative process that no other magazine had a prayer of witnessing.

The minute we touched down at O'Hare International, Del called Axl. "We're going to the Metro," directed my senior editor with the keys to the GN'R kingdom. "He wants to play us something. He sounds excited." We grabbed a cab and headed for Chi Town's most famous rock club.

Club owner Joe Shanahan, an influential player in the local rock scene, had built a rehearsal space above the concert venue. WVVX 103.1, Chicago's metal station, was known as the first station in America to play Metallica, and they were on *Appetite* months before mainstream radio hopped on the nigh train. Axl liked Chicago. He planned on hanging out there until mid-August.

Del and I entered the airy Metro around 6 P.M. and were guided upstairs, where we found the most persecuted and venerated lead singer in rock seated at a grand piano in the middle of a large room. He was noodling the ivories as Del and I quietly took our seats.

"Hey, man," said Del to his pal.

Axl lifted his head, smiled, and replied, "Hey. You guys wanna hear something I've been working on?"

We answered with enthusiastic unison, "Yeah, man. Go for it."

The fair-haired maestro then took a deep, cleansing breath, laid his hands on the keys, and in the blink of a jet-lagged eye, skated into a rhapsody that from the very first notes harkened a hero Axl and I shared, Elton John. With the exceptions of "Sweet Child" and "Patience," ballads were nonexistent in the GN'R repertoire. That was about to change drastically.

When I look into your eyes
I can see a love restrained.

These were the first lines of the artist's moving aortic anthem that would eventually emerge on disc and video as a two-part orchestrated opus of love and loss the likes of which rock had never seen. "November Rain" had been floating around in demo configuration on bootlegs since the *Appetite* sessions of '86, but the structure of the composition was never right for Axl, so it didn't make it on the band's long-form destructive debut.

"November Rain" eventually fell in the fall of 1991 on the ambitious *Use Your Illusion* double-disc package. Its companion track, "Estranged," the second part of the tragic tale of love lost, was based on a short story written by the long-haired, ten-dollar-an-hour *RIP* editor seated next to me. Axl was possessed to create something larger than life and rock, heaven and earth. "November Rain" and "Estranged" presented a moment in music history when the bar would be raised so high, even the band members lost sight.

When the song was over, Del and I glanced at each other, goose bumps rising off both his inked and my bare arms. Our golf clap in the dank room did not do justice to the awesome event we'd just witnessed, a first peek at what history may ultimately proclaim as one musician's watershed creative moment. Then he played around with a couple other tracks and announced that dinner was on him tonight. "Hey, guys," he said. *"Batman* just opened. I really want to see it. Let's grab Slash and go later."

That night, after pasta and wine, the four of us hit a suburban Chicago multiplex and watched Tim Burton's stunning celluloid comic-book adventure. One thing that stands out in my mind about that surreal night at the movies was when Axl got up to go to the bathroom. The minute he left his seat, the jingle of his bracelets acted as a magnet for about a half dozen girls seated behind us who were well aware of our presence in the theater. I wondered if he would make it back in time for reel three. To my surprise, he returned in five minutes.

Guns N' Roses' creative wave was about to crash into some dysfunctional rocks as the trappings of success began to erode the makeup of the band. The childhood buddy with whom Slash originally formed GN'R, drummer Steven Adler, proved to be the first casualty. Steven was a case study in self-destruction who dove into drug abuse like a swan into a mountain lake. A likeable kid with a warm, playful personality, he couldn't say no to anything that would alter his state of mind.

Steven's troubles started when he failed to show for the January 30, 1989, broadcast of the American Music Awards, where the band was performing their monster ballad "Patience." Eagles drummer and Axl fan Don Henley ended up replacing the absent Adler on skins. When basic recording for *Use Your Illusion* commenced, Steven was virtually absent, and even when he did materialize, he was so wasted that his drum tracks proved unsalvageable. He only made the cut on one song from the double-disc release, "Civil War."

Then came the unreal week in October of that year when GN'R joined the Rolling Stones for four dates at the Los Angeles Memorial Coliseum. As timing would have it, the third-anniversary *RIP* party was on the docket, and I pitched it to the guys to "warm up" for Mick and company at our gig, which was taking place at the Park Plaza Hotel in Echo Park near downtown. They went for it and at 1 A.M. on the night of October 13, 1989—after a thousand of my guests were thrown out by the fire department because we were way over capacity—the band rifled into what would prove to be the last formal club gig they ever played.

The next day, I was getting calls from all over town applauding us for the soiree from Hell. But in the office, Del informed me that all was not well in Guns land. Eighty thousand others were let in on the secret a few nights later when, on October 18, the ever-forthcoming Axl did some very dirty public laundering.

I hate to do this on stage. But I tried every other fucking way. And unless certain people in this band get their shit together, these will be the last Guns N' Roses shows you'll fucking ever see. Cause I'm tired of too many people in this organization dancing with Mr. Goddamn Brownstone.

In this unprecedented act of public intervention, Axl was exposing both Slash's and Steven's demons for the entire world to see with the hopes of keeping the toxic tribe together. He didn't realize, however, that his draconian control of the group was having a more poisonous effect on band unity than the finest china white. His lead guitarist apparently took the wake-up call to heart and began to curtail his drug use. His drummer, however, was too far gone to care.

The straw finally broke the donkey's back on April 7, 1990, at the high-profile Farm Aid benefit concert. GN'R was scheduled to play "Down on the Farm" and "Civil War." When Steven tripped over his drum kit in front of national cameras and increasingly frustrated bandmates, it signaled the end of the Adler era. Matt Sorum was recruited out of the Cult—the group GN'R had opened for not too long before—soon after the barnyard debacle.

Rhythm guitarist Izzy Stradlin was the next victim. The nonconfrontational fellow Indiana rocker couldn't handle the drama, even in the midst of earthshaking fame and fortune. No one was more laid back than Izzy. He had the most genuine Keith Richards' "cool" of any rocker I'd ever seen. He could have been Keef's son. They played, drank, even vocally sounded alike. I wasn't in the room when he had his epiphany, but my gut told me that he'd ridden the night train about as far as his soul could handle, had tons of cash, and just didn't care anymore. Steven's ouster and Izzy's exit pointed to the eternally fragile state of band cohesiveness that defined GN'R.

RIP was becoming the unofficial GN'R scrapbook. We were the first to announce Steven's departure for Matt Sorum, and we ran frequent quotes by Axl—who talked to no other metal magazines at this time. The Friend family had also become part of the Guns N' Roses family, and nowhere was the strength of that friendship more evident than on the evening of July 29, 1990.

Joyce, our baby daughter Megan Rose, and some friends were celebrating my thirty-fourth birthday at our tiny Culver City home when around 7 P.M. the phone rang. "Dude, is the party still going?" It was Del, calling from a pay phone somewhere in Hollywood. He sounded clear-headed and somewhat excited.

"Uh, yeah, buddy," I said. "You wanna come over? It's kinda winding down, but there's plenty of food left and my buds are still here."

"Yeah," he fired back. "I'm with Axl, Sebastian [Bach, from Skid Row], and Ian [Astbury, from the Cult] and their gals."

For a moment, I stared blankly out the back window at our suburban patio, sparsely populated with a handful of friends whose professions ranged from advertising account executive to salesgirl at Tiffany's. "You're bringing Axl, Bas, and Ian . . . here? To my house? Now?" I asked, feeling equal parts fear and elation.

"Yep," he said. "Is that cool?"

"Come on down, dude! . . . Joyce!" I shouted through the back door of our 1,200-square-foot abode. "We've got rockers on the way. Someone needs to make a run for more beer! A lot more!"

The editor's backyard birthday shifted into high gear when the rockers entered the Friend-family domain. Passing through our living room to the back door off the kitchen, the parade sauntered down the redwood steps of our back deck and into the arms of disbelief. My guests looked as if they'd just been transported to Munchkin land and the Lollipop Guild midgets were in the house. Behold the parade: Axl, Erin Everly (daughter of '60s pop icon Don Everly, and Axl's girlfriend at the time), Sebastian, Maria (Sebastian's bride), Ian, Ian's dark princess—and taxi driver to the stars, Del James.

After some modest drinking and conversation, the party warmed up considerably. The trio of rock notables—now swilling brews on my back porch—had combined sales by this time in 1990 somewhere in the neighborhood of 25 million units worldwide. Sebastian Bach had the sandpaper screech, bad-kid charisma, and an imposing six-foot-six-inch stature. He idolized Axl, walked in his shadow, and didn't hesitate to cop a move here or there while retaining a stunning individuality that fueled the multiplatinum success of Skid Row's resounding self-titled debut.

Ian Astbury was the troupe's rock 'n' roll shaman. As the charismatic lead singer of the Cult, Ian was the one who greenlighted GN'R for the opening slot on their first arena tour. Axl and Sebastian held the British crooner in deep respect for being not just a magnetic stage veteran but also the composer of modern rock songs that bridged the gulf in the late '80s between metal and alternative.

At around 10 P.M., the energy on the property shifted. That's when Axl pulled me aside. "I've got some rough mixes of the new album," he whispered softly. "You wanna hear 'em?" The band had been in the studio for months carving out the follow-up to one of the greatest debut efforts in the history of rock 'n' roll. Del had been keeping the magazine informed of the progress of the *Use Your Illusion* project, and I spoke regularly to Slash, who'd told me that they had tracked more than thirty-five songs for what looked like an unprecedented double-CD release: two entirely separate titles, hitting the market on the same day.

There were few bands in rock with the commercial authority to undertake such a campaign, and Guns N' Roses was one of them. "Uh, are you kidding?" I asked.

"I'll pull my car onto your carport and we'll listen on the stereo."

A few moments later, Axl Rose was standing six inches from my left ear, singing me the lyrics to "November Rain" as the instrumental tracks blared out of his car speakers. How far the song had come in the year since Del and I first heard the exquisite melody in that Chicago rehearsal room.

But the highlight of the evening came when Axl and Sebastian followed me into the kitchen to use the phone and refresh their drinks. Out of nowhere, the duo busted into a resounding rendition of the timeless spiritual hymn "Amazing Grace." It was better than any "Happy Birthday" (except maybe the one Steven Tyler sang to me backstage in Phoenix on the *Get a Grip* tour, summer '93).

GN'R hit the road in May of '91 with a cache full of songs but no official product in stores. It didn't matter. This was the band that never followed rules. They would jam the tracks from their upcoming masterwork live, for the fans, and they sold out every show regardless of there being no new record to promote. *Use Your Illusion I* and *II* were released simultaneously in the States on September 17, 1991, months after the original release date.

Bob Clearmountain—the legendary studio magician who'd tweaked the knobs for the Stones and Springsteen—had mixed the original master, but Axl and Slash hated it, thought it was too slick. They brought in Sex Pistols mixer Bill Price to retool (dirty up) the entire double-sized opus. Having moved several million units in a few short weeks, the band (especially Axl) was feeling pumped. He even accepted a Thanksgiving pitch to break radio silence and do the unthinkable—a live on-air interview—and I would be along for the ride.

Rockline was the venerable weekly Q&A radio mainstay hosted by seasoned L.A. DJ Bob Coburn. "B. C." had a classic FM voice and a deep knowledge of contemporary music and, like me, preferred the nonconfrontational route to conversation.

It was long established that Axl was not keen on doing press. But the band was so hot that he was compelled to speak up. Several songs from *Illusion*—namely, "Don't Cry," "Civil War," and "Live and Let Die"—were saturating the airwaves. Add to that the approaching holiday season, the time of year when record sales traditionally go through the roof, and you see why he had to do the interview. The GN'R faithful needed reassurance that Axl Rose was a living, breathing sentient being. He was the biggest rock star in the world, but you could count on one hand how many times his voice had been heard outside of a concert.

Axl's anxiety over the *Rockline* appearance was one of the reasons he asked me to coproduce the event, which amounted to me just being there, a friend and trusted journalist in the room. The night before the broadcast, I drove out to his Malibu home. I thought spending a few hours just talking would ease his mind, even get him excited for the experience. He greeted me at the door graciously, showed me around his glamorous pad, and poured me a glass of white wine. Axl was not the drinker in the band. Everyone else handled that task quite well. Then about an hour after I arrived, the phone rang. It was a fellow musician in crisis.

On the other end of the line was Jane's Addiction guitarist Dave Navarro, having some sort of a narcotic-related meltdown. He was reaching out to Axl for help. I grabbed what bits and pieces of information I could by eavesdropping while Axl counseled his friend. If he didn't want me to hear the conversation, he would have left the room. To this day, I'm not sure whether Dave was high during the call, but it was obvious that Axl cared about him.

Ninety minutes or so later, the conversation ended. Axl apologized for the distraction but none was required. I was enamored by his compassion. We chatted until after midnight. I told him that Coburn was a cool guy and not to worry. He'd take the high road and ask questions mostly about the music.

Axl's new girlfriend, supermodel Stephanie Seymour, was driving him to the L.A. Studios on Cahuenga Boulevard near Universal City. I'd been there more than an hour, chatting with B. C., producer Mark Felsot, and Global Satellite president Howie Gilman. They were understandably anxious when, with ten minutes to air, there was no sign of the rocker and his sexy chauffeur. "It's Axl. He'll be here. Don't worry," I said. He walked into the *Rockline* booth about fifteen seconds before airtime, delayed by a gaggle of autograph-seeking fans in front of the building.

The interview went off without a hitch. B. C. asked about the songs on *Use Your Illusion*, the recent death of his hero Freddie Mercury, and his relationship with Slash and the band. There was no drama. Fans called in and expressed their love for the often-misunderstood artist. That's when I realized how much Axl was enjoying himself. By shunning the press, he'd lost touch with the people most responsible for his rock 'n' roll ascension. Every artist, no matter how eccentric, needs to feel that connection, even if it's only once in a blue Hollywood moon.

A couple months later, the window of opportunity opened for me to gather some on-the-record quotes from Axl for the magazine when I made a cross-country winter road trip to see and feel the GN'R beast roar in President George H. W. Bush's backyard. We were sitting on a dressing-room sofa in Washington, D.C., backstage at the Capital Centre. The compost of that conversation appeared in my March 1992 *RIP* feature, "Guns N' Roses: From the Inside."

> I've had a mutated form of polio, a mutated form of rubella, the swine flu, scarlet fever, and strep throat in my heart. It's mostly respiratory stuff. Air conditioners in hotels circulate the same air, and on the plane everyone's breathing the same air. So if anyone's got anything, my tonsils grab it. I'm chronic like that. That's one of the reasons I've never liked touring. I also found out it is supposedly some kind of mental thing having to do with me punishing myself for expressing myself. For twenty years of my life I was beaten by my parents for expressing myself, so part of me believes I should be punished for that expression. I do this by lowering my own resistance. Turn that around, and there you have it—self-punishment. Other than that, I'm pretty healthy.

That was no excuse for those who've been bitten by his tardiness or angst-inspired verbal tirades. One night Axl called me at home because he was upset about something he'd read in *Kerrang!* According to Axl, the journalist completely missed the boat in reviewing the band's performance at Rock in Rio. "We were *on* the second night," Axl told me. "Why didn't he see that?" Our conversation rambled on about the press, and I was forced to ask Axl why a sentence in a British metal rag should matter to the lead singer of the biggest rock band in the world. "I just care," he answered with conviction. "I don't know why. I just do."

One fateful night in Montreal, Axl may have cared too much, or perhaps not enough. It was the megaband coheadlining bill of the ages: Metallica and Guns N' Roses, August 8, 1992. In a freak accident, Metallica front man James Hetfield caught fire by mistakenly walking into a pyro blast. The band was forced in that tragic instant to cancel their set as their singer was whisked away to a local hospital with severe burns over 40 percent of his body. But instead of carrying the torch, so to speak, Axl got pissed off nine songs into GN'R's set, complaining of monitor trouble, and stomped offstage, taking his band with him and igniting a torrent of violence that poured from the stadium and out into the streets.

This event signaled the acceleration of Axl's onstage dysfunctional behavior that had commenced with the infamous riot in St. Louis the previous year on July 2, 1991, at the Riverport Amphitheater in the Missouri suburb of Maryland Heights. Having just throttled into "Rocket Queen," Axl spotted a biker in the pit rolling videotape. He abruptly stopped the song and asked security to take care of the bootlegger. When arena officials didn't move fast enough, the Red Tornado decided to take matters into his own hands, diving onto the burly fan, fists flying, band members gazing on helplessly.

GN'R crew hoisted Axl out of the pit and back onstage, where he grabbed the mike and announced to the less-than-understanding Midwest throng of testosterone-and-whiskey-fueled fanatics that he and his band were done. They'd only played eighty minutes of their two-plus-hour set. That's when the gates of Hell and all its angels—two-wheeled or otherwise—went berserk. Hundreds of fans on the floor trashed the stage, destroyed Axl's piano, and looted gear. The Gunners and crew escaped with their lives. In the alphabetical liner-note acknowledgments in *Use Your Illusion I*, "Lonn and Joyce Friend" comes just before "Fuck you, St. Louis."

Axl made airing anger in public an art form, often poisoning an otherwise ecstatic performance. And it wasn't just from the live pulpit that he delivered his indicting sermons. His unprecedented vitriolic tongue-lashing of the press in *Use Your Illusion II*'s "Get in the Ring" is a classic example of his pathological inability to just do his thing and not give a shit who was out there jotting down notes, critiquing his art, his life, his flaws, or his calling. Axl never learned to use his illusion. He let it use him, which contributed to the relatively short lifespan of GN'R.

On June 6, 1992, the mutual trust we had forged resulted in a magical transatlantic tour to the City of Lights, Paris, France, for a pay-per-view concert that netted me two round-trip first-class tickets and a handsome five-figure consulting fee. Axl and manager Doug Goldstein wanted me involved, so they exercised their influence and brought me on board.

With respect to professional compensation, no rocker in my career ever stepped up for me the way that Axl did. A decade later, Jon Bon Jovi would toss me a handful of nickels for a similar consulting exercise. As for the Paris concert itself, well, that proved to be a bootlegger's wet dream.

On the ride from the hotel, everyone was in great spirits. Slash's grade school pal from L.A. Lenny Kravitz was hanging with us, doing his own gig in a couple nights. Lenny was already a god in France. It took years to equal stateside the popularity he'd accomplished in Europe with his debut LP. But something went amiss in the hours between our arrival at the venue and the time GN'R finally took the stage, involving Stephanie Seymour and her ex-boyfriend, movie star Warren Beatty. Apparently, "Bugsy" had called Paris, looking for his girl who'd run off with the rock star. This was the actual, word-for-word rant Axl laid on the fifty-eight thousand mostly clueless French-speaking fans in attendance, not to mention the hundreds of thousands tuned in on pay-per-view TV and FM stations worldwide:

I'd like to dedicate this next song to a man who likes to play games. To a man who lives his life playing games . . . pre-meditated games. A man who is so empty, that's all he can do is play fucking games. A man who is a parasite. A man who lives his life sucking off other people's life force and their energy. An old man who likes to live vicariously through young people and suck up all their life 'cause he has none of his own. I'd like to dedicate this song to a cheap punk named Warren Beatty. A man who has a family and a baby but who spends his time fucking around with other people because he doesn't know what to do with his own life. A man who uses you and uses the media and uses everybody to fulfill his fucking parasitic needs. Well, listen, home-fuck, if you think Madonna kicked your ass, I'm betting on Annette, you stupid fucking asshole. This song is called "Double-Talkin' Jive," motherfucker!

Whenever Axl was pissed, he would fiddle with the spongy head that covered the microphone. Tonight, he mangled the mike throughout the entire diatribe before catapulting into the smoldering song like a man possessed.

Joyce and I were standing at the soundboard. "What was that all about?" she asked me.

"I don't know," I laughed nervously. "But it's a good thing Warren Beatty isn't here tonight."

The band then kicked into the cover of McCartney's "Live and Let Die" from *Use Your Illusion I*, brought that much closer to home by the anger and judgment of an artist forever slave to the perception that someone was always "out to get" him. My relationship with Axl was intellectual, professional, and distant. I respected him and he knew that. He was a true artist, tormented by demons, driven by the ineffable need to express and channel what was passing through his being. Whether his musical creation was born in Heaven or Hell was irrelevant. It took insight and patience to even attempt a connection with this extraordinary individual. I believe to this day, the only true comrade Axl ever had was Del.

The front man in a rock band usually has tons of drama. Their sheer artistic day-to-day maintenance is astonishing. Del was Axl's guy, from errand boy to shrink to creative coconspirator. How else did he coauthor "The Garden" and "Yesterdays" from *Use Your Illusion* and live happily for fifteen years on the mechanical royalties from those songs alone? If the real Axl Rose story is ever written, Del will compose it. No one else could.

But Slash, he was a different story. When the band wasn't touring, we'd spend time together outside the office, go to concerts or local clubs. Slash was the yin to Axl's yang. He was always in a good mood and never complained about anything except running out of booze or cigarettes. But as affable and approachable as the friendly guitarist was, he too was wrestling with his own demons. This became clear the night I visited his home in the Hollywood Hills to conduct the interview for the exclusive February 1990 *RIP* cover story, "Slash: Under the Black Hat," the feature that led to my coauthoring (with Jeffrey Ressner) a *Rolling Stone* cover story a year later.

What is significant about the *RIP* story is what I didn't reveal in the published text: Slash's heroin addiction, something he'd freely discuss later in the *Stone* story. Both photographer Robert John and I knew something was amiss the night we met at Slash's house for the *RIP* session. Robert had accompanied me to the guitarist's Walnut Drive pad to shoot the cover and layout pix. When we got there, Slash was alert and accommodating. He'd ordered some food from a deli down on Sunset Boulevard.

I started rolling tape as we munched, but about a half hour into the session, Slash asked if we could break for a little while. "I'd like to go upstairs and take a shower," he said.

"Sure, dude. We'll just hang out in the living room and wait for ya. Take your time."

And take his time he did. An hour went by and Slash was no-where to be found. Robert said, "I'm going upstairs to check on him." About thirty minutes later, Robert returned, reporting that he got some awesome shots of Slash in the shower but that maybe I should come back tomorrow and finish the interview.

"Did he ask me to leave, Robert?" I asked.

"No, man, he's just, uh, let's say, not in real good shape right now." Robert didn't reveal what was happening, but when Slash finally returned—a full two hours later—it was obvious. He had been shooting heroin and was now extremely stoned.

Robert's remarkable photo of Slash standing naked under the water spray, cigarette dangling from his lips, eyes sliced shut, black curls gently sliding down his shimmering back, is a micro-cosmic image of what made *RIP* the iconoclastic magazine it was. No other metal mag had access or license to capture or publish such blatant invasions of artistic space.

When Slash returned to the sofa and I flipped the tape recorder on again, he could barely move his lips to speak. His voice was so soft, I had to hold my tape recorder two inches from his mouth to capture the words. I asked him if he wanted to stop, but he insisted on continuing the interview.

"No, man," he whispered. "I'm cool." What is most remark-able is how coherent and concise Slash's responses to my ques-tions were, despite how completely wasted he was.

"Nothing in what I got out of Guns N' Roses, monetarily or fame-wise, I could really give a shit about," he said. "It was, and is always, the band. If my ability to play guitar suddenly left me, or if something happened to Axl, Duff, Izzy, or Steven, and GN'R suddenly ended, I'd be in serious fucking trouble because I depend on them. I depend on them to be part of the group that makes us special . . . that keeps my life going."

Slash loved the "Black Hat" cover story. It strengthened our friendship. I didn't agree with the way he lived his life, but I ac-cepted him and never judged him for his aberrant behavior. When we hung out, he didn't force me to do anything I didn't want to. He knew I was a lightweight when it came to controlled substances and even teased me about it.

One night he went on till dawn and I tried to keep up. I was sick the entire next day, stumbling around the office in a daze, wearing my white badge of honor for having partied with the rock star. I wasn't thinking about the consequences of my own actions because I'd come from a place where one couldn't see the forest for the sleaze. Whether they were reptilian pornographers or wild-eyed rock stars, I used the illusion that they dug me to get the job done.

Truth was, Slash liked me and I liked him. We'd come from similar roots. His father was Jewish; he'd grown up in Los Angeles and was weaned on the Beatles and Bowie. His mom even dated the Thin White Duke when he was a kid. One night, we listened to *Hunky Dory* together, my favorite Bowie record, and he said, "I'll introduce you to him some time. He's like an uncle." He made true on that promise after a Jeff Beck/Stevie Ray Vaughan show at the L.A. Sports Arena. Slash counted Stevie Ray as a hero, slicing a spicy piece of "Voodoo Chile" into his *Illusion* tour guitar solo.

"David, this is my friend Lonn. He runs *RIP* magazine."

Ziggy Stardust had me in his headlights. "*RIP*? I've seen your magazine," he grinned. "It's quite a good read."

I thought to myself, *Oh, Lord, there is life on Mars!*

I had memorable encounters with Axl, but I never really knew or felt completely comfortable with him. But Slash was right here on earth, close enough that I could feel his sincerity and comprehend his character. Our friendship manifested in my proudest journalistic moment, when I saw my byline in rock 'n' roll's most revered publication.

Jeffrey Ressner started his career like I did, as associate editor of *Hustler*. He'd left the company a year before I got there. We met in '87 while he was working at the industry trade magazine *Cash Box*, and struck up a friendship. When Jeff got the gig as staff writer for *Rolling Stone* in 1988, I was excited for him. He called me midsummer 1990 and said that Jann Wenner wanted another cover story on GN'R. They'd already done three, including the Axl Rose interview penned by Del and photographed by Robert.

"Slash seems the obvious choice," he said. "I was thinking, maybe you'd like to write it with me, since you know him so well. He might feel more comfortable going into the subjects he hasn't commented on publicly yet with you there. I talked to my editor and they're hip to the idea." I was blown away and immediately called Slash to get his take. "Yeah, man. I know. I told them I wanted you to be involved. I trust you."

We met Slash at a restaurant on Melrose Avenue. I watched Jeff do his thing. A brilliant interviewer with a knack for getting to the point without fanfare or emotion, he asked Slash about his relationship with Axl, the band, the new *Illusion* records, and ultimately, about his heroin use. Slash came clean on all fronts. I peppered the conversation with comments here and there, mostly softening the atmosphere if the dialogue got too touchy.

Jeff wrote the first draft and I gave it a once-over. A gorgeous headshot taken by *Stone* staff photographer Mark Seliger graced the cover of the January 24, 1991, issue. On the inside, the headline read *"Slash: The Rolling Stone Interview*, by Jeffrey Ressner and Lonn M. Friend." When I got my copy, I felt like jumping on a stage in my underwear and screaming, "Fuck yeahhhhh!"

2

Full Metal Jacket

"THE LAW OF SURVIVAL OF THE FITTEST IS NOT BASED ON CRUELTY,
IT IS BASED ON JUSTICE; IT IS ONE ASPECT OF THAT
DIVINE EQUITY WHICH EVERYWHERE PREVAILS."

—*James Allen*, The Mastery of Destiny

The Whisky on Sunset hadn't been that crowded since the
Doors played the legendary venue in 1967. Seven hundred human sardines (the capacity is five hundred) packed in sweaty oil
were oblivious to their collective discomfort because they had
come to celebrate the sound and fury of metal and throw roses at
the feet of its greatest unsung hero. It was December 14, 1995,
and the chaotic cause célèbre was the fiftieth birthday of one Ian
Fraser "Lemmy" Kilmister. Though he was actually born on
December 24, the party was starting early for the leader of the
immortal English speed band Motörhead, who for twenty years
had rocked harder and truer than any other of his kind.

A rumor had been spreading around Hollywood that some
special guests were poised to perform, though as of 9 P.M. there
had been no confirmation of the heavyweights. As the audience
grumbled with anticipation, I was upstairs, drinking Jack Dan-

iel's in the dressing room, with my old friend, who despite the hoopla maintained his traditional unaffected demeanor.

"Are you sure they're coming, Lem?" I asked.

"Well, if they don't show up," he replied in his nonchalant British whine, "we'll just play a longer set."

Suddenly, a monstrous roar filled the building. "About fucking time!" he grinned. We marched out to the VIP balcony railing as comic actor Tom Arnold, the emcee of the evening, introduced four figures that'd just emerged through the alley door left of the stage. They all were wearing black wigs, black moustaches, leather jackets open down the middle to expose the gut, and upon closer examination, two large moles on their left cheek.

As the quartet of faux Lemmys grabbed their instruments, I leaned over and said, "Happy birthday, Lem."

He shook my hand and turned his gaze to the stage. "Fucking brilliant! I can't believe they actually made it."

For the next thirty minutes, James Hetfield, Lars Ulrich, Kirk Hammett, and Jason Newsted, known collectively as Metallica, cranked through a flaming set of Motörhead staples that brought the fans to a frenzy and the evening's honoree to near tears. Motörhead—the Ramones of metal—never sold a ton of records, but their lore is authentic. Metallica left a Bay Area garage to become the most popular hard rock band in history. They are connected by the unified field of the metal culture, a loyal, globally galvanized gang of high-volume, high-octane fans that just won't go away.

A wise man once told me the difference between fate and destiny is this: fate is what you're given; destiny is what you do with what you're given. I was given a last name, a window of opportunity, a moment in rock history, and a whole lotta serendipity. Which brings us to that chilly January night in 1988, five months into the *RIP* gig, when destiny reared its hairy head. Or should I say "heads"?

I was standing in front of the Roxy box office, next door to the Rainbow, waiting to see a band I really didn't care to see. That's when I recognized them. "Hey, you're James and Lars from Metallica," I said. "I'm Lonn Friend from *RIP* magazine."

James, long on giggles but short on words, said, "Hey, what's up?" But his shorter, more animated partner chimed in instantly. "Lonn Friend? Hey, are you the guy from *Hustler* who wrote that article about porn stars in Paris? Amber Lynn, right?"

"Yeah, dude!" I responded gleefully. "That's me."

"Fuck, that was a great story, man," he exclaimed. "I like the part where Sharon Mitchell blows that guy in his seat on the plane ride over."

The next three hours, James, Lars, and I held court at the 'Bow. And even though I'd never owned a Metallica record, common ground was revealed. I gave them some sordid behind-the-scenes outtakes from the "French Flicking" feature that Lars had found so entertaining. The porn-rock connection was in play. I had instant cred because I came from the skin world. "We started tracking our new album," said Lars. "We'll be in town for months. Maybe we'll hang out." The album in production was called . . . *And Justice for All*, and Metallica fans were waiting for its arrival like expectant parents.

I felt an instant connection to Lars, perhaps because after only three LP campaigns—*Kill 'Em All*, *Ride the Lightning*, and *Master of Puppets*—he had become a master at manipulating the metal media. He was the tireless spokesperson for the band, the appointed and anointed expert at articulating the Metallica mission statement, which was, in essence, to rock harder and faster than any other band on the planet, because that's what the fans wanted and deserved.

Lars would talk to anyone and everyone who showed Metallica the least bit of true, passionate interest. They ranged from underground fanzines, local newspapers, metal radio stations like Long Beach's KNAC 105.5 to foreign and domestic rock publications. And he had just met the newest kid on the metal-media block. I wasn't aware of it then, but Lars Ulrich and Metallica were my first real professors of hard rock.

My premier "hang" with the band came when I was invited to their publicity photo shoot for . . . *And Justice for All* that summer. Jason Newsted was still wet under the Metalli-ears and proved the shy one in the band. Lead guitarist Kirk Hammett and I connected instantly. James was funny, sarcastic, and detached from the supposed importance of photographer Ross Halfin's assignment to capture the new configuration of the group since losing bassist Cliff Burton. Burton died in a tragic tour-bus accident near Stockholm, Sweden, in the early morning of September 27, 1986. He was only twenty-four years old. Many say that Cliff was the true spirit of Metallica. His machine-gun bottom-slapping style, flopping wild hair, and reefer-driven don't-give-a-shit attitude embodied the ethos of the garage quartet that originally initiated home jam sessions to let off steam and entertain some of the kids in the neighborhood.

It was at that photo shoot where the first goofy outtake of "Lonn with rock stars" was captured. I don't know which shot was better: band mooning the editor or the editor stripped down to his boxers while the guys laughed hysterically. As obnoxious as he was, Ross gave *RIP* some of its most exhilarating images and me some of my best scrapbook material.

It was around this time that I stopped shaving and began to wear a beard that got burlier as my life got crazier. The more hair I had on my face and head, the better chance I had of fitting in with the folks who actually lived the lifestyle and embodied the metal persona.

Metallica had taken the punishing instrumental prowess of the first three LPs, honed a time-honored rock message ("Power to the people," or in more metal vernacular, "Fuck the man"), and prepared for the next step in their ascension to rock godhood. Time to hit the road to reconnect with the flesh-and-blood fans, the human coal fueling this bonfire. Arena gigs were being booked, but to warm up the chops, Metallica jumped on an interesting "festival" opportunity. They were early in the set, but when they got off the stage, no one cared about the acts that hadn't played yet.

It was billed as the 1988 Monsters of Rock, featuring Van Halen (with Sammy Hagar up front), Scorpions, Dokken, Metallica, and a Led Zeppelin clone called Kingdom Come. The British-born festival was the brainchild of Ozzy Osbourne's enterprising wife, Sharon. The formula had worked brilliantly overseas. Mass gatherings of long-haired punters spending twelve hours on their feet to be pummeled into submission by a half dozen acts had become part of the European rock culture. Sharon felt it was time to experiment on the American metal populace.

At the Los Angeles Memorial Coliseum, the bands lined up to crush a half-filled stadium. Ticket sales were not as brisk as promoters had hoped. It seemed what worked on the Continent didn't quite translate stateside. It was cultural. They lived and died for these massive musical gatherings of the tribes. U.S.

crowds were more lethargic and individualistic; less connected by the event than by the loyalty they felt for specific favorite bands.

Metallica played second on the bill at the Monsters, and that's when all hell broke loose. Fans on the stadium floor began hurling their metal folding chairs in riotous reaction to the intoxicating strains of "Whiplash," "Creeping Death," "For Whom the Bell Tolls," and "Blackened." I watched from the soundboard. So *these* were my people now, huh?

A few weeks later, Joyce and I flew to Kansas City to catch another Monsters gig. Arrowhead Stadium was the site of the carnage. Again, Metallica completely stole the show with their short but uncompromising set. We watched from the stage. It was the first time I'd ever been eye level with the artist. Looking out over the sea of fans was surreal. I'd eventually have to muster the courage to venture down into the valley of mosh, or the pit, and experience Metallica shoulder to shoulder with the fans that were making them rulers of the hard-rock kingdom.

I hit the pit on my first official Metallica feature assignment at the Veterans Memorial Coliseum in Phoenix. It was December 4, 1988, and bassist Jason Newsted was playing his debut hometown gig with his new band on their first headline tour of America, quite a step up from his last outfit, the local thrashers Flotsam and Jetsam. With my all-access laminate dangling from my neck, I left the safe confines of the backstage as the arena went black, and I watched the first three songs amidst a throng of frenetic fans.

Metal is physical music. Sitting passively in your seat with your toe tapping and head bobbing works for an Eagles or Elton John concert but not a Metallica show. Motion and contact are adventure. Lars had come up with the concept. He went to his supreme career overseers, QPrime Management's Peter Mensch and Cliff Burnstein, and they signed off on the idea, knowing I would personally oversee the project. Metallica fans were so loyal, we created an entire monthly column called "Metalli-Watch" devoted to chronicling the progress of the next LP.

That first visit to North Hollywood's One on One studios, I met the band's new producer, Canadian protégé of the great Bruce Fairbairn, Bob Rock, the single most significant factor in the transmutation of Metallica's sound from thrashing metal to mainstream heavy rock. The sonic muscle of Mötley Crüe's 1989 smash *Dr. Feelgood*, which Rock had produced, blew Lars away. It was also the record that helped lift the Hollywood glam rockers to the next multiplatinum level, and according to Lars, Metallica was poised for the same metamorphosis.

Being this close to the operation, I began to realize that the business of Metallica at this time was very much under the eyes and edict of Lars, the five-foot-seven-inch Danish-born son of a professional tennis player. When it came down to artistic creation, however, that's when James Hetfield emerged as the driving force of band's musical vision. But making a record involved immense compromise and flexibility, both challenging states of being to attain when strong egos are involved.

Not being a musician myself, I wasn't entirely hip to the technology or studio vernacular being spoken in my presence during those visits. So more than scrutinize or try to comprehend what was taking place inside the studio walls, I took in the atmosphere and reported to the best of my ability what was happening during those *Black Album* days.

For the February 1991 issue—seven months before the record's formal release—I was getting song titles. "Let's see, we've

required to truly feel the power of the songs. And so the mosh pit—a swirling whirlpool of human bodies crashing into one another—spontaneously evolved at metal shows in clubs and theaters and eventually to arenas and stadiums. The zeitgeist of metal in perfect, unchoreographed chaos. The more intense the strains, the faster you moved. Volume and fury inspired bumps and bruises and a hell of a good time.

I floated back to the soundboard for the final, spectacular sequence. I loved watching from there, sitting next to Big Mick, Metallica's 250-pound scrubby-faced Englishman. The architect and manipulator of the group's bloodcurdling audio assault, Mick looked intimidating, but he was really a gentle giant. "Now watch closely, Lonn," he advised, "and cover your ears."

A giant blindfolded statue—the Lady of Justice from the album cover of . . . *And Justice for All*—crumbled onstage as gunfire and bomb blasts married with the pyrotechnic flashes of fire and light while the band played on with bravura precision. The Justice tour illustrated Metallica's commitment to their fans by giving them more than just the riffs from the record to titillate their senses.

After the Justice tour ended on October 7, 1989, in São Paolo, Brazil, James and Lars began writing the record that would knock Planet Rock off its axis. They kept their chops sharp by performing a dozen one-off festivals in Europe. They also did two special North American gigs opening for Aerosmith. One was in Toronto on June 29, 1990. I happened to be in New York on assignment with Mötley Crüe when the rare 'Smith/Metallica double bill was taking place. We had a day off, so I pitched the overnighter idea to Tommy Lee, who endorsed the plan immediately. He and I flew to Canada on an afternoon flight, played nine holes of golf in the rain at Glen Abbey Golf Club when we landed, hustled over to the concert, hung out the entire night, and were back in Manhattan by noon the next day.

Being out there, on the road, living the life with these bands—this is where the bonds were formed, the trust between rocker and writer. Whenever I was pitched a story that involved travel, I'd go. That's when the job began to blind me to what else was happening in my life. My daughter was born on March 24, 1990. Three months later, she was still being breast-fed, and I was on a jet with Mötley Crüe, observing the decadence up close and personal.

On June 27, 1990—in the throes of their Dr. Feelgood tour at the Capital Centre in Landover, Maryland, just outside of Washington, D.C.—bassist Nikki Sixx announced backstage that I was in charge of backstage passes that night. In other words, it was my job to scope the crowd and find girls who wanted to meet the band.

Tommy had devised this captivating twenty-minute drum solo in which he'd soar across the roof of the arena on a track while banging his kit to samples of Cheap Trick and Led Zeppelin. Nikki took this time to rest in his bass tent; Vince walked around behind the riser. Mick Mars sat quietly in his tent. I walked by Sixx and he said, "Lonn, go find some girls! Tommy will up be up there for a while!" The dutiful editor and friend obeyed like a good soldier and marched into the audience with a string of VIP laminates hanging around his neck. It wasn't five minutes before two girls caught my eye, bouncing up and down in their seats like a pair of jill-in-the-boxes. One was blonde, the other brunette. I gave 'em an acknowledging nod, whereupon they dashed from their seats to my side, hugging me like I was about to hand them winning lottery tickets. "You guys wanna go

backstage?" I asked rhetorically. They let out a wail you could hear across the Potomac. A moment later, I deposited the brunette in Nikki's tent and handed the blonde over to the front man. I didn't personally witness what transpired next, but you don't have to be a brain surgeon to figure it out.

When Tommy returned to his main onstage kit, Vince and Nikki both greeted their flying friend by placing their fingers underneath his nose, where he instantly caught a whiff that affirmed his bandmates had been doing anything but tuning up during the drum solo.

I would not wear the hat of groupie gatherer again, but throughout the *RIP* years, I bore occasional witness to the carnal cliché. One night in Fort Lauderdale, Florida, while on the road with Great White, I stood in awe as lead singer Jack Russell had his back-of-the-bus way with not one, not two, but three local ladies before his Plant-like pipes soared into song number one of the band's set. I even wrote about it in my feature "Back to the Bone Age," much to the elation of the insatiable singer.

The deeper I got in league with the bands and their free-for-all lifestyles, the more I fantasized about my own false sense of celebrity and ability to enjoy some rock-'n'-roll road-sanctioned misbehavior. I deluded myself into thinking that because I was with the band, I was as cool as the band. Truth is, I was more fool than cool and never got in much trouble. The fact that I wanted to, however, illustrated how distracted I became by the temptations of the road, and that alone caused me to begin to lose touch with my wife. But I was traveling constantly and too busy to notice. The magazine was getting soul all right, while its editor was losing his.

I got the call in the fall of 1990. *RIP* had been offered the only exclusive, all-access print coverage of the next Metallica studio

got one called 'Enter Sandman,' " confided the drummer. "It's about this children's fable that if you don't go to sleep, the sandman's gonna come and put sand in your eyes. Then there's one called 'Sad but True,' the title of which has been around for years. It's not really political—most of the stuff on this record isn't, unlike *Justice*, with its attacks on the system. 'Shortest Straw' was about blacklisting, and 'Eye of the Beholder' spoke of censorship. Most of the stuff on this record is first-person perspective, inner stuff."

As the months passed, I popped my head in at regular intervals, rolled tape, and took notes. One evening James revealed to the world and me the "tent of doom." "Moving the heavy blankets aside," I wrote, "I peer at the ten Marshall amps stacked on one side, facing a half dozen small but exacting microphones. The top of the tent is open." James went on to explain to me the secret of his undeniable sound. "Basically, this design kind of boxes in the sound," he explained. "And gets those real chunky parts where you really feel the air moving." It started to hit me that night how sacred this space truly was.

Jaymz (as he signed his name when giving autographs) was a complicated man. That may have been for reasons that had nothing to do with music. He was born August 3, 1963, in the dreary Southern California suburb of Downey. James not only had a comatose one-horse stucco town to drive him to his chaotic craft, but he was the child of Christian Scientists. When his mom fell gravely ill to cancer, she refused to seek medical help and passed away in the family's home. On the day she died, James's father made him and his siblings go to school. The courageous front man would dig deep and purge that demon on *Black* with the song "The God That Failed," a ballad of pain and closure inspired by and dedicated to his late mom.

While Lars and I could talk for hours, James was a man of few words who spoke through his lyrics and unequalled mastery of the rhythm axe. This record was changing him from a wild-eyed rebellious brat bent on annihilation to one of rock's most important figures. Here was a man who believed that without music, he would have died. In other words, he owed his life to Metallica, and conversely, they owed theirs to him.

After he showed me the tent, I asked James if he wanted to go to West Hollywood. Metallica's old publicist, Byron Hontas, was working with an all-girl metal band called Phantom Blue, playing the Roxy. "Cool," he said. "You drive so I can drink. Hee-hee." As soon as the doors shut on my Mazda 626, James pulled a tape out of his pocket. "You wanna hear some shit?" he barked, that classic, playful but sinister Hetfield grin creeping to the surface.

"Fuck, yeah! Pop it in!"

A rough mix of "Holier Than Thou" cracked the night air, my first raw, reckless, uncompromising taste of *Black*. We listened to it five times before pulling into the Roxy parking lot. The song was urgent, brutal, in both its rapid beat and its lyrical message. The gospel according to James.

> *Before you judge me, take a look at you*
> *Can't you find something better to do?*
> *Point the finger, slow to understand*
> *Arrogance and ignorance go hand in hand.*

Capped off by a face-melting Hammett guitar solo, it was vintage Metallica taken to a new sonic level by Bob Rock's rich production.

On the most memorable visit of the eleven-month studio

siege, the guys said they had a surprise for me. I arrived in the late afternoon and surprisingly James, Lars, Kirk, and Jason—Metallica intact—were in the house. Engineer Randy Staub came out to the lobby to fetch me. James, Lars, Kirk, Jason, Bob, and Randy surrounded me on the sofa facing the big monitors that hung above the console. "You ready for an ass puckering?" giggled James. They were all laughing until Bob gave Randy the green light. "Cue it up. And crank it!" All of sudden, I had to take a piss.

The opening notes were thunderous, rattling the studio and every molecule in my body. Then the song paused, as if it were taking a breath. As the drums cracked, the song settled into this pummeling, seductive groove. My mouth opened, my head began to move backward and forward, and every set of proud eyes was fixated on the writer reeling in the rapture.

Hey, I'm your life
I'm the one that takes you there!

I felt like I'd been swallowed by a grizzly bear.

You know it's sad but true!

The last crushing note of the song echoed away, and I slumped there, limp, exhausted, elated. "So, Mr. *RIP* magazine, what the fuck do you think?" chimed Lars. I don't remember whether I was clever, stupid, exacting, or incoherent. My instincts had told me that rock history was being made in this studio, but it wasn't until I heard the rough mix of "Sad but True" that I was absolutely certain. *Black* was destined to be an album for the ages. Like *Led Zeppelin IV,* Pink Floyd's *Dark Side of the*

Moon, Van Halen's *1984*, and AC/DC's *Back in Black*, it defined the moment in the ride where the wheels came completely off the tracks.

The last "Metalli-Watch" segment was printed in the October 1991 issue, featuring Alice Cooper on the cover. We had a three-month press lead, so the magazine was put to bed shortly before *Black* hit the streets. In that final installment, I wrote, " 'Enter Sandman' will startle Metallica fans. While it possesses the Metallica sound in all its monstrous glory, one thing is unbelievably evident that hasn't been on past efforts. James Hetfield is a singer. When he keens the song's powerful chorus, 'Exit light, enter night!' the Mighty H's voice positively soars." For the November 1990 *RIP* exclusive with James, I'd referred to him on the cover as "The Mighty Hetfield." The label stuck, for good reason.

Lars also confessed in that final piece that Bob Rock was responsible for James's vocal transformation from growler to singer. "Bob should be given total credit for making James feel comfortable enough to take that guard down and really sing," he said. "We always thought of ourselves as big, bad Metallica, but Bob taught us a new word none of us had ever heard before— soulful."

Metallica's fifth LP, officially untitled though proclaimed and forever known as "The Black Album" (as the Beatles had their "White Album"), was unleashed in August of 1991, the same month my weekly spot "Friend at Large" debuted on MTV's *Headbangers Ball*.

QPrime Management helped me christen my new boob-tube voyage by giving me an early pressing of the Metallica "Black Album" cover, which I showed to the world for the first time. My serendipitous foray from behind the desk to in front of the camera was the fallout of a fun and successful promotion be-tween *RIP* and *Headbangers Ball* called the Megadeth Party Bus.

Like Metallica, Dave Mustaine's second speed-metal four-some was a *RIP* favorite, so the idea was pitched to MTV for a special edition of the *Ball*. A big yellow school bus was secured, we set up a faux magazine office in the back, members of my staff, the band, and a video crew hopped on board, and we headed into West Hollywood to see what kind of trouble we could get into.

Arrangements were made for us to "accidentally" run into some heavy rockers while we were cruising around Los Angeles. At the Cat & Fiddle Pub on Sunset Boulevard, we met up with Slash and Duff from Guns N' Roses. Jon Bon Jovi "just hap-pened" to be in the place too. Then we headed west toward the ocean and the Santa Monica Civic Auditorium, where Ted Nu-gent and Armored Saint were performing. The Motor City Madman took us on *his* bus, showing off the amenities of his customized mobile hotel—big-screen TV, velvet-bedspread-covered queen-size bunk.

The producer of the segment, Carol Donovan, was so happy with the end result, she pitched the idea to MTV talent execu-tive John Cannelli that I might make a cool regular addition to the *Ball*. I came up with the tag Friend at Large and the concept that I would just talk about what was happening in hard rock music without a script, and we'd see how things developed. The initial spots were shot on a dull soundstage in Santa Monica, but the location for FAL soon changed to the actual *RIP* offices in Beverly Hills.

I began to take my 8-mm video camera on the road with me, gathering bits of behind-the-scenes moments with bands doing their thing. My weekly invasion into the headbanging living rooms of America was not only popular with the fans but with the music industry as well.

I rocked the *Ball* for two years until I was unceremoniously "unplugged" by the network in August 1993. Truth be told, I brought it on myself. My ouster was the political fallout of a scathing shot I took at the programmers of MTV in my "Friend to All" column in the powerful industry tip sheet *Hits*. I accused the media monolith of not playing the Masters of Reality video "She Got Me" from their *Sunrise on the Sufferbus* LP, because the band members were "too old."

Two weeks after I revealed to the world the *Black* cover, I was winging my way to London for another Castle Donington festival. This time, I had Joyce and our fourteen-month-old daughter, Megan, in tow. This was a really exciting adventure for the Friend family. Joyce hadn't been on a road trip with me since Meg was born, and we both loved England. Having our tiny blonde beauty with us made the journey all the more sweet.

The plan was for me to hook up with Metallica in London and fly with them for the next two gigs, Budapest and Munich, while the family remained in England for a minivacation. Megan fell asleep in my arms at the side of the Donington stage while the band played "Enter Sandman." We were based at the Conrad London hotel with several bands, including Mötley Crüe. Nikki Sixx's son, Gunner, a couple months younger than Meg, gave our daughter her first slobber on the lips while the kids were playing together. Talk about the fruit not falling far from the tattooed tree.

The flight to Budapest was a blast. The guys welcomed me deeper into the fold, chiding me as if I were one of the crew. Lars, however, was becoming visibly cocky on the heels of

Black's release in America. Elektra Records was predicting enormous first-week sales. He was feeling his oats in brave new ways. When we were passing through immigration in Budapest, Lars hid Kirk's passport, which no one, especially Kirk, found too amusing. Here we were in a formerly Communist country— only months since the Wall had come down—and the millionaire rock star was fucking with the system. Tour manager Ian Jeffery did a smooth song and dance and all was soon well. I sensed that there was more going on here than just old fraternity play between band members.

Metallica was joined in Budapest by the same groups that rocked Donington: AC/DC, Mötley Crüe, Queensrÿche, and the Black Crowes, but it was now billed as the Open Air Festival 1991 tour. I rode to the concert grounds with James, Kirk, and Jason. Lars wanted to get to the venue early. On that ride, I was made privy to the inside joke that led to a chain of events that would strangely etch my name on the stone tablets of Metallica mythology.

"Have you heard about the white leather jacket?" giggled the Mighty Hetfield.

"Uh, no," I responded.

"Lars bought this white leather jacket," he explained. "Because Axl had one. He wears it out at night. It's ridiculous." Lars and Axl had curiously bonded when both bands jammed together on November 9, 1990, at *RIP*'s fourth-anniversary party.

"Ask him about the jacket," said Kirk.

"When the time is right," James laughed.

That night, my phone rang about 2 A.M. *Who in the world could be calling me at this hour?* I thought. Joyce was in England, so I knew she was asleep. The Germans could bomb London again and she wouldn't wake up. Megan was a sound sleeper too. Once out, they were gone till morning. Unlike me, who hasn't slept more than a six-hour stretch since high school.

"Hello, Lonn?" asked the subdued voice.

"Uh, yes," I responded, groggily.

"It's Dave Mustaine. I know it's really late there and you're wondering why I'm calling." I paused for a second, grabbed my glasses off the nightstand, and composed myself. "Hi, Dave," I replied. "What's up, man?" For the next five minutes, I was party to my first twelve-step confessional. Dave Mustaine had battled heroin for years, and I guess he'd finally gotten clean and as part of the process of healing, he had to make contact with those he felt he'd done wrong.

Dave and Megadeth were always great to the magazine and me. When he and filmmaker Penelope Spheeris stopped by the office on their way to the Megadeth performance shoot for *The Decline of Western Civilization II: The Metal Years*, I gave Dave a *RIP* T-shirt, which he proudly donned for the awesome concert sequence. "I think I may have been an asshole to you a couple times," he confessed. "And I want to apologize. That's all I wanted to say. Good night, buddy."

The next morning, I knocked on Lars's door. He was anxiously awaiting the fax from the States with the first-week sales figures on *Black*. "Hey, man," he said. "I got a weird call last night from Dave Mustaine."

"So did I," I replied.

We shared a kind word for a courageous metal man battling the demons back home, but no one knows but Lars how much sleep he lost over the ousting of Mustaine. Dave's teary "sour grapes" diatribe in 2004's revealing documentary *Some Kind of*

Monster was one of the film's most engaging sequences and appeared to serve as the closure the talented guitarist had long sought and prayed for.

When the fax arrived, it was time to party. *Black* had opened at number one. "Fuck, man!" he laughed. "We're fucking number one! Metallica is number one! Can you fucking believe it? Listen, Lonn, I got a bunch of calls to make. I'll see ya later, okay?" The shift was on. You could see it in his eyes. World domination was now at hand.

Whatever success the band had enjoyed through the *Justice* years was about to be forever dwarfed by the *Black* monolith. Metallica was soaring out of the metal underground and into the mainstream rock stratosphere. And no one was feeling more invincible than Lars. His self-image was expanding in direct proportion to *Black*'s unit sales and concert grosses. Ross Halfin had recently given the drummer a new nickname: "Stars" Ulrich. The next night in Munich, we suffered our first head-on ego collision.

I was sitting in the bar of the German hotel talking to Hetfield and Mötley Crüe's Nikki Sixx, who were getting off turning the tables on me by conducting a mock interview. It was playful, by no means mean-spirited, but for some reason, my skin felt unusually thin that evening. I was walking a high wire and had no idea how far the fall was.

"Where's Lars?" I asked.

"He's at some club with Angus," said James. "Ask Tony Smith. He'll tell you. Lemme know if he's got the jacket on . . . hee-hee."

Tony was Lars's affable, accommodating Guy Friday who always knew where his boss was at any time of the day or night.

"He's doing a bit of celebrating, Lonn," Tony reported. "Watch yourself." The comment soared right past me as Tony told me the name of the club.

An hour later, I walked into a dark Deutschland disco pulsing with blaring music and sexy girls. I looked around and found Lars and AC/DC guitar legend Angus Young sitting in a roped-off lounge area with one of the crew's security gorillas standing watch. I approached the rope and waved to Lars. He looked three sheets to the Bavarian wind. Angus sipped tea (he never partied). But his abstinence wouldn't deter cofounder of the number-one-selling rock band in America from hoisting a few.

I knew I was out of place, but I took a seat next to Lars and interrupted his conversation by congratulating him on the number-one record. I can't recall the exact words he spit from his intoxicated tongue but they landed hard, and even though he was probably just teasing, I was poised for a meltdown and completely lost it in that moment. It was like I was the only person in the room standing stark naked and everyone was laughing at me. My heart sank in my chest, and all I wanted to do was get the fuck out of there, away from the scene, the stars, the stupidity, and everything else I'd become seduced by over the past several years. I headed straight for the exit. I never turned around to see if he was following me or even looking my way. I didn't care.

It wasn't his rude dismissiveness that got my goat and caused me to race for the door. I'd seen him in obnoxious, inebriated states many times before. Something else was happening to me. A shift was taking place. The ribbing earlier by James and Nikki, and now my closest compatriot of all brandishing a sarcastic sword my way—it was as if I had ceased acting and was now solely reacting. It was getting to be too much to handle. In that microcosmic moment as I spilled out into the damp Munich night, I questioned the friendship of every artist I'd come to know since the day the *RIP* ride began.

I grabbed a cab, went back to the hotel, packed up my things, wrote a very succinct "Fuck You!" note to Lars, slipped it under Ian's door, and made a beeline for the airport, where I caught the next flight back to London and my family, the people who really loved me. When I arrived at Conrad London late that night, Joyce said that Lars had called twice but didn't leave a message except to say call him immediately. I ignored him, explained to my wife what had happened, and ranted the victim's rant. Joyce had made reference over the past year to my own narcissistic state. I'm not sure she empathized with me. I really can't remember what she said. The drone of my own self-pity drowned out all external chatter.

Three days later when I got back to L.A. and the magazine, *RIP* art director Craig Jones and I constructed a dummy opener for a Metallica article called "The Swelling of Metallica," featuring a shot of the band with Lars's head blown up to five times its normal size. The copy read, " 'It's got to be white!' shouted Metallica skinmeister Lars Ulrich into his hotel room telephone. 'I mean, really white. You understand, fuckhead? Not some wimpy shit cream colored crap, but WHITE. White like the first virgin winter snow of my Danish homeland. HELLA WHITE! Get it!' As the skin-bashing Mr. U. hung up the phone, he wondered to himself, 'Will this leather jacket be different than all others created before it, or will people think I borrowed it from Axl?' "

You couldn't tell that the layout was bogus. I faxed the spread to QPrime as if it were authentic. "See what Lars thinks of the opening to my article," I wrote on the cover note. The image was forwarded to the band while still on tour in Europe.

The only thing good about insufferable, bombastic, back-slapping awards programs are the afterparties. A few weeks after my faux fax, I attended the Video Music Awards postshow soiree. MTV secured the entire back lot of Universal Studios for their thousand-plus virally imprudent pests, and that's exactly where I reconnected with the guys. "Hey, man, that magazine layout was hella cool," giggled James. "Lars stewed for days. I mean, it really fucked with his head. At first, everyone thought it was real. He's been wanting to talk to you pretty bad."

I was engaged in meaningless dialogue with someone from the industry when he found me, took me aside, and started to speak from what I know was his heart. "I'm really sorry about that night in Munich," he said. "I mean, I was just fucking with you. But I guess I came off as a bit of an asshole. Believe me, you weren't the only one I was being insensitive to. Listen, man, you're my friend. Not just the fucking editor of *RIP* fucking magazine. You're my friend and that means a lot to me. Are we cool?"

"Yeah, we're cool, man." And it hit me then and there how much I loved this band—especially Lars. And not because they were Metallica and they'd let me in to ride their lightning. But, rather, because they helped me to understand the ethos of celebrity, up close and personal, Lemmy-sized warts and all.

"I think of you as my friend, too, Lars," I said. "I hope it'll always be that way. But seriously, dude, you gotta lose that jacket! I heard Sebastian just bought one."

"Fuck off!"

3

Wonder in Alice Land

"WRITE THE THINGS WHICH THOU HAST SEEN,
AND THE THINGS WHICH ARE, AND THE THINGS
WHICH SHALL BE HEREAFTER."

—*Revelation 1:19*

What's the best scene from the original *Wayne's World*? C'mon, I'll give you a hint: "We're not worthy! We're not worthy!" That's right! Mullet-headed underground cable-access-TV hosts Wayne and Garth are at a rock concert, flashing their laminates proudly as they prance cluelessly about the backstage area, until they finally come upon the madman himself, who explains the linguistic origin of the word *Milwaukee* to his guitarist Pete Freezin'. "It's pronounced 'mill-e-wah-que,' " he says dryly. Dumbstruck at the sight of their hero in the flesh, the dynamic duo drop to their knees and launch into the now-classic moronic mantra, their arms and torsos rising and falling in rapturous praise to the one, the only Alice Cooper.

That about describes my own adolescent adulation for rock's mythological maestro. I discovered Alice in high school, early '70s, thanks to my younger brother Rick, who happened upon the LP *Love It to Death* in the cutout bins of Moby Disc Records in Van Nuys. "You have to hear 'Ballad of Dwight Fry'!" he said excitedly, laying the platter on the turntable. "It's amazing. I'll get the tennis rackets! We have to air guitar!"

Alice was blasting into the mainstream with "Eighteen," but my brother and I didn't really listen to the radio. We were album collectors, and it was our mission with each new record that entered the Friend enclave to dig deep into the grooves and suck out the vim, vigor, and venom of every song. We played *Love It to Death* to death (figuratively speaking of course; you can scratch vinyl but you can't kill it) along with every single Alice LP over the next six years.

Killer, School's Out, Billion Dollar Babies, Muscle of Love, and *Welcome to My Nightmare* followed *Love It to Death*. Bob Ezrin, coarchitect of the Alice gestalt, produced every record. It represents one of the most prolific creative runs in the history of rock recording. Alice took me and mine right through college, bitch-slapping our senses over and over again with a horrific fun house of melodies, visual tricks, and unearthly escape routes that every kid growing up in the staid and sullen San Fernando Valley glommed onto for dear life.

The *Welcome to My Nightmare* tour hit the L.A. Forum in the winter of 1975. This was rock-'n'-roll theater in its purest and strangest form—guillotines and spiderwebs, snakes and spooky images designed to shake us out of our collective San Fernando stupors. Leaving the building that night after the concert, my ears were ringing and my heart was soaring. It never crossed my mind that someday I would meet the mascara'd man, play a key role when his career reached a crossroads, and beyond that, call him friend.

. . .

Our first encounter took place on a golf course in the L.A. suburb of Calabasas on a rainy day in the spring of 1989. Epic Records A&R executive Bob Pfeifer set up the round. He'd recently signed Alice to a new deal, and there was great optimism around the label that this effort possessed all the earmarks of a comeback. Not that Alice needed to come back from anywhere. For two decades, he'd stamped his legend on the forehead of rock 'n' roll with a dizzying array of iconoclastic albums and tours. He'd long established himself as the godfather of shock rock, the emperor of onstage theatrics.

But in the unit-driven, commercially conscious "what have you done for us lately" world of entertainment, Alice Cooper hadn't seen a song ride the charts since his 1978 ballad "How You Gonna See Me Now." Being a household name is one thing, having a hit is another, and the Cooper camp felt that they had a monster in the cage but could use a little help from the media to set that beast loose.

Pfeifer and Epic's publicity department made it crystal clear from the get-go. "We want the cover of *RIP*," they said. We were riding a circulation and credibility high on the heels of our exclusive Guns N' Roses and Metallica coverage. Everyone was talking about us, even the legends. Pfeifer knew that I played golf, one of Alice's passions, though still in the closet at this time. But he didn't need to romance me with eighteen holes or dangle any other carrot. Alice was one of my childhood heroes. I'd have stood on a mountaintop in an electrical storm with a five iron in my hand to make his hallowed acquaintance.

The raindrops kept Pfeifer from joining us for the round,

but that was just fine. This was about Alice and me. The Coop was on the putting green when I arrived. "I like a man who isn't afraid to golf in the rain," he said, shaking my hand. "Are you kidding?" I replied. "I'm ready for thirty-six!" The next four hours were loaded with laughs. He told jokes and stories about the wild, decadent days of old, like the time he was so drunk he passed out onstage with his head in the guillotine and almost broke his neck!

What struck me even deeper, however, was that the *man* Alice Cooper was the absolute antithesis of that deep, dark, sinister character that had welcomed me and mine into his devilish nightmare at the crack of the '70s. He asked questions about my wife, where and when I got married, how I liked running a magazine, and when I had picked up the game of golf. He popped open cans of Diet Coke every other hole and shared a package of Cheez'N Crackers with me at the turn. He was warm, funny, and utterly, humbly human.

At the end of the round we had a sandwich, and Coop handed me an advance cassette of *Trash*. "It's unmastered but I think you'll get the idea," he said. No pressure, no hype, but his eyes beheld a sense of both pride and enthusiasm. "Hey, let's play again sometime," he smiled. The next morning at the office, after spending the evening with the tape, I green-lighted the cover story, sans protest from the staff. Del asked to write the story but I assigned the piece to Bruce "Screamin' Lord" Duff, a massive Alice fan who'd made the plea first.

I gave the task of taking the cover photo to the eccentric Glen LaFerman, one of the best portrait rock photographers around and a giant Cooper fan. When Glen shot the artists that he truly loved, the real magic would materialize. Coop was having a blast as Glen cranked *Trash* on the stereo and danced about with his Hasselblad. "He's having a great time," said Coop's longtime assistant, Brian Nelson. "This is going to be awesome."

Brian was right. When the Cooper camp received the proofs of our session, they went crazy for one of the images, a beautiful, pensive shot of Alice with his head down. Both Pfeifer and Alice's manager, Shep Gordon—who had watched over the icon's career since day one—called my office and asked if Epic could procure a shot from our session for the cover of *Trash*. I was honored but conflicted. If I gave them my session, what would I use for the cover?

RIP's success was predicated on our devotion to quality of content in text, image, and graphic design. Our insistence on exclusive photography helped give the magazine its cool look and vibe. As luck would have it, noted photographer Lynn Goldsmith appeared on my radar to solve the problem. She offered to photograph Alice and turn the shots around in a day. And even better than that, Epic offered to pay for the session and give *RIP* the exclusive cover image. It was a win-win proposal.

Lynn delivered a spellbinding full-bleed facial image of Alice on a washed-out snow-white background, his hands clinched close to his chin grasping a pair of handcuffs, his eyes piercing the camera. Glen's shot adorned the cover of what became Alice's first multiplatinum release in ten years—fueled by the big-hook vintage-riff single "Poison"—and the October *RIP* went on to become the second-biggest-selling issue of 1989, a notch behind the April "Axl with Shotgun" cover.

It was the first time in my life that I felt like I'd given something back to one of the rock heroes that had given so much to me. But I didn't realize the extent of Alice's appreciation until a specially created plaque arrived in my office one afternoon. It was a framed, autographed original print run of the *Trash* cover. "Lonn, it's *your* cover. Thanks. Alice."

Cooper and *RIP* joined forces again for his next LP, *Hey Stoopid*. We did a hilarious session of Alice in a bathtub dropping an electric hair dryer into the water for the cover of the October 1991 issue. Neal Preston shot Alice in a Hannibal Lecter leather mask for the inside spread, and Del James finally got to interview Alice for the feature, "The Silence of the Coop."

Alice Cooper put the bottle down for good in the early '80s. Here was a man that rocked the bottom of a glass since fame and fortune arrived shortly after "Eighteen" rearranged the pop culture in 1971, twenty years before Nirvana evoked the same postadolescent angst in their apocalyptic "Smells Like Teen Spirit." The anthem made Alice an overnight hit, and an overnight drunk. But I never personally knew the intoxicated Alice.

Our friendship grew throughout the '90s on a foundation of the dimpled white ball. He nicknamed me "Angry" after reading my editorial in the September 1990 issue of *RIP* we devoted to censorship. "Wake up and smell the oat bran, youth of America," I wrote. "Censorship is alive and well in the great U.S. of A.! It's coming at ya in many forms from various sources, and it's affecting what you're allowed to see on TV, hear on the radio, listen to on your CD or record player and, we kid you not, read in your favorite heavy-metal magazine."

The cover of that issue featured Ozzy Osbourne with one of those old PMRC warning stickers over his mouth. Kindred spirits in the foundation of heavy, avant-garde rock 'n' roll, Alice and Ozzy always had a flotsam-and-jetsam relationship based on creative integrity and mutual respect. Ozzy had even laid down a guest vocal on *Hey Stoopid*. They had never, however, appeared together on the same radio show until May 24, 1992.

I was hosting *The Pirate Radio Friendship* in L.A., the 100.3 FM local forerunner to my syndicated airwave adventure *Pirate Radio Saturday Night with Lonn Friend*. Ozzy was live in the studio with me and in rare form. He'd brought his eight-year-old daughter, Amy, into the booth with him, so terribly shy she barely uttered a peep the entire two hours her daddy was on the air, except when the Oz asked her if she read *Hustler* magazine. "No," she giggled, "but my dad makes a very nice shepherd's pie." After ten minutes of warm-up banter, Ozzy went to the bathroom and I had my engineer, Jamie, dial up Alice at home. I'd set the call to surprise Ozzy and the listeners, having made no promotional announcement about what was about to become a historic radio moment.

Coming out of the song "Hey Stoopid," I opened the mike and let the god speak. "How goes it, Alice?" roared Ozzy. "You know I never got a chance to thank you for allowing me to sing on your record."

Alice thanked him for the comment and replied, "I think we'd met each other like four hundred times, but we were both so drunk, we never remembered it!"

Whereupon Ozzy responded, "Isn't it funny that all of sudden you get sober and say, 'Hey, I know that guy!' "

Then I asked, "Who drank more in the '70s?"

"I don't know," giggled Ozzy. "I think it was a toss-up between Alice and myself."

"When I went from beer to whiskey, I obliterated at least six years," added Alice.

"Well," fired back Ozzy, "I suddenly woke up and found out I was married . . . twice, and had seven kids . . . and had been on the road for ten years!"

Alice then commended Ozzy for the blistering antibooze

ballad "Demon Alcohol" on his latest LP and laughed, "You know, I had a blood test last week, and I haven't had a drink in ten years and I'm still legally drunk!"

When I left *RIP* in 1994, I lost touch with a lot of the rockers that'd I come to know well during that magical seven-year run. One artist, however, that I got closer to after *RIP* was Alice. In fact, it was his creative counterpart, Bob Ezrin—also known for his work with KISS and Pink Floyd—who helped resurrect my media career in December 1999. That's when I was hired by the legendary record producer and former Motörhead comanager Rob Jones to oversee the editorial content of KNAC.com, a live, streaming Internet radio station devoted to hard-rock music.

And so it happened, the unexpected. I was on a short personal trip to Phoenix. My youngest brother, Michael, had just landed the front-office-manager position at the Pointe Hilton, Tapatio Cliffs Resort in Scottsdale. Fifteen years my junior, Michael was my biggest fan. He was going to college in Virginia during the years I was on MTV's *Headbangers Ball* and called me on more than one occasion, slightly hammered, with a potential angelic conquest in his sights. "Bro," he'd slur, "tell Debbie you're my brother. We're watching you right now! Dude, she doesn't believe it!"

Whether my being on MTV or the backstage passes I gave him ever got Michael laid or not is irrelevant. He wanted to pay me back in his own way. "Come down and I'll hook you up for a nice suite, comp'd. The property has an awesome golf course, too. Call Alice. The pro down there will flip out!"

The day was perfect. Warm, slightly breezy, late spring—an Arizona postcard. It had been a while since the Coop and I had played a round together, but we picked up right where we'd left off. He was beating me and I was fine with it. What became evi-

WONDER IN ALICE LAND   65

dent somewhere around the twelfth hole, however, was that the content of our conversation had completely changed. I was confessing to my hero-turned-friend the changes that I'd been going through over the past few years, how things at home weren't that good. My wife didn't seem to understand me anymore. No one did. In midlife, I'd become more of a misfit than the kid who once lip-synced "Billion Dollar Babies" into the teeth of a hairbrush.

I told him how much I loved my daughter and how I was feeling a bit guilty about checking out of the family and not being as devoted a dad as I could. And then I mentioned what books I was reading, that I had been studying yoga under the Kundalini master Guru Singh. I could see in Alice's eyes that he was down with my struggle.

"You know, Lonn," he said, "you have to get empty."

"Get empty?" I replied.

"That's right, empty," he fired back, pulling a six iron from his Callaway golf bag for the 180-yard approach shot to the green.

"What happens after I get empty, Coop?" I asked.

"You get filled up," he grinned, whereupon the godfather of shock rock stroked it pure and sweet, landing his pill on the soft green pillow five feet from the pin. Like his golf swing, Alice's life appeared to me then as effortless. The golf swing requires two things: faith and agility. If you lack either, you're in trouble. Alice Cooper was having no trouble with this round or this life. There was something more in that big black bag than just funny-looking sticks with numbers on them.

"Hey, Coop, after the round, let's do an interview. I've got my tape recorder in the car. We haven't had a good on-the-record rap in years. I'll write it up for the Web site."

"Sure," he responded without hesitation. "Why not? But first we'll go to Cooper's Town for dinner." That's Alice's restaurant, his very own Hard Rock Cafe, so to speak, a bastion of memorabilia located across the street from the two sports venues where the Diamondbacks and the Suns play. A joint business venture between Coop and his pals—Shep Gordon, baseball legends Ryne Sandberg and Randy Johnson, Megadeth's Dave Mustaine, and legendary Arizona concert promoter Danny Zelisko—the lively eatery had become a destination for anyone who wanted to get some good eats and feel the spirit of the incomparable Alice Cooper. That spirit, incidentally, was driving this entire day.

With a stuffed belly and two nice Cooper's Town-logo golf shirts in possession, we rolled into the parking lot of the Pointe. All afternoon, I'd been feeling extremely fortunate to have a friend like Alice. And when I began to roll tape, I let go of all expectations. I'm not sure I had any to begin with. What resulted was not just the most honest interview of my entire career but also an illustration of one artist's fearless devotion to truth. Alice revealed to me—and to the world for the first time—that he was a devout, practicing Christian. Like his golf swing, the confession was effortless.

"I was pretty much convinced all my life that there was just one God, and there was Jesus Christ, and there was the devil," he said. "You couldn't believe in God without believing in the devil. I always tell bands that the most dangerous thing you can do is to believe in the *concept* of the devil or the *concept* of God, because you're not giving them full credit. When you believe in God, you've got to believe in the all-powerful God. He's not just God, he's the all-powerful God, and he has total control over everyone's life.

"The devil, on the other hand, is a real character that's trying his hardest to tear your life apart. If you believe that this is just mythology, you're a prime target, because you know that's exactly what Satan wants: to be a myth. But he's not a myth, of this I'm totally convinced. More than anything in the world, I'm convinced of that. So, here we are. We have God pulling us one way and the devil pulling us another, and we're in the middle. We have to make a choice. And everybody, at some point in his or her life, has to make that choice. When people say, 'How do you believe this? Why do you believe this?' I just say nothing else speaks to my heart. This doesn't speak to my intellect, it doesn't speak to my logic—it speaks right to my heart and right to my soul, deeper than anything I've ever thought of. And I totally believe it. That being said, I'm not a very good Christian. I mean, none of us are ever *good* Christians. That's not the point. When you're a Christian, it doesn't mean you're gonna be good, it means you've got a harder road to pull."

Alice inspired many in his long and illustrious career. There are pieces of him in acts ranging from Nine Inch Nails, Twisted Sister, Poison, and Mötley Crüe to Adam Ant, Hanoi Rocks, and W.A.S.P. But no one morphed and mangled the Cooper mystique with more arrogance or eloquence than '90s shock rocker Marilyn Manson.

"Manson has a lot of style, I'll give him that, and I have never criticized him for anything he has done onstage theatrically," Alice observed. "The only thing I've had a problem with is his view on Christianity. He's very vocal about it. I believe *Antichrist Superstar* was pointed right directly at me. I didn't volley the first shots in this whole thing. His whole anti-Christian thing, and I'm like 'Hey, I'm Christian, and I'm not going to denounce what I believe.' I can be a rock 'n' roll star, a Christian, and Alice

Cooper. But like we were talking about before, Marilyn Manson spends most of his time in character. I've never met one person in the world that could be their character all the time. You paint yourself into a corner when you say, 'I am Marilyn Manson,' or 'I am Rob Zombie,' or 'I am this guy' all the time. They're not! You know, how could Manson be Manson when he takes his girlfriend to dinner or goes Christmas shopping for his mother? The Marilyn Manson rock-star dark character doesn't go Christmas shopping, and he wouldn't be caught dead in a restaurant, you know what I mean? So you paint yourself into a corner when you say, 'I'm going to wear this mask all the time.' "

That's when I posed the question, "Christianity has always been a very private issue with you. You've rarely preached to anyone in song, except for perhaps 'My God' off *Lace and Whiskey*, which was still far subtler than, say, Stryper tossing Bibles into the audience during their late-'80s concert performances or, more recently, Creed's pretentious proselytizing. What do you think tweaked Manson about the church?"

"I think Marilyn had a really bad Christian experience when he was younger," he replied. "My guess is he got involved with some less-than-Christian Christians, and that really, forgive the expression, nailed him. You know, he's one of the greatest button pushers I've ever met. And I know that game because I invented that game: how to push buttons and piss people off. Manson clicked because he found a whole new set of buttons to push—he even pushed my buttons, which is pretty impressive since I was pushing buttons before he was born. I'd really love to sit down and talk to Marilyn, not just about religion, but about anything. I've read interviews with him. He's very bright and quite funny, too. I'd probably get along with him very well."

The entire, exhaustive Q&A ran on the KNAC.com Web

site under the title "Alice Cooper: Prince of Darkness/Lord of Light." Faith-based author Mark Joseph cited the published exchange as the inspiration for his second book, *Faith, God, and Rock and Roll*, an enlightening examination of the connection between spirit and music.

That's what that moment in the desert was all about: connection. There we sat, the hero and the fan, the rocker and the writer, the Christian and the Jew, friend and Friend, in a parking lot in Phoenix, talking about God.

4

Chicken Soup for the Rubber Soul

I emerged from my mother's womb July 29, 1956, but I was born on February 9, 1964, the day the Beatles first performed on *The Ed Sullivan Show*. If you were in front of the television or anywhere else in the world within earshot of that event, you unwittingly became part of the miracle. Our collective musical consciousness was born. We learned what it was to love music, to love a rock band, to love . . . period. I love music and have observed, composed on, and examined it both personally and professionally my entire life for two reasons: I am the son of a piano player, and I was born with the Beatles.

The first time I ever experienced the intangible buzz came during the days leading up to that big bang in popular culture. I can recall with surreal clarity how everyone on the schoolyard that Friday afternoon was talking about this band ("Band? What's a band?") from England ("England? Where's that?") who played rock 'n' roll ("Rock 'n' roll?"). I was seven years old, a class clown with a four-year-old little brother and a mother fresh from divorce.

It was 1964. No VCRs, no TiVo, no Internet, no DVDs. All we had was television, and if you missed a show, that was it. My brother Rick and I planted our prepubescent butts down on the living-room floor of our $120-a-month duplex at 7:45 P.M. My mother was oblivious to the event that was about to unfold before her and the rest of civilization. She was still grieving over JFK and the departure of my dad.

We sat on the floor in front of our black-and-white set. As showtime approached, our toes started wiggling. Then the screen went black, and boom: opening shot, that odd-looking old man with the hunched shoulders, tacky suit, and high voice is on camera. He starts talking about the craziness that's been taking place around the TV studio ever since their plane touched down. The introduction was brief because the audience was screaming so loudly. "Here they are . . . the Beatles!"

Rick and I were bouncing as Paul McCartney's face filled the screen and the first notes of "All My Loving" poured out of his smiling mouth and into the Milky Way. It was like tasting a Hershey's bar for the first time. For the next two minutes, the camera darted back and forth between Paul up front on bass, John Lennon on rhythm guitar, the frail George Harrison on lead guitar, and the silly, happy man named Ringo banging the drums. Intercut with shots of screeching females who'd lost all sense of decorum, whipped into momentary madness by this magical new music, the scene represents a snapshot of the earth knocked off its axis.

I'm not sure that I'd ever heard a song before "I Want to Hold Your Hand" exploded off the radio a few days before the

Sullivan show. A song. My father was a traveling musician, but memories of seeing him perform before my parents split up are nonexistent. For all intents and purposes, music came into my life via the Beatles. And from the very first notes I was hooked, and have been for more than four decades.

Sitting in the here and now, a half century after the doc slapped me on the ass and I wailed my first "yeah, yeah, yeah," I trace my time on this planet, trying to make sense out of why things occurred the way they did, the decisions I made, the mistakes, the successes, the failures. Throughout it all, crazy as it may seem, there is one constant: the Beatles. Through thick and thin, wherever I roamed, I have always depended on them, on their songs, to lift me when I was down or to reconnect me when I was falling apart. I know them all by heart because they are a part of my heart.

The Beatles were in love with life, fame, women, spirit, drugs, heaven, hell, earth, sea, and sky. But mostly, they were in love with love. They journeyed in and found melody's holy grail. "Michelle," "In My Life," "Wait," "If I Needed Someone." These were psalms from the right ventricle delivered in three-minute harmonious ooo-la-la-la tones. Musical poetry, warm butter on hot biscuits. Mmmm. So good that my first kiss came as a result of singing "Girl" from *Rubber Soul.*

My mother, brother, and I resided on a suburban avenue where not much happened. Carol lived across the alley behind our stucco two-bedroom dwelling. She had short black hair and chalk-white skin. There was a playhouse in her tiny backyard. The inside was dark, cloudy, gray, like the sky on this particular day. Her mom was in the house. We were playing Mr. and Mrs. John Lennon, way before Yoko. I was eight years old.

The rain was falling, a rare occurrence in Southern California's San Fernando Valley. She shut the door of the playhouse and grabbed me, wrinkling my sweater. And then, the magnificent moment, eternal as the song. Her lips were cold, wet, and wonderful. She pressed them so hard against mine. It must have lasted a minute. I came up for air and immediately went back for more. Ambrosia. Ecstasy. An early glimpse of what the boys were singing about. Love. Wow.

You rarely discover music on your own. There is usually a friend or sibling who's getting the message along with you. With Rick three years my junior and not quite as sophisticated in the early ways of rock as I, Ron Meyers emerged as my Beatle "brother," right from the start. That's where our long and winding friendship began. But Ron didn't just listen to the Beatles; he dissected them. While I drifted away into the melodies, my bespectacled friend examined the construction of the songs, the meaning in the lyrics, and the development of the personalities of the band members.

His sister Leslie had a record player in her room. She got home from school two hours after we did. One day, she burst through the front door as we were cranking the new single "I Feel Fine" / "She's a Woman." L.A. AM radio stations KHJ and KRLA were playing the songs virtually every hour, but that hadn't been enough. We'd bought the disc. Did the same thing when "Hey Jude" / "Revolution" came out.

"Guess what, boys?" shouted Leslie over Paul's vocals.

"What?" we said.

She reached into her purse and whipped out two small, rectangular pieces of paper.

"What's that?" we asked, momentarily breaking our musical hypnosis.

"Read 'em and weep, suckers!" Leslie had the goods and

she rubbed our faces in it. The Beatles, live at the Hollywood Bowl.

"No way!" we screamed. The roar illustrated both our elation that someone we actually knew was going to see the Beatles in concert, but also our extreme pain and frustration that it wasn't going to be us witnessing what history would prove to be one of the very few live performances the Fab Four would ever permit their massive American fandom.

The Beatles hated their debut touring adventure of the States. It was just too big, too insane. The fans were out of their minds; stadiums full of psychopaths so loud, John, Paul, George, and Ringo could barely hear themselves. They did thirty-five minutes at Shea Stadium. That was enough.

Between 1966 and 1969, when the Beatles escalated into their creative psychedelic run the likes of which popular music had never seen (and will never see again), we were in that room every day, holding court with our four shamans, friends, saviors. We were morphing into adolescents. The Who's *Tommy* had come out and blown our minds. Rod Serling's *Twilight Zone* was in reruns on KTLA Channel 5, and we watched it every afternoon. Our childhoods were ending, and so, as we would soon discover, were the Beatles.

The '70s birthed free-form, guitar-driven, progressive, out-there, punk, and funk musical exploration that expanded upon everything that the Liverpool quartet had created in the scant seven years prior. The decade was born with the death of the Beatles. Ron and I found out about the catastrophic breakup where we got most of my rock 'n' roll news: Moby Disc. The first Moby Disc was straight out of Nick Hornby's novel *High Fidelity*. There was a guy who worked there named Dana, the accidental model of Jack Black's character in Stephen Frears' beautiful film adaptation of the book.

Overweight and overly critical of each LP that entered the store, Dana knew what was going on with every band from Van Nuys to Vancouver. Ron and I went out to buy the new LP, *Let It Be*, but had no idea that the band had broken up. Paul McCartney had announced to the press on April 11, 1970—a month before the release of *Let It Be*—that he would not record with John Lennon again.

"Yeah, it's over," said Dana flatly. "This is the last record. They had a nice run. Still think it's been downhill since *Sgt. Pepper's*." We weren't paying attention to Dana or his judgmental babble. We walked out of the store clutching *Let It Be* like we were holding the Bible.

The '70s was the decade I discovered live music and marijuana. Ron went on an exploratory mission to Santa Cruz and I went to UCLA. I saw him once, on my wedding day in June 1986. He showed up in a black overcoat. I couldn't see his eyes, he was wearing sunglasses. We talked about the Beatles, the days in his sister's room, how lucky we were to have been there as it was happening, living the moment together. He told me he loved me and disappeared out the front door of the restaurant just as the reception was kicking into gear. I never saw Ron again, but every time I hear "I Am the Walrus," I think of him.

Running *RIP* magazine, I started to live the dream, getting paid to travel the world with rock stars. I was meeting the men who made the music. KISS, Metallica, Def Leppard, Guns N' Roses, Skid Row, Mötley Crüe, Bon Jovi, and Aerosmith, those were *RIP*'s bands, the fans' bands, my bands. I never got to write about the Beatles—at least I never got *paid* to write about them.

But as my fly-on-the-wall professional experience began to man-ifest, I did find myself buzzing about a Beatle on two occasions. The first time, I swatted myself. The second, I flapped my wings.

It was New Year's Eve, 1994. Joyce, Megan, and I were vaca-tioning on Maui, where Alice's manager, Shep Gordon, was holding his annual soiree on the beach. Shep owned a spectacu-lar property on the Kihei side of the island, and on this particu-lar evening, the place was electric with human energy. More than a hundred guests, locals and mainlanders, common folk, movie stars, chefs, and notables mingled. Alice Cooper's daugh-ter Calico was making a beaded bracelet for my daughter when I looked up and saw him, six feet away, engaged in conversation with my billion-dollar golfing buddy.

"Look, Lonn, a Beatle," observed my wife matter-of-factly. "Here's your chance. He's talking to Alice. I bet he'll introduce you." It was George Harrison all right, sipping a Coke on Shep's patio, on a rock in the middle of the Pacific, a world away from L.A. and Liverpool.

I can't explain, even in hindsight, why I simply could not talk to the Beatle George that evening. Alice walked up to me and said, "You wanna meet George?" But I couldn't. I wasn't ready. I'd never been shy about meeting anyone who'd ever wielded an axe, no matter how famous, but something told me that this was not the right time or place to introduce myself. It was seven years later, five thousand miles from Maui, in the wake of Sep-tember 11, 2001, that I got another shot at meeting a Beatle.

Anthrax's Scott Ian and I were attending the afterparty of the VH1 Concert for New York, a noble, star-studded event de-voted to raising money for the Big Apple and the spirits of its battered residents. We were holding court in a roped-off VIP enclave, chatting with friends, actors, and rockers. Jon Bon Jovi and Richie Sambora were by my side when he passed by, just two feet from me. The Beatle Paul. I remembered New Year's Eve, Maui, 1994, and the lost opportunity with George.

I swallowed hard, took a deep, yogic breath, and flashed back to Sherman Oaks, the days in my room playing the records, singing the lyrics, forgetting about anything and everything except how much I loved the music and the men who played it.

Sir Paul hugged Jon and Richie, chatted for an instant, and then came face to face with your humble narrator. I reached out my hand and we shook. It was one of those intimate shakes where one takes the hand that's not doing the shaking and joins the hand that is effectively sandwiching the hand of the individual being shook. I wanted to bottle that moment and take it with me. Eye contact, an instant of pressed flesh, and he was gone. Hello Goodbye.

I loved Paul in the innocent days of my childhood. But Lennon was the Beatle I yearned to meet, because as my life unfolded, he fascinated me more and more. As my journey got more complicated, John's songs really began to resonate.

The first *Plastic Ono Band* LP, *Imagine*, and *Walls and Bridges* are existential works, comprised of beautiful yet punishingly truthful songs that are as strong as his best Beatle efforts. But given that he was a solo artist for almost a decade before his untimely, violent departure at the hands of Mark David Chapman, Lennon's musical output was relatively sparse. Nevertheless, he remains my most-beloved personal rock-'n'-roll hero, and the day he died, millions of fans—myself included—felt a part of themselves die too.

I was home listening to the radio in my bedroom. The dial was tuned to the great old L.A. rock station KMET-FM. "A little bit of heaven, 94.7, KMET, tweedeedledee." Luminary DJ Jim Ladd was in the middle of a set when he broke in and told us that he'd just heard the news today. Oh, boy. While most of America was watching *Monday Night Football* and getting the sad scoop from TV color man Howard Cosell, I was in my room, just like the Beach Boys song. In my room, where I'd spent hours spinning the Beatles, mourning the terrible loss of John Lennon.

Later that night, I drove fifty miles southeast of Sherman Oaks to Anaheim, home of Disneyland, to join Terry Gladstone, a disc jockey for the Orange County rock station KEZY-FM. She was on air playing Lennon, angry and despairing, like so many of us were. I got to know Terry by calling the station when she was on air and talking about music with her. Our friendship was born over our mutual love of the Beatles.

I sat with her in the studio until 2 A.M., selecting my favorite Lennon tracks to share with the audience of fans who were feeling the pain just like we were.

When a legendary artist is taken, the fans have nothing left but the music to console them. That's what I did after the death of Lennon. I went back and listened to the albums, more deeply this time.

When we are faced with the challenge of darkness and loss, music can offer an explanation, comfort, a way out. So it was when the light of another Beatle faded shortly after Thanksgiving 2001. It was early Friday morning in Miami Beach. I was spending a couple days at the palatial estate of MTV/mass-media legend Les "the Garman" Garland, a mentor and friend since my *RIP* days. I was out on the back grass adjacent to the Garman's pool, doing my morning meditation, when the perfect silence of a warm Florida sunrise was broken.

"Bud," said the Garman, using the name he'd given me al-

most twelve years ago when I first met this indefinable, spectacular fellow. "It's George, Bud. He's gone." I didn't understand.
"Only two left, Bud. Very sad day. Very sad." Recognition, like a
bucket of ice water on a Buddhist monk. I sat in stunned silence,
shaking my head.

Gliding through the various cool environs of Club Garland,
I passed through the billiard room and noticed the framed
Beatles plaque with an original ticket stub from Shea Stadium.
Went nicely with the photograph of him in the late '70s passing
a joint to Paul McCartney backstage. Garland has so many magnificent mementos from an incredible career that began in radio
around the time the lads landed in New York City. He co-
founded MTV, The Box, and The Tube, and I've watched him
do his thing since we met on a *RIP* road trip in the late '80s. On
November 30, 2001—the day after George Harrison took off
for the sun—Garland was simply a friend, a fellow grieving fan,
and the afternoon's *fab*ulous DJ.

Upon returning to L.A. later that week, I played *Abbey Road*
for Megan (who was then ten years old) for the first time. This
was her virgin long-form Beatles encounter. I could feel it when
I popped the CD into my car deck after picking her up from
school and she took the jewel case from my hand to examine the
cover. This was that moment I'd been imagining for years. The
passing of the torch. I never pressed it. I had already endured
countless hours of stomach-wrenching, corporate-pop crapola.
Britney. N' Sync. Pointless, purposeless, soulless audio nothing-
ness. In the blink of a beautiful adolescent eye, the course was
changed.

"This is George, right?" she asked, pointing to his image,
half knowing the answer already. "Was he the youngest?"

"Yes, he was," I responded. "This photograph was taken on

Abbey Road in London, where the Beatles recorded—Abbey Road Studios. See how they're all walking with their left foot first, except Paul? It was part of this ingenious rumor that Paul was dead." I was in storytelling nirvana, my genetic reflection of beauty times ten listening carefully.

"They scattered clues over several records," I continued. "See the license plate on the car? 28 IF. Paul was twenty-eight when this album was recorded. At the end of 'Strawberry Fields Forever' on *Magical Mystery Tour*, you can hear John clearly say, 'I buried Paul.' And then, this was the weirdest, if you played 'Revolution 9' from the 'White Album' backward—you could do that with vinyl—it sounded exactly like 'Turn me on, Dead Man.' " My daughter was fixated. I was on a roll.

I tried to explain to Megan that everyone was a Beatles fan back then. The band connected us to one another. She didn't really get what I was trying to say until I grabbed for a piece of Hollywood symbolism, recalling the mashed-potato scene from the movie *Close Encounters of the Third Kind*, in which lots of people started seeing the image of Devil's Tower—the landing spot for the aliens. I explained how these "touched" individuals were feeling something that they didn't really understand. They just knew they weren't alone in that shared sensation. It was beyond their control. That was the Beatles. They had landed and we all wanted to see them, feel them, and most of all, hear them.

I wanted Megan to at least get a sense of how the Beatles were bigger than anything. "They were a thousand times bigger than the Backstreet Boys, who, by the way, will be completely forgotten in five years," I lectured.

"They're already over, Dad," she fired back, nonchalantly.

Thank God, I thought.

Elton John wrote in the January 17, 2002, issue of *Rolling*

Stone, "George was the sage of the Beatles. He found something worth more than fame." I was finding that, too, here in that time of professional and personal confusion.

I didn't actually see a Beatle in concert until April 5, 2002, in Las Vegas, Nevada, at the MGM Grand events center, when Paul McCartney launched his first solo tour since the *Off the Ground* campaign in 1993, which I also missed. Ditto for the *Flowers in the Dirt* trek of 1989–1990. But that was then and I had another chance, and this time, McCartney took not just the tunes to the road but the eternal memory of his fallen brothers, John and George.

The night was magical. Paul played and played and we shook, rattled, and rolled with every divine musical punch. From the melancholy performances of "Here Today" and "Something"—tributes to his departed brothers—he and his band ran through "Can't Buy Me Love," "Getting Better," "Let It Be," "I Saw Her Standing There," and so many more, culminating with the main set closer, "Hey Jude."

Throughout my life, I've celebrated the music of the Beatles. So many songs, all so beautiful, the grandest, most untouchable catalog of melodies the world will ever witness. I was born with the Beatles. I will probably die with them too. In fact, I've already written them into my eulogy. I hope I don't have to use it any time soon, but as the boys said, tomorrow never knows.

5

The Amazing Journey

"I LEARN BY GOING WHERE I HAVE TO GO."

—*Theodore Roethke*

"Why are you flying to London?"

Points two and three of the Friend family triangle knew they were asking a rhetorical question, but I reiterated for argument's sake. After six months of unemployment and a dwindling bank account, they deserved an explanation. "I have $500 credit on British Airways," I explained. "I found a sixty-dollar-a-night flat in Paddington." Those were logistical adjuncts. I swallowed hard and coughed up the real reason. "I'm going to see the Who," I confessed. "They're playing the theater in Portsmouth, where the movie *Tommy* was filmed. I can't explain. I just need to be there."

It was four months after September 11, and I was in a cataclysmic funk. Most of my days were spent sitting out back in the guesthouse, composing existential missives for distribution to my e-mail list. The only thing I hadn't lost faith in was rock 'n' roll. When the Towers fell, I sought comfort in the bands of my youth. And one of the bands that made me who I am was the Who.

They arrived in my life on the heels of the Beatles. The record that introduced me to these four new lads from "over there" was a mind-blowing double-sized concept LP simply titled *Tommy*. A year after John, Paul, George, and Ringo had ignited my senses with their double dose of psychedelic rock, the "White Album," here was something even more ambitious because it had a theme, a thread, a story, that Ron Meyers and I could really sink our curious minds into.

It was as if Ron and I had met an imaginary new friend, a deaf, dumb, and blind boy who would hang out with us after school in sleepy Sherman Oaks and take us far, far away from ourselves. The music was the spaceship and Tommy was the pilot. "Come on the amazing journey," they sang, "and learn all you should know." Our skinny arms did not need twisting.

Looking back, I realize that "We're Not Gonna Take It," the closing anthem of *Tommy*, may have provided me with my first, unconscious experience with mantra. "See me, feel me, touch me, heal me," cried vocalist Roger Daltrey. He crooned like the man in the talus who sang the Hebrew prayers in temple during high holidays.

> *Listening to you, I get the music,*
> *Gazing at you, I get the heat.*
> *Following you, I climb the mountain,*
> *I get excitement at your feet.*

Two Jewish kids from the Valley had no clue how big a picture the prophet Pete was painting. Rock stars weren't human back then. They were mythological creatures who had no contact with real people.

We read the liner notes and producer credits, and knew that some sort of process was taking place, but it was irrelevant to the end result—the music and what it was doing to us, where it was taking us, how it was changing us. If you had told me at age fourteen that someday, in the future, I'd not only meet the prophet but also break bread with the cantor, well, I'd have called you some kind of wizard.

Elaine found me from across the Atlantic in 2000 while I was working as editor in chief of the streaming hard-rock Web site KNAC.com. She fancied herself a writer and began sending me intelligently scripted e-mails attesting to her devout love of music. I took Elaine under my wing. She came to the States that summer and interned at the online station, brightening the studios with her UK accent and headbanging enthusiasm. I had little doubt that when I got to Heathrow, Elaine would be waiting for me.

"This is Jamie, Lonn," she said with a shy smile. I'd gotten the advance profile via e-mail. New Jersey born, he was very good with computers, loved rock, and apparently, loved Elaine. The ten-hour flight from L.A. for me and the six-hour train ride from Glasgow for them were the main legs of the trip, but we still had another two hours by ground to get to Portsmouth.

The damp, cold wind blew strong off the Channel as we disembarked at our seaside destination. It was 4 P.M. We didn't know what time the show started, where the venue was, where we'd be staying for the night, or even if my friend Rod Smallwood, chairman of Sanctuary Group in London, was able to procure last-minute tickets. I'd sent the charismatic Cambridge graduate (who had built an empire on the managerial shoulders of one of metal's most enduring institutions, Iron Maiden) an e-mail just the day before. He forwarded my note to his assistant, Dan McKinley, with the accompanying directive: "Dan, the Who boys visit Sanctuary all the time. Suss Lonn out for the show." The note was passed onto the company's "it girl," Angie Jenkison, who also happened to be a longtime friend of the Daltrey family. We had, as the Brits would say, "no worries."

"Where would the Who be playing tonight?" I asked the cabdriver who picked us up in front of the bus station. "Only one place, the Guildhall." We got out of the taxi in front of a Tetley Hotel boasting "Single Room, 36 pounds per night," which comes out to about fifty-five dollars. Worked for us. We secured two rooms, rested for a bit and rendezvoused in the lobby at 6.

The three of us strolled out into the Portsmouth night. We cased the venue first, a brief ten-minute walk from our hotel. The Guildhall is a glorious old Gothic building in the town's main square. It looked like a place where politicians rather than rock bands would perform. The steps in front were scattered with early arriving fans. A door to the right of the entrance appeared to be the guest window. "The list will be here at six-thirty," reported the portly sir in charge of the gateway. "Let's have a pint and some dinner," I said. We agreed and floated into a pub across the road where I ordered the British Isles beverage of choice, the indefatigable Guinness.

We were united in the kingdom of proof. The culture here is pub, not pop, where life is played out in smoke-filled, wood-paneled caverns where accents merge, genders collide, and the melting pot percolates in dialogue of a hard day's work giving way to a hard day's night. After dark is when Britain bristles. I take note of a blonde in tight leather pants with the sliced bells at the bottom, doing her dance for a captivated crowd of tweed-coated gents with pink-hued cheeks and yellow-tooth smiles. They're not concerned what time the gig starts because they're not going. This is the event—countless sips on flapping lips—like it is every evening.

An occasional drink before a historical rock concert is one thing; making the pub your nightly stop on the way home from work is another. But who was I to judge? Walk a mile in someone else's shoes and you shall know of their struggle. Rock a mile in mine and you'll understand what I was doing half a globe away from home, broke and with an angry wife, waiting for the band to hit the stage.

My glass was empty and showtime approached. An envelope with just my first name on it was waiting at the window. Tenth row. Dead center. The inside decor was '70s drab and drafty, complete anathema to the Gothic, glorious external architecture. I wondered if the architects were knocking back the ales across the street when they got around to the interior.

"This looks like the place where my mum and dad used to go dancing when I was a kid," observed Elaine, who was only twenty-two but possessed the wit, wisdom, and musical heart of someone years older.

"The balcony is cool," I observed. Then I glanced at the stage and saw the instruments laid out across the platform. Entwistle's four-string machete caught my eye first. And next to it, the prodigious six-string wand of the Wizard.

The lights dimmed and the crowd wailed. "I Can't Explain" started it off. The set list was wondrous. This was the tri-

umphant return of the Windmill, the single most significant de-
marcation of Townshend's onstage rebirth.

They smoked through several songs from *Who's Next*. In
the exhaustive and analytical liner notes for the twentieth-
anniversary commemorative reissue of his seminal solo endeavor
Who Came First—released by Rykodisc in the fall of 1992—
Townshend explained the film project that inspired the recording sessions that spawned the tuneage perfecto that would
eventually become *Who's Next*.

"The *Lifehouse* idea was very simple," he wrote. "It was a por-
tentous science-fiction film with Utopian spiritual messages into
which were to be grafted uplifting scenes from a real Who concert. I was selling a simple credo: Whatever happens in the future, rock 'n' roll will save the world." I'm still not sure if rock 'n'
roll is capable of saving the world, but as I watched that show
unfold that night in Portsmouth, I was thankful that it had at
least saved me.

"How many of you were here in 1974?" Townshend asked
the Portsmouth crowd. The band performed a free show in this
building for the local extras that week as a thank-you. From the
thunderous applause, one could assume everybody around me
had been in the room that night. How magnificent for these
hardworking, loyal local rock fans to relive the bells, buzzers,
and whistles of that night. But beyond that—as Pete whirled
into the cataclysmic opening riff of "Pinball Wizard"—how incredible that the strains off the stage were as strong and sweet as
they'd ever been.

The machine-gun intro to "Pinball Wizard" is cemented in
rock culture. Townshend's acoustic wrist play sucks us in like a
vacuum, but the song—no, the ride—doesn't begin until the
first, bombastic bang of Entwistle's mighty bass. It is so fat, so

authoritarian, so goddamn heavy, it almost stops the song before it starts. But therein lay a critical fact about the Who: John Entwistle did not play the bass guitar, he invented it.

The Ox in performance was a perfect balance of stoic beauty and blinding speed. Entwistle manipulated the instrument with digital precision while holding redwood stature. Once he took his position stage left, that is where he stayed; his feet never strayed from their spot. All movement took place at the ends of his insanely long arms, which ended in two of the most fluid, cantankerous hands to ever caress a four-string. He was "Flight of the Bumble Bee" fast, surgically precise, yet completely free form.

"Keith taught Zak to play," said Simon Daltrey, son of Roger, who was seated directly next to me in the Portsmouth theater. Don't ask me how the lead singer's flesh-and-blood off-spring got planted right where the wandering journalist on no particular assignment could bend his ear. Must have been my rock karma. Simon was, of course, referring to Zak Starkey, Ringo Starr's son, the latest in a long line of Who drummers going back to the departed Moon. "When he was a kid, Keith and Ringo were best mates. I watched it. Zak and me are the same age—thirty-six. Keith was always showing Zak how to hit the kit."

It was during Entwistle's mind-boggling bass solo for the sleazy epic "5:15" from *Quadrophenia* that the teacher-student dynamic truly revealed itself. John danced off a series of notes with ageless perfection, and Zak answered, confident, concise, and cool.

Here, so long since the amazing journey began, Pete Town-shend proved again why his rebellious imprint is as indelible as the scarred stages that played victim to a thousand shattered guitars, slammed home at the close of every show in a climactic clank of revolutionary theater that sent parents and principals racing for the exits. But the violence was merely a manifestation of the intensity boiling within the artist, played out for a post-'60s civilization that was in the throes of metamorphosis.

In late 1967, Townshend was introduced to the teachings of Hindu avatar Meher Baba. "One minute, I was freaked out on acid," he further confessed in the *Who Came First* liner notes, "and the next minute, I was into Baba." At age twenty-two, Townshend began to write music that lifted the spirit while rocking our world, constantly reminding us that love, surrender, devotion, and sacrifice were what life was all about.

Pete Townshend pushed the mod-music envelope by daring to compose what no other had ever attempted: rock symphonies. He was the genre's first Beethoven, a visionary rebel who led us by moped and magic bus to the outer reaches of modern musical theater. He literally bled mind, body, and spirit for rock 'n' roll, touring with scraped, scarred, bandaged fingers from 1967 to 1980. The whirling arm of twang whipped the strings with the precise fury of a fencer or bullfighter.

Still floating from the two-hour dream sequence, Elaine, Jamie, and I drifted around to the back door of the venue, where a small gathering of fans waited for the band to exit the building. A time-machine scene, twenty-five years past, the rock stars in early development, signing a ticket stub for the locals. They were so friendly, chatty, warm with the kids, who were no longer kids, but still very much all right.

I stood quietly as Roger and John made their way to the respective cars that would drive them, not to some five-star hotel, but home. This was their home. Those of us who'd walked the Sunset Strip had encountered Entwistle at the Rainbow, where one of his guitars hangs proudly from the ceiling. He and Roger both loved L.A., but the Who was born here, in these woods, by this Channel. This was a world away from my home, but this was still my generation.

Townshend was the last to exit. As he gently traversed the small crowd, I waited for the perfect moment to make contact. His back was to me, six inches away, as he signed the last photograph placed in his hands by a fan. The car door was open, awaiting his arrival. Townshend the magnificent, a breath away, in a brick alley in Portsmouth, England, on a cold, damp night in January. "Pete," I said softly, "I came from Los Angeles." He stopped, turned around, and caught my glance. "Well, you came farther for this gig than I did, mate," he grinned. Then he took my hand, shook it, and I felt the calloused strength of a million windmills.

A few weeks later, I was in the kitchen of Anthrax's Scott Ian and his girlfriend, Pearl. Scott's far better half is the child of Mr. and Mrs. Meat Loaf. "I've been writing about the Who, Scott," I said, launching into a recap of my trip to Portsmouth.

"Really?" he replied. "Pearl's mom just had dinner with Roger last night. They're best friends. He's in town for a couple weeks. You might be able to meet him."

Five days later, there was a message on my voicemail. "Lonn, it's Scott. Listen, Saturday night, me, Pearl, and Leslie [Pearl's mom] are going to dinner with Roger. We want you to come. Call me back."

My fingers danced on the keypad like an Entwistle bass fill as I dialed Scott's number.

I picked up the couple a half hour early. *Live at Leeds* was cranking in the car. We arrived at the Chadwick Restaurant in Beverly Hills—owned by my friend Benjamin Ford, a brilliant chef and eldest son of Harrison "Indiana Jones" Ford. Leslie was fetching Roger in the San Fernando Valley.

With the cosmos in control, the lead singer of the Who found himself seated directly to my right. Same place as his son was in Portsmouth. "What's going on here, Lord?" I asked myself. I was no stranger to celebrity. I never consciously changed my demeanor, not anymore. I was a fan of rock, and the rockers that made the rock roll. I also knew that, basically, they were no different than you or me. Whether they're heroes like Townshend and Daltrey or the kid in the apartment upstairs who keeps you awake playing his Gibson at 2 A.M., they breathe the same air and suffer the same slings and arrows as the rest of us.

When the scandal broke about Townshend's alleged downloading of underage Internet porn, I tossed it out with the rest of the gutter press news o' the day. I had fielded from the inside enough scandalous rumors about Guns N' Roses and Mötley Crüe during the *RIP* days to fill a tabloid tabernacle. Hey, were you there in the room when so-and-so was beating his wife? You weren't? Well shut the fuck up then!

Townshend was eventually absolved of all charges, but that incident illustrated that the greatest pratfall of fame is maintaining the public perception of purity, which by its own definition is problematic. Even at the peak of my career, I never had much stomach for the superstar mystique.

After an hour consuming California cuisine with Mr. Daltrey—where I related sitting next to his son in Portsmouth, soliciting a "he's a good kid" from Dad—I began to feel quite comfortable, enough so to don the journalist's hat, unofficially of course. Roger was so likeable, I figured what the hell? "Pete's songs would never have acquired the immortality if it weren't for the presentation," I said. "He didn't sing 'Love, Reign O'er Me' [the closing anthemic ballad off *Quadrophenia*], you did. No one else could have. He must have known that deep inside."

Part of my comment was ego stroking, part was true personal belief that the Windmill without the Pipes would have had very different results, different history. Roger nodded, obviously pondering three decades of a relationship of unspeakable chemistry, good and bad. Then someone cracked a joke, probably Scott, and everyone laughed. Roger never really answered my question because I hadn't really asked one. I was just paying homage to one of my heroes who happened to be enjoying a slice of pâté.

Roger Daltrey and Pete Townshend affirm the great balance of vocal undulation and instrumental dementia. Pete wrote the songs and played the riffs, and Roger stood up front and swallowed the white-hot spotlight, interpreting the message, delivering the goods, track after track, night after night. It could not have happened any other way.

Dessert was approaching, so I reared back for a proper volley. I figured I would never get a chance to interview a member of the Who again, so I'd better get at least one exclusive fly-on-the-wall tidbit for the archives. "Roger," I said, "I just got the remastered *Who's Next* rereleased from '95 with an alternative mix of 'Behind Blue Eyes.' It's fucking unbelievable. The track bleeds with more soul than the original. Can you tell me about the recording?"

"Okay, Lonn, I'm going to tell you something I've never told anyone," he said. His eyes were glassy, possessing a warmth unbecoming a legend in social conversation. "The day we cut that track, my dog died," he said with an almost bittersweet grin.

"That dog was my best friend in the world. I loved him more than anything. He got killed, hit by a car. And I had to go to the studio and lay down that vocal."

"But why didn't you call Pete or [producer] Glyn Johns and say, 'I can't track today, my dog died'?" I asked, giddy at this tender revelation.

He shook his head. "We never stopped working, not for anything. That was not an option back then. There's a lot of pain in that vocal. My pain."

We returned to small talk. "You know I really love Southern California," Roger said.

"I grew up here," I replied.

"Really?" he said. "Whereabouts?"

"Sherman Oaks, in the San Fernando Valley."

His eyes widened, his smile returned full force, and the mouth that wailed the immortal "yeahhhhhhhhh!" before the final verse of "Won't Get Fooled Again" proclaimed, "That's where I bought my house! Sherman Oaks!"

When he told me the name of the street where his new L.A. retreat was, I almost lost my chocolate mousse. Roger Daltrey was living five minutes from where Ron Meyers and I first listened to *Tommy* and a rolling stone's throw from my high school. Or to put it more eloquently, a healthy jog from the suburban flat where a nearsighted student once sat in awe of a deaf, dumb, and blind boy.

6

That
'70s Chapter

"COME, SAID THE MUSE,
SING ME A SONG NO POET YET HAS CHANTED.
SING ME THE UNIVERSAL."

—*Walt Whitman*

I had an odd, impish friend in high school named Van Alpert who had a colossal album collection and the most expensive stereo system in the San Fernando Valley, accentuated by a pair of towering, ear-shattering speakers. Van came up to about woofer height, and when his folks weren't home, we cranked those babies for all they were worth. It was in his room after class every day from the winter of 1973 to the summer of 1974 that I flew at warp speed into the stargate of progressive ("prog" as it came to be known) rock.

Van, my brother Rick, and I were getting into futuristic groups like Pink Floyd, Strawbs, Curved Air, Roxy Music, Barclay James Harvest, Supertramp, the Moody Blues, Camel, Caravan, Yes, Van Der Graaf Generator, Jethro Tull, Triumvirat, Nektar, Blue Oyster Cult, Kansas, Kayak, Can, Renaissance, PFM, Hawkwind, and Be Bop Deluxe. Another friend, Mark

Henteleff, was tripping out over a renegade outfit from San Francisco called the Grateful Dead. The air-guitar sessions at his house after school, rockin' out to the live double-LP *Europe '72*, went on for hours. The Dead led Mark to fusion—Chick Corea's Return to Forever and John McLaughlin's Mahavishnu Orchestra—and Mark led them to me.

Music was flying at me from all quadrants of the galaxy, and it was always playing. At home while doing my homework, in the car while cruising around the Valley, at night before finally falling asleep, usually after reading a short story by fantastical author Ray Bradbury, whose freaked-out fable collection *R is for Rocket* whisked me as far away as Yes's *Close to the Edge* LP. Also on my nightstand were Anthony Burgess's *A Clockwork Orange* and Kurt Vonnegut's *Slaughterhouse-Five*.

Grant High is where I had my first close encounter with real live musicians. They were called Still Life and played regularly in the school gymnasium. I hung out after their sets and got to know their guitarist, who was in my geometry class. His name was Steve Lukather, an axe prodigy who had lightning fingers, like Be Bop's Bill Nelson. After he graduated, the group changed their name to Toto and went on to sell millions of records. Luke and I have known each other since 1974. He was the first rock star I ever called my friend.

I wasn't quite ready to leave home after Grant, so my education continued in September 1974 at the junior college across the street. Los Angeles Valley College had a bad rap. Kids called it UFO—University of Fulton at Oxnard (the two streets that bordered the campus)—or worse, Grant with Ashtrays. But truth be told, I grew enormously at Valley, thanks in large part to three professors: Tom McGuire, Bob Barlow, and Dick Raskoff.

McGuire had greasy gray hair, wore shabby clothes, and

spoke in jagged, succinct sentences, often shoving his index finger in the face of students seated up front. He officially taught English, but unofficially, he was drilling into us what it meant to be an artist. His lectures were long, drawn-out anecdotes about magnificent figures in history whose sense of expression was never co-opted.

The chain-smoking, dry-witted Bob Barlow taught astronomy in the campus planetarium and gave us essay tests. Answering these long-form cosmic questions about the makeup of the universe is where I cut my compositional teeth.

Barlow had the wicked personality and detached demeanor of a rock star. He would tease us relentlessly, crack jokes incessantly, and conduct his lessons without notes, virtually from memory. He had a bohemian, Bukowski brilliance about him. Mark and I were infatuated with Barlow and thought he was probably more twisted than he let on to his students. One night after class, we stayed around, like a pair of fans by the backstage door. Barlow affirmed our suspicions by kicking our ass with a ribald tale about the time he had wild sex in an abandoned lumberyard. We marched home about midnight, our guts aching from the scurrilous postshow soliloquy.

Raskoff taught an enhanced geography course that ventured into geology, the study of the earth. In other words, rocks! He was "bent" like Barlow but in a different way. A music freak who made cassette tapes with songs ranging from Zeppelin's "Your Time Is Gonna Come" to Beethoven's "Ode to Joy," he wore a close-cropped goatee and spoke in a very slow and succinct cadence. One might have thought he was dropped on his head when he was child. Maybe he was. I connected with him big time. He took us on a field trip to a ghost town and hiking in local canyons. I got to know Raskoff, baby-sat his kids once. He also gave essay tests—and a term project.

Our assignment was to create something experimental using music. It had nothing specifically to do with geography, but Raskoff didn't care. He wanted us to be creative. There were no rules. I went out with my reel-to-reel tape recorder and collected sound bites of the city. Strangers' voices, traffic noise, things like that. Then I recorded at various tape speeds a bizarre poem I'd written called "I Scream with Nuts," splicing in sound clips from Gentle Giant's *In a Glass House* record. At the end of the term, I presented my audio experiment to the class in the planetarium, using the starry dome overhead and big-ass speakers for ultimate effect. I got an A, but my untrained manipulation of the dome's night-sky dials threw the star positions off by three hundred years!

The inventive music of the day was feeding my own creative spirit and keeping me busy to boot. My social calendar wasn't exactly sizzling. Lanky, four-eyed prog rockers didn't get a lot of dates. Girls were more into muscular jocks that drove red Camaros and listened to Led Zeppelin. I had a 1961 Mercury Comet that couldn't break fifty-five if Sammy Hagar were behind the wheel.

On January 24, 1975, the skies were azure blue over Van Nuys. I woke up and turned on the radio to find my senses stimulated by the most wondrous aural textures. The rock opus ebbed and flowed for almost half an hour. I didn't move from my speakers. I didn't care if I was late to class. This was far more important.

John Clark was on the air, the whisper-throated jock for the tiny progressive rock station KNAC-FM 105.5. The airwave enclave would a decade later change its format to metal and become a close ally in my career media endeavors. "That was 'Supper's Ready,' " he said. "Genesis, from the LP *Foxtrot*, in its entirety this morning to honor the band's show tonight at the Shrine Auditorium in support of their new LP, *The Lamb Lies Down on Broadway*. Don't miss our exclusive interview with Peter Gabriel this afternoon at five."

I didn't walk to class that morning, I hovered, with no other purpose but to find Peter Weiss, the only son of a rabbi whom I'd just met and bonded with over our mutual love of—you guessed it—rock bands. I couldn't wait to tell him about my morning's musical baptism. "Dude," I buzzed, "I heard Genesis this morning! 'Supper's Ready'! I can't believe I hadn't gotten into them yet. It was amazing. Like nothing I'd ever heard. And they're playing tonight at the Shrine Auditorium."

But Peter was ahead of me. "I know, dude," he said. "I'm going! They're playing the entire new album."

I got the blow-by-blow report on the show from Peter the next morning, a visual feast that included a thousand slides and a dozen costume changes. Within days, I had the entire Genesis catalog. They were waiting for me in the used bins at Moby Disc. *The Lamb* carried me through the summer of 1975. I bought a Genesis shirt at Moby Disc Records and had "Imperial Aerosol Kid" printed on the back, a lyric recalling the LP's protagonist from the album's title track.

Gabriel became my mentor, compatriot, chief storyteller, and most mystical of all rock heroes to date. And then, at the peak of their chemical majesty, without a warning shot across the bow, Peter Gabriel and Genesis bid each other adieu and went their separate artistic ways.

In the spring of 1976, the stripped-down Genesis released

A Trick of the Tail, having converted their drummer and former background singer, Phil Collins, into a front man. I bought the record the day it went on sale, took it home, but didn't listen to it immediately. That evening, I was getting together with a new kid I'd just met named Barney. He was elfin, like Van, and dug the same music as me. We met in the library at Valley, where Peter and I first hooked up. "Come on over and hang out tonight," he said.

"Sure! I'll bring the new Genesis!" I fired back.

Barney didn't have a lot of friends. In addition to being short, he had kinky black hair and bad skin. He did have one thing, however, that elevated his cool factor—something I'd heard about but as of yet had never experienced firsthand. Barney had pot. An hour after I arrived at his dreary Victory Boulevard apartment, he pulled out a joint and I pulled out *A Trick of the Tail*. "You wanna smoke?" he said.

I paused for moment. I knew that Peter and Mark had tried marijuana, and as for Van, well, he'd already eaten mushrooms and dropped acid. I didn't like to drink because the hangover sucked. But I was curious about pot. An altered state with few side effects. Everything happens when it happens, right? "Fire it up!" I said.

Naïve to the power and effect of weed, I took four monster hits of Barney's Acapulco Gold. Before track one on the record, "Dance on a Volcano," had finished, I was not only dancing but damn near hallucinating. There was something different about everything. The images in the room took on extreme proportion. Barney got uglier, the lights got brighter, and the music— oh, man, what was going on with the music? It was like I could detect the beats inside the beats. Not only was I hearing the songs, I was really feeling them.

"You high?" he asked with a glassy-eyed grin.

"Uh, I don't know what's happening, buddy. I think I'm freaking out. But it's cool. Are you hungry?"

We melted into the rest of *A Trick of the Tail*, hypnotized by its progressive majesty, as accentuated by the pot, and then drove to Casa Vega, the Mexican restaurant on Ventura Boulevard frequented by local rockers. Years later I would meet Slash there so he could sign a Gibson guitar we were giving away in *RIP*. I couldn't stop laughing long enough to order a burrito, making a complete idiot out of myself with the waitress. The next day, I was remorseful, vowing to never smoke that evil weed again. I had enough trouble with reality. Fall session at UCLA was starting and the punks were waiting for me—with open arms, a catalog of chaotic music, and a satchel full of goodies. It was the perfect environment for a fly about to buzz.

UCLA was twelve nautical and a million sociocultural miles from Valley College. When I landed on the Westwood campus in September of 1976, I was instantly overwhelmed by its size, age, and aura. I started my junior year as a geography major, inspired by Raskoff, but quickly changed to geology. Both subjects had too much math and science for me, so I struggled through my first quarter. When I told my dad that I was a geology major, he didn't get it. "Geology? Why are you studying rocks? How are you going to make a living doing that?" Actually, unbeknownst even to me, I'd begun my undergraduate work in the field of "rock." And this subject would not be a struggle.

Almost instantly, I fell into a clique of sophisticated music freaks who took little time ripping the prog-rock cape off my back. There was a more urgent sound rattling the brain stems of post-teen America—it was the punk/new wave movement, and like so many musical tides before, the initial swell crashed directly on my beach. The folks getting drenched with me this time, however, were not geeks but avant-garde hipsters. We made the North Campus Student Center—the loud and bustling lunchroom adjacent to the massive Young Research Library—our hang.

Liz Heller, Claudia Puig, Debbie Kamins, Nancy Gottesman, Jodi Lunine, Perry Watts-Russell, Scott Sigman, Lyn Healy, Dave Burg, Greg Sowders, Janet Grey, and Patti Clark—they were my peeps, the North Campus crew. Lyn was the leader, a sexy, cynical smartass who rode the cutting edge of punk fashion like a Thoroughbred jockey—riding crop and all. A different miniature naked-baby toy earring hung from her sexy lobes each day. The girls envied her cool, and the guys wanted to fuck her, me included. And I almost did the night she invited me over to watch *Harold and Maude*. I'd scored a couple of quaaludes. The relaxing happy pill had me snoring before Ruth Gordon died.

As far as controlled substances went, I sampled from the dessert tray and found to my surprise that only pot fit my character. It was organic, not manufactured. Coke made you feel great for twenty minutes until it wore off and your nose and brain needed a refill. And another, and another until your whole face was numb. It's a seductive lie that I watched several souls fall victim to later on when my career put me in league with the powder brigade. Mushrooms didn't sit well with me either. They made me feel discombobulated, like a man walking on Mars who couldn't speak Martian.

Among the NC clan, only Scott was a Genesis fan, though not to the extent that I was. When Moby Disc's doors opened for business on February 25, 1977, the day *Peter Gabriel*—the self-titled solo debut—went on sale, I watched Dana unlock the door. The album, produced by Bob Ezrin, didn't sound like a Genesis record. It was more personal, more Gabriel, a logical extension of the seeds of introspection planted in *The Lamb*.

The ad appeared announcing two shows at the Roxy. My brother and I got to the club twelve hours early! Our commitment was rewarded when we took our seats at the very first table next to the stage, dead center—no easy feat by the way, since this was the return of one of rock's most revered figures and everyone was dying to witness what wonders the long pause had wrought upon our once noble and proud prog hero.

The room was not electric, it was atomic. When the curtain rose on the man and his keyboard—the instrument he taught himself to play while on the mountain—the roar could be heard all the way to Jerusalem. He laid his fingers on the ivory keys and a hush fell almost instantly. You could hear a gum wrapper dropping to the asphalt outside. Gabriel was three feet away. When he opened his lips to sing for us, you could feel the building begin to float off its foundation.

When the night shows, the signals grow, on radios
All the strange things, they come and go, as early warning.

His power, his wisdom, and his beauty mesmerized us. "Supper's Ready" was the New Testament in prog-rock loincloth that featured characters taking part in a multi-act play. The story was told outside the storyteller. Gabriel had come back, and his message was personal, emanating from within, offered with poetic,

My first rock star photo. Fellow North Campus peep Greg Sowders stares in amazement as I get familiar with Talking Heads bassist Tina Weymouth, UCLA, November 1978.

Althea Flynt circa 1983 at some Persian nightclub in West Hollywood. We'd begun our nocturnal rock adventure by seeing the punk band the Cramps at the Country Club in Reseda.

Jon Bon Jovi invited me down to an L.A. studio while he was producing his friend Aldo Nova's record *Blood on the Bricks*. Gotta love the sweat pants.

The infamous January 1991 *RIP* "broken bottle" cover.

This shot was taken in the kitchen of Lars Ulrich's just-purchased mansion in Tiburon, California, sometime in 1993, before he'd purchased one piece of seven-figure artwork.

On the street in Westwood Village after the premiere of the movie *The People vs. Larry Flynt*, me and the former Mrs. Cobain. Oh, that's Melissa Auf De Mer in the . . . Hole.

My thirty-fourth birthday backyard bash with Skid Row's Sebastian Bach and the Cult's Ian Astbury. I think the unidentified girl worked at Tiffany's.

Axl on a Hollywood sidewalk the day he and Slash appeared (at no charge) in a *RIP* subscription TV commercial.

New Year's Eve 2005. Megan flew into Vegas
and celebrated the holiday with her dad and "Uncle Slash."

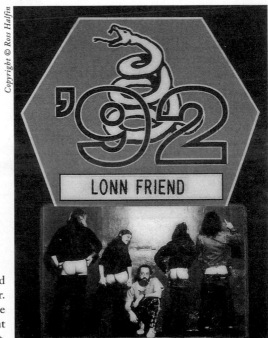

This is my personalized
laminate for Metallica's 1992 tour.
The Ross Halfin outtake was the
framed shot on my office wall that
offended Kurt Cobain most.

Aerosmith tour photographer Gene Kirkland shot this in Steven Tyler's dressing room, Donington, England, an hour after the Chuck Berry bus ride, August 1990. I had an 8-by-10 print made, signed it, and presented it to Mario Maglieri as a gift. It's been hanging in the entryway of the Rainbow Bar & Grill since Christmas '90.

Flying high over Planet Rock on Mötley Crüe's private plane.
No one wore seat belts.

Motörhead's maestro and radio promo "dude" Mike Schnapp flank me at Lemmy's fiftieth birthday bash at the Whisky about an hour after Metallica's tribute set.

Local San Francisco photographer Jay Blakesberg (known for his extraordinary work with the Grateful Dead) visited The Plant recording studio in the winter of '95 to snap this promo shot of the Bogmen with producer Jerry Harrison and engineer Karl Derfler. Who's the blonde? Don't ask me!

The infamous Seattle *RIP* party, October 1991, boasted an unprecedented Temple of the Dog jam featuring Soundgarden's Chris Cornell (left) and Pearl Jam's Eddie Vedder. Marty Temme's photo captured the rare and exhilarating moment.

My dinner with Roger Daltrey ended with this photo taken in front of the restaurant. That's the happy rock couple, Pearl Aday (Meat Loaf's daughter) and Scott Ian (of Anthrax) flanking Daltrey. But who is that gray-faced man on the far right? Take a guess.

melodic grace for anyone possessing the awareness to hear the word.

For the bluesy and prophetic "Waiting for the Big One," he surfed the audience—a breathtaking gesture of connection that would later be emulated by a generation of fearless rockers that would include Bono, Eddie Vedder, Chris Cornell, and others. The crowd became one. After a seven-minute jam that traversed the five-hundred-seat commune so every single patron could lay their hands on the man, Gabriel floated toward the stage to the waiting arms of two brothers who lovingly hoisted him back up to his spot behind the microphone.

When it was over, we were ten seconds from being kicked out when Gabriel's saxophonist, Timmy Cappello, came through the side door that guarded the upstairs dressing rooms.

"Timmy, you guys rocked tonight," I said.

"Thanks, man," he responded on the fly.

My instinct told me to go for the jugular. What was there to lose? "Hey, Timmy, can we say hello to Peter?" I chirped nervously.

He then paused and addressed us directly. "Well, let me go upstairs and check it out. Wait here, fellas."

Rick and I stared at each other in momentary shock. The fact that there was a possibility was far more than we'd hoped for. "We need a gift in case we get in!" I said. "I'll run next door and buy a bottle of champagne. Oh, my God, Gabe!" Five minutes later, I returned from Gil Turner's with a fifth of Asti Spumanti, a bubbly cider of some kind, cheap stuff. Twenty minutes passed and Timmy finally reappeared. "Let's go, boys," he commanded.

We entered the dressing room as he was removing his eye makeup. There were other individuals in the room, but we never looked at them. His persona was always larger than life. Yet in this moment, in this tiny, dimly lit room—in the wake of a flood of new and magnificent song—he was just a man called Peter about to accept a fifth of cheap champagne from two young fans.

"Bearing gifts," he said, taking notice of our humble offering.

"Yes. It's an honor, Peter. Thank you for an awesome performance—and welcome back." He smiled and shook our hands, and we were returned to the real world.

Prog whisked you away to outer space, where your mind was free to embrace other possibilities. Punk was about attitude, holding your space, your integrity when the Man told you to get straight, vote Republican, abandon your dream, and turn down the stereo. Punk brought you back to earth to confront head on man's inhumanity to man. I related to both because half of me was always out there, and the other half, down here. The '80s were right around the block. Joe Strummer knew it. The kids in school knew it. Society was on course for a narcissistic train wreck. You could almost smell the vapid stench of disco in the distance. In four years, I'd be reviewing porn films for a living.

"I'm so *bored* with the U.S.A.!" Lyn shouted that Clash chorus ten times a day. Some of us laughed, some of us sang along. We were all bored: bored with our stupid professors, our shitty part-time jobs, and the sorry state of television. *Charlie's Angels* and *The Dukes of Hazzard*—meet Johnny Rotten and Sid Vicious! I was watching *Twilight Zone* reruns. I will always watch *Twilight Zone* reruns because those stories stuck. They had a message. Like the music I grew up on, it survives. No, it thrives.

Three or four times a day, the NC clan would meet and talk about the new albums we were listening to, and there was a lot to chat about. We were munching our burgers and fries while

Planet Rock was giving birth to a movement. Between May 1976 and August 1977, debut records were dropped by the Ramones, the Buzzcocks, Blondie, Devo, the Clash, Elvis Costello, the Sex Pistols, and the Jam, just to name a few. We had every record and saw every tour when it passed through L.A.

Being there was the rush. Seeing it live. Watching the angry, bespectacled Elvis Costello flail about the Hollywood High School gymnasium was not just entertaining, it was cathartic. Seeing Joe Jackson tear up a copy of the Sunday *L.A. Times* on stage at the Santa Monica Civic was invigorating. When Blondie played the Starwood, I was pressed right up against the stage. Debbie Harry's skirt was so short you could see her pubic hair. Underpants weren't punk. Again, I managed to talk my way into the tiny dressing room area behind the stage and exchange a word with the divine Mrs. H. Perry was there, too. He worshiped Debbie, had photos of her all over his apartment. She dug his British accent.

In the winter of 1978, during my endless senior year, a quartet of New York art-school rockers known as Talking Heads came through town in support of their second LP, *More Songs About Buildings and Food*, released the previous July. It had scored massive points with the entire NC contingent. Everyone loved the band's debut LP, *Talking Heads: 77*. "Psycho Killer" had become a quirky standard thanks to the support of local radio station KROQ. We had waited patiently for the band to hit L.A., and so they did. I went with Lyn and Patti.

In the same room that Gabriel had elevated the year before, the Heads delivered a stunning performance. We sat in the VIP balcony and stared straight down on the band. "I saw Tina's tit," chortled Greg Sowders. The real encore didn't take place onstage but in the dressing room afterward, where David Byrne fell head over high heels for Patti. Five feet tall with a massive head of kinky red hair and a smile as wide as the Brooklyn Bridge, Patti had mastered the art of being aloof. Like her best mate, Lyn, she radiated an alternative savoir faire. To put it simply, she was adorable, and evidently she had pierced the heart of one of modern rock's most enigmatic new stars.

Over the next couple weeks as the band gigged up the coast of California, Patti was closer to David than his road case. And that access got us access. We were invited out to see the shows and hang out with David, keyboardist Jerry Harrison, drummer Chris Franz, and his wife, bassist Tina Weymouth. Scott loaded up the car and the four of us drove to Santa Barbara and then onward to Sacramento and San Francisco. I came up with the moniker Headhunters for our caravan. Scott had a dozen T-shirts made with the logo.

Sitting in the dressing room at one gig while the band was onstage, Patti told me how odd and wonderful David was. "He considers the intersection of the San Diego and Santa Monica freeways a work of art," she giggled. "I wish I had a tape recorder rolling for all the bizarre and beautiful things that constantly float off his tongue." The California trek was magical, but the best was yet to come.

Greg did a daily shift on the campus radio station, KLA. He and Patti helped lobby David and the band into performing a free show for the students on the massive Janss Steps on the west end of the campus. Ten thousand new-wave Bruins turned out that day. Greg interviewed Chris and Tina on his radio show an hour before the set began and happily helped the rockers empty a vial of coke on air, which ratcheted up the conversation to near psychobabble levels. I gave Chris my UCLA '75 T-shirt, which he wore onstage. And Tina, Greg, and I took the very first "Lonn Friend hanging out with rock star" photo.

When I finally got my diploma in March of 1979, I still had no clue where I was going in my career. But I wasn't worried. Something would arise, and sure enough, two months later, a wild opportunity came my way, because I was where I was supposed to be: watching a rock show—several shows, as a matter of fact.

Todd Rundgren was doing a weeklong stint at the Roxy— seven nights, two shows a night between April 17 and April 25. I'd gone through a serious Todd phase at Valley and was into the new solo LP, *Hermit of Mink Hollow*, which featured the single "Can We Still Be Friends." Todd was a visionary artist who'd been making records under his own name and with the prog quartet Utopia since the turn of the decade. He always charted his own path, experimenting with new sounds and technologies. *Initiation* was released in May 1975 and delved deep into synthetic audio textures and lyrics based on Eastern philosophy and transcendental meditation. The opening track, "Real Man," was aimed right at my solar plexus. "Way down inside me, there's a real man," he sang.

Todd never listened to anyone but himself. He was a McGuire kind of artist, independent, who had flashes of mainstream success, but like his iconoclastic contemporary Frank Zappa, he turned away from the marketplace and guided his creative gaze inward.

I'd bought tickets to three shows, the opening set of the first two nights and the late set of the third. That's all I could afford. Exiting the lobby on the third night, Mario Maglieri, the coowner of the Roxy, Rainbow, and Whisky since the Doors days, grabs me by the arm. "Hey, kid!" I thought I'd done something wrong. Mario was an ex–Chicago cop with an old-school, harmless yet intimidating style. Until he got to know you. Then you were like his adopted godchild.

Mario lived for the rock fans on Sunset. His clubs were like home to us because in the '70s, no one in town was booking cooler or more important acts on a regular basis than the Roxy. The Boss of the Boulevard said he'd seen me all three nights and asked if I planned on going to every show. I told him I didn't have any more tickets. "Come down tomorrow night," he smiled. "I'll let ya in." So I did. And the night after that, and the night after that. In fact, thanks to Mario and "Steady," the Roxy doorman, I didn't miss another performance of Todd's entire run.

As the Runts (hardcore Todd fans—they loved my handmade "Todd Is Godd" T-shirt) poured out onto the street post the final encore of the historic residency, a guy with laminates around his neck who could've passed for Todd's younger brother stopped me on the sidewalk. "Hey, you, what's your name?" he asked. I gave him the handle. "Friend, huh? Cool name." His was Danny O'Connor, the official merchandiser for all things Todd Rundgren. He'd also caught my recurring face, and after meeting and talking to me for fifteen minutes, he offered me a job!

"How'd you like to go on the road this summer and sell T-shirts? Utopia's going out in June." The pitch blindsided me. "I live in Livonia, Michigan. We've got two club dates left in San Francisco this week, and then I'm heading home for a break before the big outdoor tour starts. Come up to the Bay Area and try it out."

Welcome to my first big career decision. Was my job in the campus registrar's office enough to keep me from accepting Danny's offer? The more I thought about it, the more it felt like a dream. This is what I'd been waiting for.

The dream turned into a nightmare in early July 1979 because I wasn't mentally, emotionally, or physically ready for life out of a road case—not this way, at least. My thin Southern California skin started to peel one torrid afternoon in Legend Valley, Ohio, a massive hole carved out of a forest forty miles from the nearest indoor plumbing that twenty thousand dedicated rock fans poured into. We'd spent sixteen hours in hundred-degree heat and humidity in the midst of moonshine-toting maniacs, half of whom were probably delinquents with weapons stuck in their belts—the other half reefer-smoking, incense-burning Runts who would go anywhere, even here, to see their hero rock.

We had the shirt concession for the entire festival bill, including Cheap Trick, the Cars, and Eddie Money, who was riding on a hit song called "Two Tickets to Paradise." I'd have happily taken one because this place sucked. Danny and one of his muscular assistants spent much of the day running off bootleggers with a baseball bat, which left me manning the booth alone. These shady characters that peddled cheaply made, unlicensed shirts for half the price cut into Danny's take. This was a business, not fun and games. I had a far more romantic picture of life on the road with a rock band, and this wasn't it.

When we finally got back to the roach-infested Holiday Inn, I stunk like a pig, my allergies were bothering me, and I was dead tired. All I wanted to do was sleep. Here's where I learned the distinction between crew hotel and band hotel. The band was in town at some sweet, upscale inn, ordering room service and entertaining city girls in the bar. We were sprawled out in our rooms with a case of Coors from the 7-Eleven entertaining two hillbilly groupies with low-cut tops and buckteeth. All I wanted to do was shut my eyes, stop sneezing, and drift away.

The road crew, however, had other ideas. It was time to party! They'd worked nonstop for twenty hours and needed to blow off some steam. I finally lost it when just as I was about to nod off—having found a sofa in the corner of the chaos to lay my weary brow—Eddie Money slammed through the door and threw up all over the bathroom.

"I thought he was at the band hotel!" I cried.

"Eddie likes to party with the crew," someone laughed. I didn't see the humor. All I could see was the United terminal at LAX. It was time for the Runt to crawl back home.

I rode with Danny to Toledo the following morning, where the next gig was at a motor speedway. We checked into our hotel and while he was out scouting the location for where to set up the merch stand, I wrote him a heartfelt "thanks but no thanks" note, placed it inside his Halliburton briefcase, and grabbed a cab for the airport.

That experience with Danny gave me a preview of what was to come. In a few short years, I'd be invited out on the road again, not to sell shirts, but to gather stories. And I would soar across Planet Rock on starships fueled by success and privilege, guided by some of rock 'n' roll's craziest captains. Amazing what a sociology degree can get you.

7

Dr. Stanley and Mr. Simmons

"WHEN YOU PEEL OFF THE MASK THAT HIDES
YOUR VULNERABILITY AND YOUR HUMANITY, YOU'LL COME
FACE TO FACE WITH YOUR TRUE SELF."

—*Debbie Ford*, The Dark Side of the Light Chasers

I was walking through the lobby of the Shrine Auditorium during another boring VH1 Music Awards in the fall of 1999 when I noticed Gene Simmons sitting alone in a chair near the entrance. I sidled up to say hello. Before I could complete my introductory sentence, he directed my eyes to the wristwatch on his left arm. It was an officially sanctioned KISS timepiece—evidently, the brand-new model right off the assembly line. "Cool," I said, half-expecting him to remove the ticking novelty and award it to me (like he didn't have a hundred more at home in a drawer).

"Go to kissonline.com and you can buy one," he said, unflinching.

"Are you kidding, Gene?" I laughed. "Buy one?"

"Yes, Lonn," he responded, his legendary serpent's-length tongue not so firmly in cheek. "Buy one."

If you were to poll the artists who rose to success in popular music over the past two decades and ask them who their heroes were, a good percentage would put KISS at the top of their lists. From Anthrax to Pantera, Lenny Kravitz to Garth Brooks, and hundreds more from across the musical spectrum, if it hadn't been for KISS, they probably would have chosen another path in life. Nirvana even covered "Do You Love Me?" on the very first KISS tribute album in 1990. The four masked marvels of metal inspired a generation. Sitting in a freestanding, fully reclining leather lounger soaring across America, however, Gene and Paul were far from mythical. In fact, the visionaries who started it seemed all too human.

My first encounter with the bass player from the fabled glam rock band KISS took place in August 1987. I was transitioning from *Hustler* to *RIP*, having not yet completely abandoned my editorial duties at our more "sophisticated" publications.

The invitation was to an "intimate" schmooze at a small Hollywood recording studio designed so Gene Simmons could have some up-close-and-personal time with the local rock scribes. He'd just inked a deal to launch his own label imprint, Simmons Records, and wanted to plant some early seeds in the heads of the oh-so-important metal media. The bass man was also a businessman, and I'd just become a new addition to the influential rock press pool.

Simmons Records—their logo was a bag of money with an *S* on the side—would not drop their first release for several months, but Gene was beginning his promotional massage mission early. At the time, I wasn't conscious of anything except meeting the cofounder of the almighty KISS. I wasn't a big fan and had never seen them play live during their original makeup years, 1973 to 1983. But I was now the editor of a nationally distributed hard-rock magazine, and if there was one band of the genre that I needed to get to know, it was KISS.

I brought along a girl (we'll call her Cheryl) who worked in the Flynt "talent" department and was a huge KISS fan. She was a sexy brunette with brand-new breasts. *Gene will love those*, I thought. I had heard the rumors about how much he dug the ladies.

Since the late '70s, he and Paul Stanley—his creative reflection and musical partner—had been writing and recording salaciously silly songs and cashing in big. When he wagged that enormous oral appendage while proclaiming, "They call me Dr. Love," he was doing more than singing a song. He was telling the world exactly who he was under the mask. That night at the schmooze, Gene was about to permit me that first private peek beneath the paint.

After we were properly introduced, he took me aside and offered some cogent advice on what he believed would set *RIP* apart from the competition. He'd done his homework on who I was and where I'd come from. "This is metal, Lonn," he said. "You worked for *Hustler*. Don't be afraid to unite those two attitudes. And remember, the biggest bands will sell the most magazines. So make sure you have a lot of KISS features." His tone was half-serious, his stature somewhat intimidating. But the message was obvious: You get big, *we* get bigger. And as I would come to learn in the months and years ahead, with Gene Simmons it was all about size.

When my brief lesson was over, he turned his attention to Cheryl, morphing into the goddess enchanter without missing a beat. Gene flirted with exacting precision and confidence. He loved this game. The dinner bell had rung and Cheryl was the main course.

I drifted about the room and rapped with some local writers. After twenty minutes had passed I was ready to bail but couldn't find Gene or Cheryl—until I peered through the glass and onto the soundstage of the recording booth. Nestled in a corner was Gene with his reptilian tongue halfway down my coworker's throat, his famous four-string fingers floating across her silicone frets.

RIP's first big coup with KISS under my watch was to support 1989's *Hot in the Shade* LP. The video for "Rise to It" opened with Gene and Paul putting on the old makeup, something they hadn't done since 1983 when they exposed themselves in the clip "Lick It Up." The lineup during these "revelation days" was Gene, Paul, Vinnie Vincent on guitar, and Eric Carr on drums.

I was contemplating who would appear on our June 1990 cover when an exciting pitch came from the KISS camp. "We'll give you the only shot of Gene and Paul taken in makeup in seven years if you'll run it on the cover," offered the band's publicist. "You got it!" I responded. What happened during the production of that issue proved to be the most embarrassing moment in my tenure as editor of the bible of bang.

We had one image, taken at the "Rise" video shoot, of Gene and Paul in the classic original makeup. When my art director, Craig Jones, designed the cover, he decided to flop the photo to accommodate the *RIP* logo on the upper left hand side of the page. It was standard practice to flop shots, which reversed the image to better fit the layout of a given spread. The trick didn't work with guitarists because a right-handed player would become a lefty. What Craig didn't notice—and neither did I—was that flopping the image of Gene and Paul now put the familiar star over Paul's left eye instead of his right.

Amazingly, no one on my staff caught the mistake until it was too late. Even when the proof came back from the separator for color correction and final editorial scrutiny—before it ultimately went to the printer—not one person realized that the great *RIP* magazine had reapplied Paul Stanley's star to the left eye! And what's even funnier, neither the band's manager, Larry Mazer, its label, Mercury Records, or even Gene or Paul mentioned it when they received the published issue.

A few hardcore fans sent us letters—nothing earthshaking—but I was ashamed of the error. I needed to beef up on my KISS studies. I was long overdue for a good old seat-of-the-pants road trip, and that window of opportunity opened on October 26, 1990, for a leg-ending gig of the *Hot in the Shade* tour at the Centrum in Worcester, Massachusetts. Winger and Slaughter were the opening bands, two hairy happening outfits with platinum debuts and tons of female fans.

Just before KISS hit the stage, I walked into Slaughter's dressing room and asked lead singer Mark Slaughter if he wanted to watch the show from the pit with me. A fan since before he was potty trained, the affable front man smiled and fired back, "Lead the way, Lonn! I haven't missed their set once on this entire tour! But I haven't done the pit, yet! Let's fucking rock, man!"

As soon as the lights went down and the band launched into their smash-and-trash set list, Gene caught sight of Mark and me pummeling our way to the front and starting flicking picks at our heads while the fans, mostly female, throttled Slaughter's sexy singer with hugs, tugs, and high fives. It wasn't nearly as gnarly as a Slayer or Anthrax pit, but we were slammed, bumped, and rocked the entire set. I never had so much fun getting bruised in all my life. And remember, these were the nonmakeup days. When the war paint returned in 1996, the stakes, the crowds, the bank accounts—everything went through the roof. But in this moment, there was an odd intimacy to the KISS thing.

After the show, Gene and I were talking in the dressing room. "So, are you leaving tomorrow?" he asked.

"Yes," I replied. "Just a quick transcontinental overnighter."

He glared at me for a second and said, "How would you like to fly back to L.A. tomorrow night with me and Paul on MGM Grand?" The exclusive air carrier catered to high-end celebrities and business moguls and had only one route: LAX-JFK.

I'd gotten a taste of the good life they offered at thirty-five thousand feet with Guns N' Roses. It was like a flying hotel lobby, replete with all manner of decadent amenities. "Fly home with you and Paul?" I responded. "I'd be honored."

"We'll take a town car from Boston to Manhattan and fly from there," he explained. "You'll be very impressed," he added. "It's how the rich and famous get from coast to coast."

Gene did most of the talking on the flight—not a stretch since he was far and away the more sociable. Paul and I exchanged a few pleasantries, and then he took a nap. It was almost scripted. Let Gene loose on Lonn: the spider on the fly. We all know how that fairy tale ends. I dug breathing this kind of rarefied air, and Gene figured if we bonded like real bros, I'd be inspired to carry the KISS torch high and proud—in other words, I'd support him and his band on all media fronts. More press meant more exposure; more exposure meant more bucks in the KISS coffers. I was being played like a Stradivarius, but it didn't matter because my ass was flying ultra first class on the dime of superstars.

Funny thing was, I liked him. A lot. The first thing we talked about was the Beatles. He told me that when he saw them on *Ed Sullivan* in 1964, it changed his life. He called it "an awakening." "KISS was modeled after them," he confessed boldly. "All four members of the band sang, and there were two separate but distinct 'leaders.' A comic-book Beatles was the idea. Throw masks and platform heels on John, Paul, George, and Ringo and what do you get? KISS!" Then we shared our favorite Fab Four songs. Like me, he knew the entire catalog.

We were somewhere over the Great Lakes when the dialogue left Liverpool for other waters. He reiterated what he'd said many times before that the New York Dolls and Alice Cooper had a powerful effect on him, Paul, Ace, and Peter. Seeing Alice live blew Gene's mind. He related instantly to the power of the makeup. They created their own unique characters based on things that turned them on. Gene loved horror movies, hence the scary God of Thunder visage.

As I enjoyed a shrimp cocktail, Gene explained how KISS became the first band to up the ante of fan adulation to sycophantic levels through aggressive merchandising—KISS dolls, lunch pails. While I was hanging out in North Campus listening to the Clash, KISS was selling out stadiums and building their brand. Collectors were born en masse. They had a name, too.

"I take it that you're a member of the KISS Army?" he asked sarcastically.

"No, Gene," I responded. "I heard the songs on the radio but never bought any of the albums and had never seen you perform live until last night."

"Well, you're a member now," he smiled.

"I just missed the draft in college," I laughed. "Will you take a Jewish kid with bad eyes and allergies?" I knew he and Paul shared the same faith as me. There was friendship developing here, or at least that's how I perceived it, even beyond the Grand Air schmooze. Maybe I was being set up. It didn't matter because I would get as much out of KISS as they would out of me. Gene not only knew that, he respected it.

"We'll probably put the makeup back on again," Gene confessed nonchalantly as we started our descent into L.A. "When the time is right . . . or more importantly, when the money is right." It was a perfectly placed bread crumb that I was sure to nibble . . . when the time was right.

A few weeks later, I was at a White Zombie show at the Palace nightclub in Hollywood, the legendary venue that played host to a network variety program in the '60s called *The Hollywood Palace*. Lead singer Rob Zombie was an Alice Cooper/KISS offspring who married hard-edged beats with midnight-movie-inspired lyrics.

In the *Hustler* '80s, I was at the Palace practically every weekend, catching cutting-edge Euro imports like the Eurythmics, Magazine, and Shriekback and flirting with the venue's spectacular waitresses. Something else Gene and I had in common. We liked to flirt. On this particular evening, the hard-rockin' industrial-metal hybrid from New York was lighting up Vine Street and summoning creatures of the rock-'n'-roll night.

The venue was a multilevel building boasting a downstairs and upstairs lobby. Upon entering the building, I made my way up, where the industry folks usually gathered. The first person I recognized was Gene, holding court with several women. I said a quick hello and drifted back downstairs as Zombie was about to hit the stage. The minute my feet landed in the lower lobby, I saw another familiar face creeping slowly through the front door.

"Hi, Trent," I said. "I'm Lonn from *RIP*." Trent Reznor, the principal force behind the groundbreaking industrial group Nine Inch Nails, was out to get some air and space from the claustrophobic confines of his recording studio, which just happened to be the Benedict Canyon mansion where the Manson murders had taken place.

"I'm having a writer's block," he said.

"Listen," I replied, "come upstairs. Gene Simmons is hanging out. Have you ever met him?"

Trent's face went white. "Oh, no, I couldn't do that," he mumbled.

"Why not?" I fired back. "He's really quite cool and easy to talk to."

I could see that Trent was uncomfortable. "Lonn, on my recording console at the house, I have two dolls," he explained. "They stand on either side of the board. One is Jesus Christ and the other is Gene Simmons. You get my point?" Of course I did.

"Trust me, Trent, it'll be cool. C'mon." He followed me up the stairs, and the moment Trent saw Gene, he was a deer caught in the headlights. Gene recognized his brilliant prodigy immediately and disarmed the introverted Reznor with breakneck speed. "Hello, Trent," he said. "Have you come out to see the band, or are you here to get laid like I am?" I walked away and left them to bond.

In April of 1992, I received an advance cassette of the new KISS record, *Revenge*. Magazine editors got new releases two to three months before the official records hit the stores. We needed the material early because of the long lead times required to produce a monthly publication. I had just landed a local radio show on 100.3 FM dubbed *The Pirate Radio Friendship*—fallout of the growing popularity of *RIP* and my "Friend at Large" MTV spot on Saturday nights.

Ignoring industry protocol when it came to airing new releases, I took the cassette down to the studio one night and spun the playful track "I Just Wanna," an act that garnered the immediate wrath of KISS's label, Mercury Records. They sent me a cease-and-desist letter that threatened legal action if I aired the song again. Record companies don't like it when new music gets on the airwaves unless it's through their own promotion departments. This is how they balance relationships with the various stations in competitive markets. I made a cause célèbre out of the event by inviting the guys—Bruce Kulick, Eric Singer, Gene, and Paul—onto my show to have some fun.

Paul Stanley read the actual cease-and-desist letter on the air live just before I had him intro the song for another unauthorized spin. We even got Mercury metal promotions director Cheryl Valentine on the phone from New York to take part in the folly. "You're not supposed to be playing that!" she laughed. The evening turned into one big promotional carnival for the band's brave new LP, *Revenge*, the record I proclaimed on air as "the best KISS album in ten years." The record birthed two of Gene's surliest vocal performances ever on "Unholy" and "Domino," as well as the anthem "God Gave Rock & Roll to You II."

On July 11, a week after my program went into national syndication, changing its moniker to *Pirate Radio Saturday Night with Lonn Friend*, KISS returned to the airwaves with another coup when Paul broke the news to American audiences that he was engaged. We turned that evening into a live on-air bachelor party, and Gene and Paul spent two hours with me in the studio taking calls from assorted fans and teasing each other about matrimony. Paul chided his same-gender significant other several times, saying, "You're next," although privately he knew that was never going to happen. Gene also got me in trouble by blurting the word *fuck*, one of the greatest no-nos in live radio.

Gene and B-movie actress Shannon Tweed had lived together for years, bringing two children into the world. But Gene did not believe in the marriage contract because he felt it was financially and sexually constraining. Without his John Hancock on a formal legal document, he was free to run roughshod through the garden of groupies lying in wait from coast to coast while still maintaining the integrity of his family unit. He had the best and worst of both worlds and never seemed to have any issues of conscience. In a way, I admired him for his candor. He had it all out on the table. No secrets. I struggled with temptation. He welcomed it.

A couple of days after the airwave soiree for Paul, Gene hosted a confidential get-together to commemorate the soon-to-be-hitched Dr. Stanley at the rooftop pool of L.A.'s most notorious rock hotel, the Hyatt on Sunset. A small but elite collection of freaks and friends looked on as a pair of hired professional female porn stars did the nasty on the concrete. The girls were robotic and cold; the guys looked either excited or uncomfortable, depending on their individual sensibilities for such activity.

The one who looked least enthralled by the action was Paul. It was almost as if he showed up to humor his partner for going to the trouble to organize the frat-house cliché. Gene was enjoying the scene immensely. Here was the dichotomy played out. The light and the dark had collided to create something extraordinary, and KISS was that creation. But in real life, the eminent Dr. Stanley and his true eternal other half, Mr. Simmons, were as different as night and day.

How the planets aligned to allow for the big-bang delivery of

KISS is one of the great mysteries of the universe. Gene Simmons and Paul Stanley were two Hebrews, one born in Israel and the other in Brooklyn, who somehow met, mind-melded, and birthed the most popular four-letter word in music history. KISS wasn't the solo, horror-movie trickery of Alice Cooper or the satanic sarcasm of Black Sabbath. They had a precise, well-developed, and completely original theme.

Four characters, each with its own singular look and thing. Gene was the tongue-flapping, leather-and-spiked, fire-breathing, bass-playing God of Thunder. Paul was the androgynous, Bowie-in-face-paint, guitar-strumming, "starry"-eyed, trash-talking Minister of Love. The Spaceman, Ace Frehley, noodled the flame-throwing lead guitar, and Peter "the Cat" Criss played drums. They all wore absurd foot-tall elevator platform boots, giving them a bigger-than-life image on stage.

At the close of 1995, KISS secured the managerial services of rock's P. T. Barnum, the one and only Doc McGhee, the far-sighted entrepreneur who helped bring Bon Jovi from the streets of New Jersey to the stadiums of the world. The synergy between Gene and Doc was the likes of which the modern music business had never witnessed.

In February of 1996, KISS eased into their triumphant Reunion in Makeup tour with a guest appearance on the Grammys. As Doc and Gene—with conscious, creative input from Paul—designed the plans for the biggest comeback in the history of rock, nerves were jumpy around the KISS camp. That is, until tickets went on sale at the end of April for the first date of the tour.

I was playing golf with Doc in Palm Springs the morning he got the call from the promoter in Detroit. "You're kidding," giggled Doc, placing his tee in the ground with the cell phone to his ear as he received the news. "That's fantastic." Tiger Stadium had sold out faster than you could say "Black Diamond." The circus was back in town, and this time it was bigger, louder, hotter, and more expensive than even Gene Simmons could have possibly imagined.

In the late '90s, I had no press platform with which to professionally approach KISS and the gigantic prosperity that the second time around in makeup was affording them, so I just popped in to see the shows when they passed through L.A. When I reentered the world of hard-rock journalism at KNAC.com in December of 1999, KISS was soaring and I was reconnecting with the superstars who had paved my previous path. Through my long relationship with Doc, I'd never lost the laminate to the inner sanctum where the kings of the nighttime world did their dirty work. But my head had changed since those frolicking *RIP* days, and if there was anyone I wanted to go toe to toe with again—rock scribe to rock star—it was the irascible Mr. Simmons.

I didn't have to wait long for that assignment. On March 17, 2000, I found myself in Gene Simmons' hotel room at the Mandalay Bay Resort and Casino in Las Vegas. We had seen each other six days before when I flew into Phoenix for the show that my old friend Danny Zelisko was promoting. That night, Beatle offspring Sean Lennon was in the crowd, and like that evening a decade ago with Trent Reznor at the Palace, I was the one connecting the rock tissue. And this time, the hero was far more modest.

"Hello, Sean," said Gene, in full concert regalia outside the dressing room just minutes prior to taking the stage. Lennon's beautiful boy was wide eyed and, dare I say, starstruck. "I loved your father very much," commented the eight-foot-tall leather-studded masked marvel. It was the second time I'd gotten a glimpse of the "doctor" inside Mr. Simmons. Seemed like a healing moment for both men. "Come back after the show so we can talk some more." I'm not sure but under the makeup, I believe Gene was actually blushing.

Three hours before showtime with tape rolling in Las Vegas, I did my best to take the conversation to higher ground, but Gene consistently returned me to earth and the core values that had driven him since childhood: sex and bucks and rock 'n' roll. He told me in no uncertain terms that he did not believe in karma and dismissed even the faint possibility of judgment from any higher power other than himself.

"God gives you a wallet," he postulated, sitting on the sofa of his hotel suite clad in a bathrobe and slippers. "He's giving you a choice of having more money or less money in your wallet. Which do you choose?" I fumbled for an answer, not wanting to buy into the premise that God had anything to do with the size of Gene's or my wallet. "More or less?" he pursued. "It's not a loaded question. What you do with that money—buy your mom a new hip or blow it in Las Vegas—has nothing to do with it. The question has to do with free choice. You can throw it off a building or use it for good. But if you don't have the money at all, there's no choice. You're happier with more money than less. And without money, you can't eat. You're not happy if you've got nothing to eat. What about the spiritual argument? Fuck the spiritual stuff. You can't shit if there's nothing digesting down there, and that takes money."

Gene was in rare form, so I kept my commentary to a minimum, letting him take the conversation wherever it was meant to go. "Does that statement make me a whore?" he asked. Before I could respond, he answered his own question. "Whores are more ethical than wives," he continued. "Because before the blow job, they're going to tell you exactly what it's going to cost. How much will this relationship cost me? Well, God gave man two balls, and the minute you're married she's ripped open your sac and taken one of 'em out. Again, you have a choice. The secret is never have joint bank accounts and never get married. Period. And where did fifty percent come into it? My mother gave birth to me and she's not getting fifty percent. She's getting ten percent."

"Where does your clarity come from?" I asked.

"I've never gotten high or drunk," he replied emphatically. "I've always been confident. My mother survived the concentration camps and still has a positive sense of life and humanity, and if she can do that with all the horrific moments she endured, what right do I have to complain about anything? The way I look at it, any day above ground is a good day."

Then, in October of that year, the following press release hit the wires. When it crossed my desk, something inside me sort of snapped. The release read as follows:

KISS online today unveiled the KISS coffin, a colorful casket emblazoned with the KISS logo and images of the band members that allows fans to rock in peace forever with their favorite band.

"This is the ultimate KISS collectible," said Simmons. "I love livin', but this makes the alternative look pretty damn good." Simmons appeared on the Howard Stern Radio Show this morning to pitch the product, saying, "Most caskets go for $3,000, but ours will sell for $4,500," prompting Stern to chastise him for not giving fans a deal even in death.

KISS is offering the item in conjunction with Signatures Network, Inc., and White Light, and it will be available only through the band's official website and through your local funeral homes. . . . KISS and Signature Networks will continue to develop and distribute more outrageous and innovative KISS products, including KISS GIRL's Intimate Leather Apparel, KISS Kola, KISS Virgin Red paint, KISS Gaming Machines, KISS Party Cruises, etc.

The KISS brand had become one of the strongest in the history of rock 'n' roll, and one of the most prostituted and diluted as well. The catalog of crazy songs, bombastic performances, and a multigenerational army of fans worldwide were in danger of deteriorating into an apocalyptic banking exercise. Billionaire George Soros once said, "The cult of success can become a source of instability in an open society, because it can undermine our sense of right and wrong."

Gene Simmons was not unstable. On the contrary, he was grounded, focused, and insufferably consistent. The gospel according to Gene said, "Take care of your *self*, make *you* number one, gather everything God's green earth has to offer you, be fearless and absolutely truthful, and society will be just fine." How can one's sense of right and wrong be undermined in the light of such personal clarity? "Thank you for making my life possible," he would often say to his fans.

Do fans really care about the inner makeup of their rock heroes? Or how many millions they've got socked away? Is Gene any less a rock hero than Bono or Coldplay's Chris Martin, who have humanitarian agendas that are as ambitious as their musical ones?

I was told that Gene and Paul contributed handsomely to

charitable organizations but chose to do so privately. I found this oddly inconsistent with Gene's timeless need for public expression and personal exposure. If the man pulls no punches about how many birds he's shagged or how proud he is of his growing fortune, why not let people in on the more noble pursuits?

When I went back and listened to that Mandalay Bay interview, I stumbled across a very telling moment in the conversation. I missed the comment completely the first several passes, but for some reason it jumped out this time. I asked the question, "Are you ever going to act again?" I really liked Gene as the villain in Michael Crichton's 1984 futuristic thriller *Runaway*. Without pausing, he responded with, "I'm acting right now." It was either a throwaway quip or the first truly honest thing he'd ever said to me.

And when this book is finally published, I will make sure that Dr. Stanley gets a free copy. As for Mr. Simmons, well, Borders has stores everywhere. Hey, a man has to eat, right?

8

Nirvana at High Noon

"THE WORLD IS ALWAYS BURNING, BURNING WITH THE
FIRE OF GREED, ANGER, AND IGNORANCE; ONE SHOULD FLEE
FROM SUCH DANGERS AS SOON AS POSSIBLE."

—*Buddha*

Friday morning, April 8, 1994, I awoke to bright sunshine and a warm desert breeze. I was due at 9 A.M. on the tee at La Quinta's famed Stadium Course, located thirty minutes east of the Southern California resort community of Palm Springs. I'd be playing in a foursome that included Geffen Records A&R executive Gary Gersh and the label's head of business affairs, David Berman. We were one of four groups of industry guys united for our annual weekend of fun in the sun under the auspices of Interscope Records president Tom Whalley. He called it the Spring Break Golf Classic.

I've been playing golf since I was twelve and have watched the game I've long held sacred become nouveau chic amongst the movers, shakers, hookers, and slicers of the music business. During the peak days of my media career, it was the best access to the titans. Where else could you spend four hours with powerful men that you couldn't normally get five minutes with on the phone?

Upon entering the beautiful PGA West clubhouse of the celebrated desert resort where Frank Capra wrote *It's a Wonderful Life*, I noticed Berman talking on the telephone with a most disturbing look on his face. This was a man who constantly smiled and was always wisecracking. Berman could have done Jewish stand-up in the Catskills in another life. There was definitely something up in Geffenland.

"Hey, bud," I said softly. He shooed me away. *Probably dealing with another Guns N' Roses legal nightmare*, I thought. I shrugged it off, walked outside, and began warming up on the putting green. Ten minutes later, Berman joined me. His face looked like he'd just seen a ghost.

"I was just on the phone with David Geffen. Kurt Cobain's dead."

I stopped putting. "What?"

"He shot himself," Berman continued. "It hasn't hit the newswires yet. Authorities just discovered his body. Apparently he's been dead for several hours, maybe days. Geffen is really upset. This is incredible. Just incredible."

I immediately called my office. Kristina and managing editor Richard Lange were the only ones in that early. "Listen," I said, swallowing hard, "they just found Kurt Cobain's body in Seattle. He's apparently committed suicide. I don't know much except that it's true. Watch the news later today. It's going to be everywhere."

It was shocking, but not severe enough for Berman, the editor of *RIP* magazine, or Gary Gersh—the man who signed Nirvana to Geffen—to cancel their round. Nero fiddled while Rome burned, and the Tom Whalley bunch played golf as the world found out another rock star had bitten the dust. But this wasn't just any rock star. This was Kurt Cobain, lead singer of Nirvana, the band that changed the course of rock 'n' roll, and he didn't overdose from smack, like Andy Wood from Mother Love Bone, or accidentally overdose, like Jim Morrison. And he wasn't assassinated in cold blood by a mentally deranged fan, like Lennon. Kurt Cobain had swallowed the barrel of a rifle and shot himself. I wondered who in the bunch had the intestinal fortitude to fire a low round today.

I first heard Nirvana at a lowbrow Metallica-hosted beer party somewhere outside of London the day before the August 17, 1991, Monsters of Rock Festival at Castle Donington. Lead singer James Hetfield was cranking a cassette by some comical metal outfit called Haunted Garage. Halfway through the soiree, guitarist Kirk Hammett shut the Garage and slapped another tape in the boom box. "Have you heard Nirvana?" he asked excitedly.

"Nope," I replied. "Put it on." Out came the opening riff to "Smells Like Teen Spirit." And down went my lower jaw.

Kirk made me a copy of the tape before I returned to the States a week later. The minute I got back in the office, I introduced *Nevermind* to my staff and began making dubs of the cassette for spontaneous distribution. The *RIP* writers had been hip to Nirvana since their indie days. Most of 'em dug *Bleach*, their 1989 Sub Pop Records debut.

When I finally received a proper CD advance of *Nevermind*, I carried it with me like a bar of gold, sharing its glow with everyone I could. One afternoon, I brought it with me to a *RIP* cover shoot with Skid Row. The multiplatinum Jersey-bred metal band was riding the top of the charts with their just-released sophomore crusher, *Slave to the Grind*. "I've got something for you guys to hear," I said. "It's going to blow your minds."

Three songs into the impromptu listening party, the boys were collectively flipping out. "Holy mother of Jesus!" screamed lead vocalist Sebastian Bach at the top of his ample lungs. "This shit rocks! We gotta take this band out with us!" Little did anyone with a screeching wail and shoulder-length hair know—no less the flamboyant Sebastian—that those infectious grooves would soon derail the entire decadent metal locomotive.

Soon after the LP hit the streets, I was looking for ways to promote it. On my October 5, 1991, "Friend at Large" segment for MTV's *Headbangers Ball*, I held up the now-famous naked-baby-in-blue-water cover and said, "This is the first CD to replace the Guns N' Roses *Use Your Illusion* discs in my deck in the past three months. This band is gonna be huge." Huge wasn't a strong enough word to describe the place Nirvana was heading.

Nevermind produced four massive airplay video singles—"Smells Like Teen Spirit," "Come As You Are," "Lithium," and "In Bloom"—and went on to sell ten million copies. The week after their breathtaking January 1992 performance on *Saturday Night Live*, the album sold a staggering half million units. But what is so impressive about this accomplishment is the competitive environment at the time.

The year 1991 was one of the most potent and prolific years for rock record releases in history. That twelve-month period saw the release of GN'R's *Use Your Illusion I* and *II*, Metallica's *Black Album*, Van Halen's *For Unlawful Carnal Knowledge*, Ozzy Osbourne's *No More Tears*, Tesla's *Psychotic Supper*, Skid Row's *Slave to the Grind*, R.E.M.'s *Out of Time*, U2's *Achtung Baby*,

Michael Jackson's *Dangerous*, Smashing Pumpkins' *Gish*, and Pearl Jam's *Ten*, just to name a few. Nirvana's rise to marketplace eminence was a miraculous feat.

But its commercial impact paled in comparison to its role as the kerosene on the grunge bonfire that rearranged the pop culture. Teenage girls who once dressed to the nines and dumped on the mousse to keep the 'do high and proud were now donning flannels and greasy mops. Metal's support systems were imploding across the map. The Cathouse, the revered Hollywood club that defined the GN'R generation, would close its doors in 1992 after five years of continuous operation. The foot traffic in front of the Rainbow diminished as the eatery transformed into a metal memorial where die-hard hair farmers who didn't give a fuck about teen spirit would commiserate and recall the days of decadence with a shot or two of Jägermeister.

Practically overnight, MTV shifted its programming focus from glam to grunge. You couldn't find a Winger video if you had a search warrant. The network that broke '80s metal worldwide was now breaking the back of its artists and fans. Alice in Chains, Soundgarden, Pearl Jam, and Nirvana were marching across rock's landscape like the four horsemen of the ripped jeans, and the rider holding the lead reins in his fragile southpaw-strumming hand was Kurt Cobain.

Not long after my nationwide *Nevermind* proclamation, the band showed up at MTV's Santa Monica studios for an interview with Riki Rachman. Kurt was dressed in a lemon-yellow wedding gown. I finished cutting my spots and was preparing to head back to the magazine when the band passed me in the driveway. *Hmm, Kurt Cobain in a wedding dress*, I remember thinking.

I got in my car and cranked *Nevermind*. With the influence

of *RIP* growing from covering an eclectic mix of bands from across the edgy rock spectrum, I was certain it wouldn't be long before Nirvana would be doing their whirlwind press junket and I would have my personal hang. That materialized two weeks later when Geffen publicist Lisa Gladfelter called to ask me if I wanted to have lunch with Nirvana.

I invited them up to the Larry Flynt Publications edifice on Wilshire Boulevard in Beverly Hills. There was an awesome gourmet Chinese restaurant around the corner called Tse Yang, where I'd taken lots of cool rock folks. It was extremely upscale, but the management loved it when I brought in musicians.

I was anxious the morning of our lunch. This was not Mötley Crüe or Ratt. I worried that the *Hustler* connection that had served me so well within the community of follicle freaks and fun boys might not wash with this new breed of somber rocker. I wondered how I should handle these guys. Should I be Lonn Friend, free-spirited, mildly pornographic, familiar dude about town? Or should I don a more serious hat? I resolved to just be myself and go with the flow. How weird could it get?

The mere contemplation of role playing defined how important it was for me to connect with the rockers. Fact is, I *was* Lonn the metalhead. I was also Lonn the prog rocker, Lonn the punk, Lonn the grunge rocker, Lonn the mosher, Lonn the thrasher, Lonn the hippie, Lonn the glam ham, Lonn the idiot, Lonn the savant—whatever the moment called for, that's what I was. As for *who* I was, I'm still working on that one.

It had become customary to take visiting dignitaries on a tour around the magazine. Since *RIP*'s editorial offices shared the same space as *Hustler, Chic,* and the most popular rag with the metalhead contingent, *Busty Beauties*, the highlight of the go-round was usually the X-rated photo department. Rockers used to drop by the office unannounced just to catch a peek at the next month's *Hustler* honeys. But my gut told me Nirvana wouldn't appreciate such eye candy, so we went directly to the *RIP* side of the building. Little did I realize that the flesh depicted on my own office wall would prove my undoing.

It was a balmy Southern California winter day when the trinity called Nirvana—Kurt Cobain, Krist Novoselic, and Dave Grohl—entered the house that Larry built.

Kurt's demeanor immediately made me uncomfortable. His eyes were fixated on the photographs that dotted my walls. I chatted it up with the easygoing Krist and Dave but kept a polite distance from Kurt, who I could tell was somewhere else. He just kept gazing blankly at the framed photos on my wall. *God, I hope he likes Chinese food*, I mused.

Tse Yang was a five-minute walk east on Wilshire to Doheny, a nice stroll to get acquainted before sitting down for a meal. I remember taking Red Hot Chili Peppers vocalist Anthony Kiedis out to lunch one time, and during the walk I started to laud the kung pao shrimp. "I don't eat shrimp, Lonn," he fired back succinctly. "They're bottom-feeders. They consume the feces from other creatures that fall to the sea floor." I was Lonn the vegetarian that day.

When we got to the restaurant, the rhythm section immediately started hammering back one Tsingtao beer after another while the laconic Cobain offered little commentary, content to remain in his private world, disconnected from the blather and bullshit that often spews freely during the initial bonding session of press and artist. I don't think Kurt took one bite of whatever Far East delicacy he ordered.

I truly enjoyed the lunch with Krist and Dave. They were disarming and fun, especially Grohl, who was a big fan of the magazine. Raised on Motörhead and Sabbath, he was an authentic metalhead and made no bones about his headbangin' roots. We were connecting and it felt good. Kurt, on the other hand, was visibly detached. I had a strong sense that he genuinely disliked me. But it wasn't until two years later that I realized just how badly that lunch at *RIP* rattled the fragile feathers of rock's darkest angel.

In 1993, Michael Azerrad's biography of Nirvana, *Come As You Are*, was published. When I reached page 210 of the book, I was floored by what I read.

Part of playing the game is going out to dinner with powerful music magazine editors and pretending to be friendly with them so they'll give the band an article or a favorable review. On one of these junkets, the band went out to lunch at a swank Beverly Hills eatery with *RIP* magazine editor Lonn Friend.

Before lunch, Kurt, Krist, and Dave visited Friend's office. "I looked up on his wall and I noticed that Lonn has a fetish," says Kurt. "A rock 'n' roll butt fetish. He has to have all these pictures taken with him and up-and-coming bands where either he's naked or the bands have to drop their pants. He's pinching their butts. There are all these pictures of him with naked rock stars that have been in this magazine. He's in the bathtub naked and they're standing around him and it started to scare me."

The bathtub shot Kurt was referring to was of me and Alice Cooper posing for a *RIP* subscription ad from the October 1991 Neal Preston cover session. The photo depicted the lighthearted prince of darkness holding an electric blow dryer over a bathtub with me in it. It was an innocent, satirical image that was actually Alice's idea. But Kurt didn't see it that way.

The next depiction that curdled Cobain was the Halfin photo of Metallica and me with their bare butts showing. The other shot was of veteran metal icons Geoff Tate and Chris Degarmo of Queensrÿche flanking yours truly clad in a bath towel with the Queensrÿche *Q* inked on my chest. The 'Rÿche hailed from Seattle, but apparently Kurt didn't recognize them from the old neighborhood.

I was riding a wave of media visibility at this time predicated on the "heavy metal dude" character fans were getting to know via the magazine *MTV* and syndicated radio. Alice Cooper always referred to "Alice" in the third person, the alter ego that made him famous. The "Lonn dude" I showed to the outside world was occasionally misunderstood. Being a chameleon is one thing. Being aware that you're a chameleon is another. I adapted to my environments, not to survive like a lizard in the desert, but to thrive amongst the weird array of creatures I encountered on a daily basis. I knew there were snakes in the grass. In the rock business, they're everywhere.

It was obvious from the Azerrad tome that my instinct that day was correct. I didn't need to waltz Kurt into the *Hustler* photo department. I had enough skin in my office to corrupt whatever relationship may or may not have had a chance to develop that day. I was completely unconscious of this, simply tickled to have silly shots of my rock star buddies on display in the well-trafficked *RIP* offices for all visitors to enjoy or, in this case, be repulsed by. Whether the rockers in the photos saw me as the "butt" of the joke or the friend in the frame never crossed my mind. It was fun. Simple as that. But that wasn't what ticked me off most about the passage. Kurt's quote continued:

It was a disgusting scene because we were basically pimping our personalities to this person to see if he liked us before he decided to promote us. It was the most sickening thing I ever experienced. I just decided to not say a word and sit there and be pissed off and act really insane. The only words he said to me after he got up to leave were, "Kurt, you shouldn't talk so much." He was really offended, totally pissed off.

My office was the most disgusting thing that Kurt Cobain had ever seen? Whoa, hold on for a sec. More disgusting than the bruises on his arms from shooting smack? More disgusting than the evening news, corporate America, or Courtney Love first thing in the morning? Okay. Kurt may have exaggerated but the last part of that sentence, that I was "really offended"—this is indicative of how severely we misunderstood each other. I wasn't pissed off at all, just disappointed that I was unable to connect with a significant artist whose songs had sincerely rocked me. It wasn't often that my personality did not jibe with those of the musicians who appeared in the magazine. But I never allowed my personal vibe with a band member dictate how *RIP* would cover that act. But this is where Azerrad really flies off the mark:

Sure enough, *RIP* didn't support Nirvana until it practically had to, at the height of Nirvana mania. When the band refused to cooperate anymore with *RIP* after the magazine ran a special edition on the band without their permission, the letters page just happened to feature more and more anti-Nirvana screeds. "If we were smart," says Kurt, "we would have played the game a little bit longer to get the acceptance

of the *RIP* readers, to where they liked us so much that no
matter what we said, it wouldn't matter. But we blew our
wad too soon."

Nirvana happened because of planetary timing and the
fact that their message reflected Kurt Cobain's keen sense of
self-expression and his ability to channel those sensations and
observations into perfect riffs and remarkable songs that the dis-
enfranchised, disillusioned youth at the turn of the decade could
relate to. Similarly, *RIP* happened because we were there to document the moment, connecting with that same transmuting
youth culture.

I had always attributed my success in this business to the fact
that artists trusted me. I earned the respect of bands and developed relationships because I never violated confidences or exploited scandal for the short-term reward of selling a few more
magazines. Damn, we probably would have sold an extra hundred thousand mags a month if I had published one-tenth the
dirt I knew about GN'R alone.

Our coverage of *Nevermind* ranked with any on the news-
stand, including *Rolling Stone*. *RIP* scribe Steffan Chirazi au-
thored the magnificent June 1992 cover story, "The Year of
Living Famously," which echoed the sentiment put forth in my
cover line "Nirvana! How They Made It . . . and Why They
Hate It!" Our layout also included a revealing sidebar titled
"Head Full of Hate: The World According to Kurt Cobain" by
Mike Gitter. Cobain told Gitter:

I don't feel much sincerity from people my age at all. Just
look at how many people just sit there and watch TV all day,
and it's really obvious that all it does is exploit macho-sexism

24 hours a day. . . . I just feel really ashamed of my generation. I seriously want a revolution. Wouldn't that be really exciting and fun?

As far as publishing a special Nirvana issue without permission, we had done quarterly specials on bands for years. They were the best photos and articles we could find, fanzine-style keepsakes, which we took great pride in. And as far as the anti-Nirvana letters, *RIP* ran the good and bad from our readers (our rants, if you will) with great attention to balance. Keep in mind, during this period the hard-core metal community was looking at Nirvana as the Grim Reaper. MTV was wiping the hair bands off their network faster than you could say "mullet head."

The grunge movement was in full flower. Metallica was crossing over to mega-acceptance, and decadent glam metal was being shoved back underground after a decade of chart-topping, multiplatinum prosperity. But my mission as a magazine editor was an eclectic one. *RIP* was expanding its focus, adapting to the changing landscape of aggressive music. It was a rock magazine, wide in its scope, fearless in its journalistic approach, and always just a bit heavier than the competition.

"Heavy" was defined by the attitude of the articles and the photography. Sebastian Bach was a pretty-boy pinup in *Metal Edge* and *Hit Parader.* We put him on the cover in an alley with a broken bottle and a "fuck you" smirk on his face. Our features were long form, sometimes up to three thousand words, unheard of for a metal mag. And we did our best to run the stories uncensored, blotting out a couple letters in *fuck* so the more conservative retailers would keep us on the stands.

Nirvana belonged in *RIP* and we did them right. But I never got to know the artist Cobain personally, so my perspective on who he was and what made him tick comes from outside sources rather than the one I've always trusted the most: my own impressions. Because the fly never made it onto Nirvana's wall, I am destined, like so many moved by his presence and musical purpose, to hypothesize on the mystery man. Kurt played the part of the tortured artist like he was bred for it.

Growing up under the cloudy skies of Aberdeen, a hundred miles from the streets of Seattle, Cobain picked up his guitar at an early age and began to channel the punk avatars with an authentic sense of violence, anger, antiestablishment angst, and almost ethereal disillusionment with society, but more so with himself. "Rape Me," "Heart Shaped Box," and the excruciating 1993 B-side "I Hate Myself and I Want to Die" resonate like the prophetic preachings of a doomed poet. Fact is, as I look back in midlife after my fair share of peaks and valleys, I empathize with Kurt far more than I ever did back when I was handing out assignments on the heroes of the day for a hard-rock magazine.

I finally got some inside perspective on that lunch and on author Azerrad and his book years later when Kurt's widow, the sometimes fabulous, ofttimes flammable Courtney Love and I spoke at the 1996 premiere party for *The People vs. Larry Flynt*, the Milos Forman motion picture in which Mrs. Cobain portrayed to a magnificent and haunting tee my old boss, Althea Flynt. Courtney introduced me to Kurt's mother that night. Shaking the hand of the woman who bore Kurt Cobain was somewhat bizarre, as was the obvious affection Kurt's mom had for Courtney.

I saw my chance during the Flynt dinner to engage Courtney in conversation about *Come As You Are* and how I felt about the page that took my beloved magazine and me to task. I wasn't looking to salvage my reputation or that of *RIP*, but rather for some perspective. I blew it with Cobain, never made the connection; maybe I missed something.

"Michael Azerrad is an asshole, Lonn," she said emphatically. "And as for that lunch, well, let's just say, Kurt wasn't in his right mind around that time." I felt somewhat vindicated, even if it was the fair-haired firebrand pot calling the kettle black.

9

Band of Golden Words

"I ASPIRE TO INSPIRE BEFORE I EXPIRE."

—*Kinky Friedman*

I'm goin' hungry!

The duet cried, their voices united by song and the memory of a fallen friend. Eddie Vedder and Chris Cornell traded vocals and marched across the Hollywood Palladium stage as four thousand fans from far and near stared at a jam for the ages. It was the encore of Soundgarden's dazzling one-hour set, the grand finale to an evening that had also seen performances by their fellow northwest countrymen Pearl Jam and Alice in Chains.

I'm goin' hungry!

They bellowed again, tossed their mikes to the floor, and took flight like a pair of flannel-clad pigeons over a sea of sweaty bodies moshing in the pit below. Into the crowd they soared as intoxicated, hypnotized fans reached for a touch of infamy. The song setting the house ablaze was "Hunger Strike" from *Temple of the Dog*, the one-off record produced by members of both bands as a tribute to Andy Wood—lead singer of Mother Love Bone—who had died of a heroin overdose the year before. Soundgarden drummer Matt Cameron along with Pearl Jam guitarists Mike McCready and Stone Gossard and bassist Jeff Ament, the latter two remnants of Love Bone, were also on stage, strumming their heavenly riffs.

I was watching from the wings, stage left, as the magic unfolded. The date was October 17, 1991, and this was *RIP*'s fourth-anniversary party, what urban legend would someday crown the "Seattle party." The previous year, we'd made history with a soiree highlighted by Motörhead and the last Guns N' Roses club performance the world ever saw. But Planet Rock had changed drastically in the span of twelve months.

There was a seductive new sound emerging from the rainy streets of Seattle, a town better known for its Boeing aircrafts than for its badass beats. Though the bands that would be kings were still yet to be crowned on a global scale, it was obvious to all in attendance that the shift was on.

My relationship with the extraordinary individuals that would fuel the movement that the mainstream media would lamely label grunge rock began with an overnight road trip to Seattle in August 1990. Just a few weeks prior to my departure, the *RIP* advertising department had negotiated what would have been our first promoted concert tour. The bill featured Mother Love Bone and Kill for Thrills, a local outfit featuring guitarist Gilby Clarke, who would later go on to replace Izzy Stradlin in

GN'R. Love Bone was the headliner. They were from Seattle, were local heroes, and had just been signed to PolyGram Records by A&R rep Michael "Goldie" Goldstone.

But the tour never played even one date because before it launched in the spring of 1990, Love Bone's lead singer, the charismatic star child with a penchant for heroin, Andy Wood, passed away on March 19. His body was discovered by his fiancée, Xana La Fuente, on the couple's bed. He'd been clean for 116 days but fell off the wagon one night, hard, when he scored some bad smack. *RIP*'s first tour was abruptly cancelled, and I soon found myself walking the boulevard where Andy had lived and died.

Columbia Records A&R rep Nick Terzo and label publicist Kevin Kennedy invited me to take a road trip with them to get a first glimpse of the band Nick had just signed. I was often privy to peeks at new bands and product before the competition. I loved making a visit to a recording studio to hear tracks from a forthcoming LP—and having the guys in the band play me the material personally. Or getting an all-expense-paid minivacation to a foreign place to catch an indigenous act live before they broke out of their neighborhood and hit the big time.

"They're very dark and very heavy," said Kevin on the phone, giving me the details of our proposed road trip.

"What are they called?" I asked.

"Alice in Chains," he responded.

"Alice in Chains?" I fired back. "Sounds like a good title for an Alice Cooper album."

We arrived around 6 P.M., got a bite to eat on First Street, Seattle's main drag of clubs, and headed over to the venue, a nice-sized theater known to most of the local talent that had built up enough of a following to escape the one-hundred-seat-capacity club scene. The mood at the show that night was

gloomy, with local fans plodding about the drafty venue like extras from *Night of the Living Dead*. Bodies listlessly milled about
the building as Alice introduced to these virgin ears strains that
would soon be known from Bellingham to Boston as grunge.
The dirgelike sadness of the band's music was only overshad-
owed (emphasis on the word *shadow*) by the long-sleeved and
knit-capped crowd, whose aura was as damp and cold as the
weather outside. But they paid attention. They hung desperately
onto every painful note that poured forth from the stage that
night.

My senses took hold of two things: the deliberate, authentic,
inventive grind of guitarist Jerry Cantrell and the hypnotic, gut-
tural vocals of singer Layne Staley. There was one song that
stood out during a rather grueling seventy-minute set. "Man in
the Box" was punishing, perfectly cast, the evil and seductive villain of that evening's poisoned theater. Layne delivered it like a
sickly seasoned veteran, diving to bowel depth to dredge up the
Edgar Allan Poetry of the song's lamenting lyric. "Jeeeeeesus
Christ!" I had no idea then that this was not just the chorus to a
song but also a cataclysmic cry for help. Layne was a junkie from
a dysfunctional family. He was drowning in this black well of addiction, and the music was his only light.

Seattle was still mourning Andy, four months after his death.
You could see it in the eyes of the local kids and feel it in the fog
moving in off the bay. Everyone loved the pudgy blond singer.
His charisma had been as infectious as the smack-induced highs
that ultimately killed him. Evidence of his potential is in every
note of the band's one and only long play, *Apple*, the unsung masterpiece of the era that had just hit record stores in July. "Crown
of Thorns," the epic, purging track on the record, like Alice's
"Box," was a lament of desperation, a plea for faith from across

the brown River Styx. Monkeys jumped from vine to vine in this soon-to-be-discovered northwest burg. You could score heroin sitting at a bus stop or standing on the street in front of a club.

Love Bone bassist Jeff Ament and guitarist Stone Gossard approached me, extended their hands, and introduced themselves. They were easy to talk to, though somewhat shy, and took me under their wing instantly, educating me on the ways of the 'hood in the wake of their friend's death. "You really should talk to Xana," they said. "She was Andy's girlfriend. She's going to be here soon."

On the avenue after the show, a gathering of the tribes ensued. Nick and Kevin introduced me to Alice in Chains. Drummer Sean Kinney and bassist Mike Starr were affable, even comedic, cracking wise about the "visiting rock journalist." (Why is it that the rhythm sections are so often the fun guys in a band? That might be a stupid stereotype, but keeping the beat seems to possess some sort of magical balancing power. I mean, wasn't it Paul and Ringo who were always smiling and John and George who wore the frowns?)

Guitarist Cantrell was distant, removed, guarded in his words and demeanor, as if he carried the burden of an imminent future that would see this little township of devoted, uncorrupted artists suddenly incorporated into a gigantic image-and-marketing campaign that would spawn millions of records by a handful of acts making their mark on rock history.

I stood in the parking lot for two hours, engaged in conversation by Gossard, Ament, Cantrell, and a bizarre but beautiful young girl who'd claimed the heart of the fallen Wood. She introduced herself as Xana, "Andy's girl," and commenced to chatter effortlessly on the immense loss of her beloved. She openly spoke of Andy's light while my tape rolled, freely proclaiming his legacy and their devotion to one another while gently indicting the so-called friends who kept his veins flowing with H. I was almost certain she was stoned herself.

At the end of the night, Jeff approached me with three people. "These are our managers, Lonn," he said, introducing Kelly Curtis and Susan Silver, partners in Curtis/Silver management, who provided artist representation for Mother Love Bone, Alice in Chains, and Soundgarden, the band fronted by Susan's husband, Chris Cornell. Chris was well respected and regarded by the street folk as the leader of the local music scene.

Our small group walked and talked while Kevin and Nick went to a local bar with the Alice boys. Susan wanted to connect with me about something. From the instant I made her acquaintance, I trusted her. Her honesty was unfiltered, rare for anyone engaged in daily battle with the demons of the recording underworld. She told me that night of Layne's addiction. The dialogue was uncharacteristically open for two people who had just met.

The pall of Layne's addiction had been exacerbated by the drug-induced death of his friend and musical colleague. Success, this savvy lady knew in her heart, would only further corrupt the fragile artist's already tenuous state. But it was too late to stop the locomotive of song and culture that was about to run over the hair farmers, making future millionaires of a bunch of shabbily dressed, angry young men whose mission was, not to entertain us, as the cynical Cobain sang, but rather to make us stop dead in our tracks and take a look at what was going on around us.

"So, can we do something with Alice and *RIP*?" asked Kevin and Nick on the plane ride home.

"Absolutely," I responded. "And thank you, guys, for this trip. It was far more than I expected." I had a feeling that a lot of record weasels were going to be descending on Seattle very soon.

"Lonn, I want you to hear something first," said Goldie, the PolyGram talent scout. It'd been months since I'd heard from him, but he was up to something with Jeff and Stone, who had confessed to Del James in the December 1990 *RIP*, "We've come to the conclusion that we are not going to continue as Mother Love Bone. The main reason being that the MLB image—and for that matter, name—was so closely related to Andy's trip that it would not feel right to just try and replace Andy." The grieving was over and it was time to create again, in a new context. What Goldie brought to my office that day shook the earth like a good old West Coast quake.

He passed through my door holding a cassette tape with two songs on it, rough mixes off a debut album by a new band he'd signed to his new label, Epic Records. "Just put the tape in, crank it up, and then I'll tell you the story," he said.

The next several minutes were as surreal as any I've ever experienced in my lifetime as a music fan. My office was shaking. It was one of those career-launching hooks. Like the Edge's locomotive grind that opens "I Will Follow" or Ray Manzarek's seductive keyboard at the outset of the Doors' volcanic first volley, "Break on Through."

Then the voice.

Son, she said, have I got a little story for you.

Cognac-smooth yet unspeakably strong, the vocal presentation was completely captivating. So many bands, so many front men, metal screechers like Dickinson and Halford or glorious growlers like Hetfield and Danzig, or those that trekked somewhere in between, like the indefinable Axl. But this, this was new and breathtaking in its boldness. Part lounge croon, classic, Mel Tormé velvet fog; part Morrison throaty, bowel centered, brave, and brutal. I was ready to cross over completely. "Let there be chorus!"

Oh, I, oh, I'm still alive.
I, oh, I'm still alive.

Goldie sat quietly on my sofa and stared at my face as it faded to white, smiling that smile, the kind that said, "I know, brother. I know." As the song ended, I stopped the tape. "Oh, my God, dude," I fumbled. "What the fuck was that? And *who* is that singer?" Whereupon the talent scout began to humbly recount the talent on the tape.

"This is Stone and Jeff's new band," he explained. "It doesn't have a name yet, but we're calling it Mookie Blaylock for the time being [referring to Ament's favorite basketball player, from the New Jersey Nets]. It's pretty good, huh?" Shift the gift of understatement to Goldie. "Good?" I replied. "Dude, this is amazing. Michael, *who* does that voice belong to, and how did you find him?"

He paused for a second, like he was preparing to tell a story that he knew he would recount a thousand times throughout the course of his life.

"His name is Eddie Vedder," he began. "And I didn't find him.

I had nothing to do with it. The guys found him. He's a surfing buddy of Jack Irons." Irons was the drummer for the Red Hot Chili Peppers who later went on to do a stint with Pearl Jam after the departure of their original skin basher Dave Abbruzzese.

"Eddie was born in Chicago and lives in Escondido near San Diego," Goldie continued. "It's one of those magical things, Lonn. Jeff and Stone met him and it just happened." No one ever saw Seattle coming. There was no script or grand promotional plan. Grunge rock was never meant for the masses. Its success, like all authentic rock creations, was an aberration. Fans discovered it and passed it along like a joint among friends. But this secret toke would not stay secret for long, no matter what course the kingmakers would map out. And Goldie knew that.

"Dave Glew [the president of Epic Records at the time] is really behind this," he continued. "But we're not going to over-promote it. The band doesn't want that. They want to tour and let it happen naturally. They have no expectations. I mean, who would have thought that after Andy died something like this was even possible?"

After Goldie played "Even Flow," the second song on the tape, I sat there trying to retrieve the breath that had just evacuated my lungs. "Look, buddy," I said, "this is going to be huge, no matter what you or Epic or anyone else does. It's a foregone conclusion. Congratulations! I hope you still take my calls in a year."

He hugged me and left. It wasn't long after that day that Eddie hit on the name Pearl Jam for the band, inspired by his grandma's homemade jelly. And so their most uncommon journey began, uncommon because Pearl Jam did everything in their

power *not* to be enormous. They had no choice in the matter. The debut LP, *Ten* (Mookie's number), operated under forces of nature unbeknownst to the record industry.

RIP began to cover the Seattle scene diligently with Alice in Chains and Soundgarden as Pearl Jam was shredding rock radio, thanks in great part to the timeless efforts of Epic hard-rock promotional dude Michael Schnapp. Mentored by Epic's guru of radio promotion, Harvey Leeds, Schnapp became an influential force of nature in hard-rock radio. A born-and-bred New York stoner good guy who called everyone "dude," Schnapp miraculously convinced skeptical rock programmers that Pearl Jam was as heavy and right for their format as the other act he was working at the time, Ozzy Osbourne, who was then riding high with his most successful solo effort to date, *No More Tears*. Schnapp was not a record guy. He was a music guy. There was a huge distinction.

Through Schnapp's relentless effort, "Even Flow" lived at rock radio for months as low-budget live clips for it and "Alive"—both accentuating the power of Eddie's onstage allure—saturated MTV. This was about the time that my staff and I were beginning to plan the 1991 fourth-anniversary *RIP* magazine party. We had secured the Hollywood Palladium and a date in October, but I'd just begun to slate the bands that would come out and play live, for free, to celebrate the publication and the passage of another successful year.

That's when Susan Silver called me. "Lonn," she said, "do you have any bands booked for the *RIP* party yet?"

I paused for a moment, allowing my toes time to tingle. Susan was not about small talk. "We're just getting into it," I replied. "What have you got in mind?"

"Well, how would you like Soundgarden to play? I've talked to Kelly and Chris and they're into it."

I was blown away by the proposition. "Soundgarden?" I responded. "Are you kidding? Yes! Done!"

I could hear the elation in her voice. "They have to headline. Is that okay?" she asked.

I didn't hesitate. "Of course," I replied. "Oh, Susan, listen, if you have any other thoughts, the bill is still pretty open and I'm all ears."

A week later, I received the phone call that took the kinks out of my beard. It was Susan. "So, Lonn, how would you like to have Pearl Jam, Alice in Chains, and Soundgarden all play your party?" I was numb. "Eddie and Chris are even talking about a *Temple of the Dog* jam at the end. Would that be cool?"

The *Temple of the Dog* LP—the hybrid project written and recorded in a remarkable fifteen days by members of Soundgarden and Pearl Jam—had been released on A&M Records (Soundgarden's label) that past April. The tracks "Hunger Strike" and "Say Hello 2 Heaven" were making inroads at rock radio, but no one there was working the record too hard out of respect to Andy. They didn't want to come off as whores by overhyping the project. Seattle bands wielded tremendous influence on their record companies. The music had to come first; it was organic, cultural, and owed little to the image makers of the big music industry machine that, up until recently, would spend untold hours figuring out when to drop the power ballad and hair metal, MTV's bread and butter. Grunge ultimately assassinated the power ballad and dismantled the wind machines, but more on that later.

The Seattle *RIP* party delivered everything promised and more. I even got Chris's favorite faux icons of metal, Spinal Tap,

to do a set, aware that Soundgarden loved to cover "Big Bottom" in concert. On top of that, Epic A&R exec Bob Pfeifer helped secure supershredding axe prodigy Joe Satriani to sit in on lead guitar with the Tap.

Pearl Jam played second on the bill, following the unknown Australian rockers Screaming Jets. After the set, I walked backstage and told the guys how awesome they were. That was the first time I met the man whose vocal style would influence a generation of pipes. From STP to Creed to Nickelback and a hundred others that borrowed (sometimes shamelessly) from Eddie's tender yet triumphant technique, he remains the postmodern archetype.

That night, he was toting a bottle of red wine, an early passion, something that connected him to the spirit of another great rock original. Eddie was Morrison-esque to me that first performance, thirty minutes of heart and soul, slightly dysfunctional yet real.

For the jam that followed Soundgarden's house-crumbling, one-hour set, Eddie joined Chris onstage for "Hunger Strike" and both men took flight, launching off into the four-thousand-capacity grunge-mad audience, a stage dive for the ages.

Susan was beside herself and so were the bands. The great American satirist Harry Shearer recalls that gig with huge fondness, being it was the only time the Tap was on the same bill as grunge-era legends and on the same stage as Joe Satriani. I adored these groups and the dedication they had to their music and did what I could to further the cause.

After the *RIP* party, Pearl Jam hit the road. MLB never really saw much of America outside Bellingham, Washington. Jeff was relishing the experience and shared that feeling by sending postcards to the magazine from the road. The first one, postmarked

November 25, 1991, read, "Hello from beautiful Normal, Illinois. . . . The Peppers is rocking most of the nation. See yuz at the Sports Arena. . . . Thanks again for the amazing time at the *RIP* party. Unforgettable. Jeff A. Pearl Jam."

He wrote us again on December 30, and when the band hit Europe in 1992, he fired us off a jubilant note from the Sheraton Copenhagen. But while Jeff was knocking out postcards from the road, Stone was checking in with me by phone. There was one afternoon, however, during a break in the tour, when I learned something about myself, thanks to the honesty of a rock guitarist.

Stone had shown a tepid interest in golf, so I hooked him up for a set of sticks through my friend Steve Mata at TaylorMade Golf. Then when he hit town, I put together a foursome that included Mötley Crüe drummer Tommy Lee and Warrant guitarist Joey Allen. It never struck me that the chemistry of this bunch might have been less than perfect.

I picked up Stone at his hotel and met Tommy and Joey at the Westlake Village house on the hill once shared by Lee and then-wife actress Heather Locklear—the same pad long occupied by Heather and her rock-star beau, Bon Jovi axe Richie Sambora. We teed it up at North Ranch Country Club, a swank, private layout that Lee somehow managed to buy his way into. Throughout the day, the dialogue was as glam metal as Lee's and Allen's lifestyle, from off-color jokes about women to what new high-priced, four-wheeled toys the guys had bought.

It was role-playing to a certain extent. Shoot whiskey all night on Pantera's tour bus and rap like a redneck? Sure. Sit with Tori Amos in a coffee house and discuss angels and fairies? No problem. Wax on the wonders of groupies with Hollywood metalheads? Piece of cake.

It was not so easy for Stone, however. He kept up a good front all afternoon, holding his own with a slightly scandalous tale or two, mostly manufactured to keep the crowd engaged. I was out of my mind, a cartoon character, Lonn the metal dude, friend to all, luckiest fucker on Planet Rock. When the day was done, Stone came back to my office with me, and we sat and played a golf video game on my computer. He really didn't dig the sport, but he wanted to hang out a bit longer. I sensed there was something on his mind.

"Lonn, why do you act that way?" he asked, knocking me a bit off guard.

"What do you mean?" I responded.

"Those guys, they're fun and all, but that rap and their decadent lifestyle, that's not you. You're being phony when you play into their world. It's not real. I know that you're a special guy, you care about music, and you care about this magazine. Be yourself, man. Always, be yourself."

I thought a lot about what Stone said that night, but I wasn't in the correct space to make any drastic alterations in my personality or behavior. I was being myself, or at least, one of my selves. His words, however, stuck with me, and in hindsight, I'm thankful for the honesty he showed me that day. If Cobain had been half as candid with me, maybe things could have different between us.

When Pearl Jam returned later in the year for the U.S. leg of the *Vs.* tour, I had one of the wackiest spontaneous ideas that ever popped into my longhaired head. It was 4 P.M. in our Beverly Hills office and Pearl Jam was playing the old Aladdin Hotel in Las Vegas at 8. I called my wife and said, "Get Megan ready. I'm taking her on a quick road trip."

Joyce was incredulous. "She's not even three years old and

has preschool at nine o'clock in the morning," came the response. "And where is it you plan on going?" The Empress was not happy with the Jester. I must have been nuts. "Vegas, to see Pearl Jam. I'm booking two tickets for a 6 P.M. flight, we'll get a hotel room for the night, and I'll have her back in time for preschool."

Looking back, I realize how much my wife supported these wild and crazy days that took me across the globe, most of the time leaving her at home alone to raise our daughter. After Megan was born, she lost interest in hangin' out. The rope she gave me was long, and she never tugged too hard to reel me back in. If there was such a thing as having too much freedom of movement, this was the case, because Joyce and I eventually floated so far apart, we couldn't get back together again. I should have taken her and Megan on the overnighter to Vegas. Somehow, it never crossed my mind.

I grabbed a cab, headed for the Mirage, found the hotel president Bobby Baldwin's daughter, Stacy—whom I had met earlier in the year at the Metallica Snakepit show at the Thomas and Mack Center—in the gym working out. She hooked me up with a room. I gave Megan a bath, fed her, dressed her up, and headed for the venue after calling my brother, who lived in Las Vegas, and telling him to grab Aaron, his five-year-old, and meet us at the Aladdin. Backstage, the whole band came out to greet the angel Megan.

She was unimpressed. "Dada, I'm tired," she said.

"Meg, we're at the Pearl Jam concert in Las Vegas!" I preached to my divine offspring of love and rock. "They're going on in just a couple minutes."

We lasted through "Release," "Go," and "Animal," but by the opening bars of "Jeremy," father and daughter were done. I could see Aaron on my brother's shoulders having a blast. His face glowed like he was standing beneath the burning bush. This was his live-concert deflowering, and no matter how old you are, you never forget your first time. Meg and I were back at the Mirage snoozing away a half hour later. Was she conscious of the event, the miracle journey of father and child for love of rock and rocker? I got my answer the next morning when I dropped her off at school. Her teacher said, "Good morning, Megan, how are you?" whereupon the slightly-worse-for-wear three-year-old replied, "I went to Las Vegas with my dada to see the Purl Jam show."

As *RIP* continued to cover the Seattle scene, I got a bit caught up in the media madness surrounding Seattle and green-lighted a special one-off issue called *Grunge* that the bands, especially Eddie, perceived as pulp prostitution of the scene to sell magazines. Pearl Jam had exploded with the video for "Jeremy," sending their debut, *Ten*, to multiplatinum sales and the band into the realm of superstardom far quicker than expected. In fact, they so detested the size and speed of their success that they did what no band before them—with the exception of the Grateful Dead—had done. They flipped the middle finger to MTV. "No more videos," they said. And for all intents and purposes, that was it. "Jeremy" was the last time Pearl Jam's fans got to see them in a slickly produced video.

It took unprecedented courage to say no to MTV, the musical media monolith that was writing me a monthly check at the time for my "Friend at Large" segments on Saturday night's *Headbangers Ball.*

One item came back to bite me in the ass. I did a segment hyping the *Grunge* issue of *RIP:* first mistake. Then I compounded the misstep by showing the poster of Eddie Vedder we inserted into the issue and doing a *Wayne's World* "we're not worthy" up-and-down bow before the photograph. This kind of behavior would have been fine for, say, Mötley Crüe or Iron Maiden, but it did not fly with Pearl Jam. I discovered the error of my ways on a *Vs.* tour overnighter to Phoenix.

We were backstage at the Mesa Amphitheatre, November 7, 1993—second show of a two-night stint being promoted by Danny Zelisko and Evening Star Productions. The rotund and wonderful Danny Z—mentored in concert promotion by the legendary Bill Graham—was not just a great businessman and fierce storyteller, he was the consummate party animal and as pure a rock fan I'd ever known. He was also my friend.

"Eddie's pissed off at you," he said as I arrived backstage, naïvely prepared to greet the guys. "You better make nice or he'll take away your flannel pj's and burn 'em. Seriously, go talk to him before they go onstage. I don't want a shitty show because of you!"

I had brought along a gift for the lead singer—my original vinyl foldout collectible copy of Jethro Tull's *Stand Up* LP. Rick Krim, talent relations VP from MTV, was also backstage. He'd flown in from New York to make his umpteenth in-person plea for the band to reconsider delivering a video for the new LP, *Vs.* Krim failed in his agenda. I, however, succeeded. It was about heart and the authenticity of uncorrupted communication.

"Lonn, that wasn't right," said Eddie, pulling me aside near the back door adjacent to where the crew and band buses were parked. "That issue, the poster, that shit on MTV, that's not what we're about."

I lowered my head, took a breath, and processed his words. "I had no idea, Eddie, really," I replied. "I just think the Seattle bands are so important and wanted to give the fans something cool. But I understand what you're saying, and I apologize."

My delivery disarmed Eddie. He smiled. "Cool. What do you have there?" he asked, sighting the LP in my hand.

"Oh, that's for you. My original *Stand Up*. I know you love Tull. This record is almost as old as you. I bought it when it came out in '69. I signed the inside."

His smile widened. "Wow," he responded. "Thanks, man! You're a good guy, Lonn. Enjoy the show."

You can say that Eddie's attitude was all about protecting their image, a vanity play, but I choose to look beyond the obvious and believe that he was sincerely trying to teach me something, from his point of view, about how the Seattle movement and its reluctant heroes were being perceived by the public. Every man creates his own reality. Sorry for the pun, but maybe these guys were just trying to make me a . . . better man. Or at least a better journalist.

The most beautiful song on Mother Love Bone's delicious *Apple* is called "Man of Golden Words." It is a touching piano ballad that praises the inspirational power of music. Andy Wood sounds almost as if he's praying, rather than singing. Perhaps he was.

> *Tell me, Mr. Golden Words, how's about the world?*
> *Tell me can you tell me at all?*
> *Words and music, communication*
> *Let's fall in love with music.*

I will always be an idealist when it comes to the individuals who create the music that connects us to something bigger than ourselves. Some musicians become assholes when they go from rocker to rock star. But the guys in Pearl Jam have clutched firmly onto their integrity while navigating the treacherous waters of fame and fortune.

The best concerts are the ones that remove you from your body and allow your soul to roam free on the astral plane for a couple hours before returning you to real life. And when you actually know the dudes up there operating the transporter machine—well, that rocks even harder.

After the show, I headed for my hotel, located directly adjacent to the concert site, a short stroll under the starry desert sky. I was feeling . . . connected. Getting in the elevator with me was a roadie wheeling a road case, laminates dangling from his neck, a walkie-talkie on his hip. "How's it going," I said, not paying attention to the image on his passes.

"Not bad," he replied in an obvious English accent. "Fucking tired, though. Can't wait to get to bed. So who played here tonight?"

"Pearl Jam," I replied. The elevator stopped at his floor first and as he exited into the hallway, I asked, "Hey, who are you here with?"

With the door closing behind him, he blurted, "Jethro Tull."

10

Live and
Let Clive

"POUND ON THE EARTH: DULL AND EARTHEN ITS ECHO,
DEADENED AND MUFFLED BY WHAT WE UNDERTAKE."

—*Rainer Maria Rilke*

Geoff Bywater worked in the marketing department of MCA
Records. I'd supported several of his label's acts and we had developed a friendship. When he landed a senior position with Fox
Music Group and saw the script for a green-lighted heavy-metal
comedy that took place in a radio station, he thought I would be
an excellent candidate for the motion picture's music supervisor
and executive producer of the soundtrack for the new imprint,
Fox Records.

The film's producers, Robert Simonds and Mark Burg, were
very high on the script, penned by a young screenwriter named
Rich Wilkes. Simonds came by *RIP* one afternoon to check me
out and got off staring at the photos on the wall of me with rock
stars and their pants down (Cobain would have hated this guy).
The hundred or so laminates hanging off the corners of my bul-
letin board also intrigued him. "These are cool!" he crowed.

"We should use them for the opening credits, like a montage. Can we borrow them?"

I got the gig and began working on acquiring music for the soundtrack with Fox principals Elliot Lurie—former lead singer of the band Looking Glass who composed and sang the 1972 smash "Brandy (You're a Fine Girl)"—and Matt Walden, a slick, Ivy league, energetic attorney. Elliot handled all things creative while Matt did the legal dirty work, such as negotiating licensing fees and clearing songs for use in the film and on the soundtrack.

The film's director was Michael Lehmann, known primarily for having helmed the 1989 black comedy *Heathers*, about a high school clique of murderous blondes all named Heather. *Airheads* starred Steve Buscemi (an independent cinema hero); Brendan Fraser, who was getting raves for his performance in 1992's *School Ties*; and *Saturday Night Live*'s Adam Sandler in his first big screen role.

The list of co-stars was also impressive. They included Michael McKean (from the movie *Spinal Tap*, who'd played the infamous "Seattle" *RIP* party), Joe Mantegna (nephew of Rainbow/Roxy owner Mario Maglieri), David Arquette (younger brother of Rosanna; remember Toto and Grant High?), and Michael "Kramer" Richards (from TV's up-and-coming situation comedy *Seinfeld*), an alum of Valley College who'd taken astronomy with Barlow.

Getting to know Adam Sandler was the highlight of the *Airheads* experience. One afternoon on the Fox lot, I sat with him in his trailer and he told me about his other dream, besides acting—the rock-'n'-roll dream.

"I had a meeting with [President] Mo Ostin at Warner Brothers Records," he reported to me in confidence. "I think he's gonna offer me a record deal. I got the shakes sitting in his

office. Eddie Van Halen, Neil Young, Paul Simon, Prince—
damn, I thought, if those walls could talk. I like Mo, Lonn. We'll
see what happens."

My first coup was securing a brand-new track called "Feed
the Gods" by White Zombie, who were buzzing big via the repeated appearance of their "Thunderkiss '65" clip on MTV's
top-rated animated show *Beavis and Butt-Head*. In the script, a
club scene called for a live band to perform while a rookie cop,
played by the late, great Chris Farley, interrogated crowd members—and Zombie fit the bill.

Todd Singerman, manager of Motörhead, came by *RIP* and
played me a track called "Born to Raise Hell," which had seen
release only in Europe. It screamed *Airheads* in riff, word, and
attitude, but it needed to be, for lack of a better term, fucked
with. Sting, Rod Stewart, and Bryan Adams had been riding the
charts all fall with a sappy ballad called "All for Love." The three
musketeers of adult contemporary gave me an idea. We could do
the antiballad. I pitched Lemmy on rerecording the vocal tracks
to "Hell" with a pair of mischievous guests: Sebastian Bach and
Whitfield Crane from Ugly Kid Joe, whose 1991 hit single,
"Everything about You," had become a troublemaker's anthem.

Whitfield and Bas—like so many other second-generation
hard rockers—idolized Lemmy, but when it came to closing the
deal, Sebastian's label, Atlantic Records, nixed the idea, not because of Motörhead, but rather, they didn't think it was good for
Skid Row's poster child for adolescent excess to share a mike
with the less-worldly Mr. Crane. Bas was in the middle because
he didn't really care. He wanted to do it. On December 16,
1993, he sent a fax to my office. "Dunk! I don't have a problem
with it, man! I'll do it. How does Lemmy feel? Lemme know.
Rip it, Baz."

But artists can be overruled, especially by managers or executives holding the purse strings to their career. Bas was axed from the project and I needed a replacement, so I called up Jorge Hinojosa, manager for rap artist Ice T, who had found favor with the metal crowd through his hybrid side project *Body Count*.

He called me back the next day. "Ice loves Lemmy and has no problem with Whitfield. He's in." We cut the track with producer Howard Benson and everyone loved it. Michael Lehmann gave Lemmy a cameo in the big demonstration scene outside the radio station, where members of the throng are spouting up to make Brendan Fraser's character, Chazz, feel better about having grown up a geek. "I edited the school magazine," cried the deadpan metal god. Classic.

Fox decided that White Zombie and Motörhead would be the LP's two singles and videos. "Feed the Gods" was an edgy-effects-laden concert clip, while "Born to Raise Hell" had a big-budget, comedic storyline woven about a killer soundstage performance. On the set of the downtown L.A. video shoot, Singerman pulled me aside and said, "Lonn, no one has ever spent $200,000 on a Motörhead video. Not even close. This means so much to Lemmy. Thanks for stepping up."

During the months I worked on *Airheads*, all memos regarding the soundtrack were cc'd to Roy Lott, general manager of Arista. Roy answered directly to label founder and industry icon Clive Davis. About three months into the project, sometime during the summer of 1993, Roy flew into L.A. from New York, the executive hub of the company, to meet with Lurie, Walden, and Bywater for a progress report on the soundtrack. I was invited, too. As the distribution arm for Fox Records, Arista would be responsible for shouldering 50 percent of the marketing and promotion costs on the release, so Roy wanted to make sure the ship, in his estimation, was sailing straight.

Roy was businesslike yet approachable. I did my song and dance on what I had in the hopper and he seemed impressed. "4 Non Blondes is going to cover Van Halen's 'I'm the One.' That rocks," I said. At the end of the meeting, we took a short walk down one of the faux Fox streets outside Lurie's office. "If you need help with anything, just ask," he said. "You're doing a great job. Keep it up. We're very excited about this soundtrack." Little did I know, Roy and Clive had begun hatching a plan to romance me out of journalism and into the record business. The debut volley came from my attorney friend and golfing buddy Eric Greenspan, who had negotiated several recording contracts with Roy and whose pedigree was business affairs.

In March 1994, Eric invited me out to play eighteen holes at Brentwood Country Club, where he was a member. "Have you ever thought about working for a record label?" he asked.

"What are you talking about?" I replied.

"Roy Lott called me the other day inquiring whether you'd consider taking an A&R position at Arista. They've been desperate to develop a rock roster. It's the weakest part of the company. They're huge in R&B and pop but can't break a rock band to save their lives. I think you could write your ticket on this. Roy really likes you. He wants you to meet Clive when he comes out for the Grammys in two weeks."

My first reaction was "no fucking way!" I preferred being on the outside of Babylon looking in. Eric pushed a little harder. "Lonn, you should meet with Clive, just for the hell of it. He's Clive Davis. Be a good experience for you." I enjoyed being a media personality, but I still wasn't making enough money to get the Friends out of the 'hood. In a couple years, Megan would be ready for preschool, and then private school, and then . . . maybe I should give this some thought. What harm could one meeting do?

The Chameleon met the King the morning after the 1994 Grammy Awards ceremony. "Mr. Davis will meet you at 10 A.M. in his suite at the Beverly Wilshire Hotel," instructed Rose Marino, veteran keeper of the Clive calendar. "He usually stays in a bungalow at the Beverly Hills Hotel, but they're remodeling." Right. Whatever. I rang the bell and waited two minutes for him to answer. The door finally opened, and a sixty-something man wearing a cardigan sweater and tinted glasses invited me in. I took a deep breath and crossed the threshold.

We exchanged pleasantries and he offered me some breakfast. "I'll have a bagel," I said. I was nervous but did my best to act aloof.

"Last night was marvelous for us! Did you watch the Grammys?" he asked, excitedly.

"Uh no," I replied. "I hate award shows. Like Woody Allen." The *Annie Hall* reference escaped him, and he lit into a recap depicting his company's victorious evening. Not one artist he mentioned was on my current personal playlist. I did my best to act interested.

"So, Roy is very high on you. He believes you could help us build a rock roster. We need assistance in that area. Have you ever thought about scouting talent? Let me ask you, who do you believe are the most significant rock artists making music out there right now?"

My mind went blank for a second and I blurted out, "Well,

Metallica, Pearl Jam—I really like Beck. I think his major-label debut is brilliant. He's going to be around for a while." Clive looked puzzled. "Beck? He's a novelty. Geffen couldn't even follow up 'Loser.' I wouldn't put my money on Beck."

He asked me how I decided what bands to cover in my magazine, and I told him I relied on input from my editors and writers, as well as my own instincts. "Your greatest ally in A&R is your gut," he responded emphatically. "You have to know the goods when you hear it. Be able to identify a star. It's a gift. Do you think you could recognize talent at its earliest stage of the game? Unpolished, raw, young?"

I was starting to feel comfortable. He wasn't so intimidating anymore. "I bought my first record when I was seven after seeing the Beatles on the *Ed Sullivan Show.*" He grinned wide at that comment. I think he was starting to like me.

Ninety minutes later, he was playing me demo tapes from crappy bands that had sent their virgin wares to his senior director of A&R in New York, Michael Barackman. "Tell me what you think of this one," he directed, cranking up his expensive portable stereo to *Spinal Tap* levels. I'm sure the volume didn't bother anyone. The suite was bigger than my house.

"That sucks, Clive," I said. "The lyrics are cliché and the guitarist can't play."

He grinned, obviously enjoying my candor. Another half hour passed and it was time to wind things up. "Lonn, one more question. If you were to use a phrase to describe yourself, what would it be?"

I paused for an instant and the words flew off my tongue. I'm not sure they even stopped at my brain before exiting the gullet. "I guess you might call me a pragmatic rebel."

There was a message from Eric waiting for me when I got

back to the magazine. "You blew him away," reported my esteemed legal counsel.

"Really?" I responded. "No shit. So, now what?"

"Well, are you empowering me to initiate negotiations? I know that Michael Lippman has represented you in the past. I don't want to overstep his authority." Michael and I hadn't done a deal together since *Airheads*. We never had a formal contract. Besides, he was busy now with this buzzing new band called Matchbox 20, which his brother Terry had discovered.

"You started this thing, Eric. It seems only right that you take it to its logical conclusion, if there is one. I'm still not sure I even want to work in the record business. Clive's kind of strange."

Enter the universe, once again. Westwood One was pulling the plug on *Pirate Radio Saturday Night* because the L.A. affiliate, KQLZ, had been sold and the station was changing to a Spanish-language format. There were signs that KLOS program director Carey Curelop was going to pick up my program, but at the last minute, he backed out. And even though I had monster ratings in Baltimore, Boston, and Indianapolis, you can't have a syndicated rock show if you're not on the air in Los Angeles.

In April 1994, Eric started talking money with Roy, and I went about my business as a rock journalist with the recently added offer to cohost a syndicated morning show for two weeks with Alice Cooper produced by the Satellite Music Network based in Dallas. Z-Rock, a division of SMN, was beaming metal out into space and bouncing it back to affiliates around the country. *Alice's Attic* was the brainchild of FM programming guru Lee Abrams, who would later cofound the revolutionary XM Satellite Radio network. Cooper and Friend hit the airwaves April 11 for an eleven-day run. Eric talked turkey with Roy while I talked metal with Alice.

After several go-rounds where both Eric and I agreed the offer still wasn't serious enough for me to abandon a well-earned media career, he called me in Dallas on April 14. "Okay, let's just ask for the moon and see what they say. They really want you. You couldn't be in a stronger negotiating position." I had done some digging in the meantime, calling certain record executives whom I trusted and who had a history with Clive to ask them what they thought about the opportunity.

"One person cannot change a culture," cautioned Sony executive vice president Michele Anthony, a former attorney who'd never missed a *RIP* party.

"He's the greatest teacher in the business," offered Columbia president Donnie Ienner, arguably Clive's most successful protégé. "But you'll probably have a tough time because he won't give you the autonomy you'll need to develop a roster."

Even Michael Lippman, who worked for Clive in business affairs at Arista in the '80s, had reservations. "I know you and I know him. He's controlling and you're a free spirit. It could be very frustrating for you."

The last person I polled was Clive's former head of marketing who'd risen to top of the industry food chain to become president of Madonna's new label, Maverick Records. "Don't do it, Lonn," pleaded Abbey Konowitch. "Trust me. Don't do it."

Arista's final offer was huge, at least for me. My annual salary at Flynt after thirteen years was $81,000. I didn't have the *Pirate Show* anymore, which had been netting me $60,000 a year, or the *Headbangers Ball* gig, worth $30,000 a year for the two years I was on the network. From 1992 to 1993, I composed the "Friend to All" column for the influential industry tip sheet *Hits* magazine and edited the "Peddle to the Metal" section, where I took a percentage of the ad revenues placed by record labels in my pages. That moonlighting adventure put about $30,000 in my pocket. Then when I jumped ship to edit the "Rawk" section of *The Album Network*, a competing smoke-and-mirrors industrial rag, my take doubled to almost $60,000 over about eight months.

My income outside *RIP* was pretty impressive, but Arista was throwing out numbers I'd never seen before. Three-year contract: $175,000/$200,000/$225,000, with a $30,000 annual expense account, yearly executive bonus commensurate with label performance, guaranteed business-class travel in the continental U.S., and a $150,000 signing bonus—the ticket to a new neighborhood. "Okay, let's do it," I said to Eric. "But before I sign the contract, I need to meet with Clive personally. I have a couple concerns."

Arista flew me to New York, and I sat with the big man in the office he keeps at 55 degrees (the staff called it the Meat Locker). "Clive, I'm very excited about the offer and coming to work for Arista, but I have to ask you something point blank."

He stared me straight in the eye. "You can ask me anything, Lonn." I was completely forthright.

"Donnie Ienner, Michele Anthony, Abbey Konowitch, and Michael Lippman all told me that you wouldn't give me signing power on bands. Is that true?"

He looked ruffled but didn't hesitate for a second in his response. "I mentored those executives," he said defensively. "They learned the business from me. You will have signing power and a great company behind you to help build a rock roster." With that, I shook his hand and entered into a pact that would change my life forever. The pragmatic rebel had just made his first Faustian deal.

Joyce had been skeptical throughout the Arista courtship. "You may regret this, Lonn," she said. "You love being a rock journalist, flying around with bands. You hate suits. I hope you know what you're doing." But her tone softened when the check for the signing bonus arrived. "Before we start looking for a house, let's do some traveling. My contract doesn't start for a month." First stop was Maui, where we spent two weeks in a condo directly adjacent to Shep Gordon's property in Kihei. I swam every day with Megan, some days in the pool, others in the emerald ocean just steps from our veranda.

On Monday, June 13, just before heading back to the mainland, a news story broke. Football star O. J. Simpson's wife, Nicole, and a Brentwood waiter named Ron Goldman had been found murdered in front of her Bundy Drive condominium, a block from my friend (and *Rolling Stone* coauthor of "Slash") Jeff Ressner's house, who'd recently jumped Jann's ship for a staff-writer position at *Time* magazine. Had he not been attending a Pretenders concert with Joyce's Chico State pal Holly, Jeff may have broken the story of the decade. I liked to think that my friend was saved the karma of that media fiasco by rock 'n' roll.

Returning to L.A., Joyce and I attended a party in Pacific Palisades in honor of our friends Karen and Ned Nalle, who'd tied the knot back East earlier in the month. That's when a dark-haired young man in his late twenties tapped me on the shoulder and said, "You're Lonn Friend. The new A&R guy at Arista." *News travels fast*, I thought. "My family's from Philly, old friends of the Nalles." His name was David Wike, tall, handsome, well spoken. He described himself as a part-time drummer, part-time actor. But it was his younger brother, Mark, who he wanted to tell me about. "He plays bass in a band from New York called the Bogmen. They're the biggest unsigned draw in Manhattan. I have a demo tape here with two tracks. Just give it a listen and call me."

The songs on the cassette were called "Raga" and "The Doubter's Glass." And they were like nothing I'd ever heard before. The rhythms were tribal but with an early U2 sonic sophistication. The singer's voice soared and fell. There were hooks everywhere. This blew away the drivel Clive had played me at the Beverly Wilshire Hotel. I listened to the cassette ten times. "They're really cool," opined my wife. "You should check it out."

I called David the next day and expressed my enthusiasm. "They're playing the Limelight on the twenty-seventh," he informed me. That was in less than a week. "They're going to sell it out. The actress Penelope Ann Miller is a big fan. She's doing *Letterman* that night and then going to the show. The tape is nothing compared to the live performance. They're insane. [Lead singer] Billy Campion is a superstar."

Again, I wasn't looking for this, but it demanded proper attention. I booked a flight to New York, informing the label that I wanted to start my gig a few days early. There were no objections.

At midnight, June 27, 1994, a thousand fans wailed as Billy Campion, Bill Ryan, Brendon Ryan, Mark Wike, P. J. O'Connor, and Clive Tucker took the stage. David was in the balcony with the girl who'd once tamed the hearts of Al Pacino and Matthew Broderick both onscreen, in the films *Carlito's Way* and *The Freshman*, and off. I pushed my way to the middle of the floor, shoulder to shoulder with the throng, half of whom had traversed bridge and tunnel from Long Island—birthplace of

O'Connor, the Ryan brothers, and leader Campion—to witness their blue-collar heroes raise the roof of the building that once was a church but now harbored the spirits of rock 'n' roll.

For seventy minutes, I was spellbound. Campion stalked and whirled about the stage like a deranged Sufi dervish. He was part hypnotic Bono, part idiosyncratic David Byrne, part lounge-lizard Sinatra. He commanded every eyeball in the room as the five competent musicians behind him created a tapestry of melody that reached down into the solar plexus and stole the breath away.

They closed the set with a bizarre and infectious breakup ballad called "Suddenly," which drove the audience nuts. I wasn't thinking about my past or my future. These unknown musical entities had me fixated on the present moment.

After the performance, David walked me back into the tiny dressing room and introduced me to the guys, as well as to Penelope, who was absolutely gushing. "When you guys get signed, I'll talk to David Letterman. He'll love you!"

The band was all smiles and fully charged after delivering what they knew was a slam-dunk set. They teased me about my new job. "So, what do you say we break in that new expense account?" laughed the Captain, the band's nickname for Campion.

"Why the fuck not?" I responded. An hour later, we were in my suite at the Parker Meridien hotel on West Fifty-seventh, ordering food and drink as if the boys hadn't eaten in a week. Maybe they hadn't.

Around 2 A.M., I estimated the party tab was approaching a grand, but I was feeling omnipotent and falling in love at the same time. These boys were so genuine, alive, untainted by the trappings of fame and fortune. I'd spent the past eight years observing and cohabitating with artists who'd already gotten their chance to show the world what they had to offer and, in many cases, had broken though. There was something refreshing and exhilarating about being here at the beginning, before the journey had even begun.

After hours of conversation, I found myself standing in the middle of the room clad only in my boxer shorts, an illustration of how comfortable I felt, when the urge to get up on stage hit me. It wasn't the Forum on my birthday in front of twenty thousand mad-eyed Guns N' Roses fans. It was the morning before the first day of my new job in a $250-a-night Manhattan hotel room, and the audience was considerably smaller but far more attentive. "Listen, fellas, I need to tell you something. I haven't even started my gig yet and I've no fucking clue what I'm doing, but I don't believe in accidents. What do you say I try to sign you guys to Arista Records?"

"More beer!" cried Bill Ryan.

"Listen, Lonn, I know who you are. You were editor of *RIP* magazine." The drummer, Clive Tucker, was the only metalhead in the band. The others didn't know or care where I came from. "I saw you in the Red Hot Chili Peppers *Funky Monks* home video. You're telling Anthony that the whole *Blood, Sugar* record is about sex. 'There's a boner in every groove'—awesome line." That's when I looked around the room and noticed the Captain was no longer on the bridge. "Where's Billy?" I asked.

"Try the bathroom," said P. J. with a smirk.

Sure enough, that's where I found the eccentric and clothed young Mr. Campion, faceup in a tub full of water. He looked unconscious and it freaked me out for a minute. "Billy! We just met, man. Don't pull a Cobain on me!"

One eye cracked open. "Lonnie, I'm just napping. It's nice

and warm in here. Don't worry. I ain't going nowhere." No one but my mother ever called me Lonnie.

Most of the boys crashed out in various parts of my hotel room, with the exception of Campion, who was still out cold in the tub, though the water had been drained. I, on the other hand, didn't sleep a wink. In the morning I went downstairs to use the telephone in the lobby and called the New York office, asking to speak to Roy. "He's on holiday in the Hamptons, but I'll make sure he gets your message." Four hours later, the phone rang upstairs. I informed Roy of my magical evening and asked him if I was insane to want to sign the first band I saw.

"Well, not if they're the real deal," he replied. "It is unusual, but if you believe in this band, go for it. I suggest that you call Clive and articulate to him your thoughts. He's on vacation in Capri, but Rose will find him for you. When Clive and I return in a week, we'll figure this out. In the meantime, get to know the managers, gather up all their demos—follow your instincts."

"Tell me about this group that blew you away, Lonn." Clive was on an island in the Mediterranean, vacationing with the rich and famous, and I was interrupting his rest with what must have sounded like the rantings of a lunatic. Nevertheless, he listened to every word I said about the Bogmen and did not dismiss my excitement. He asked me if I thought Billy was a star, and I replied, "Unquestionably." "Do you think their songs fit into the modern-rock format? I would love for your first signing to be a modern-rock band, Lonn."

I felt pumped up after talking to Clive and spent the next week in New York getting to know the people at the label. Arista's West Coast branch had a couple dozen employees. Besides me, the only other vice president back home was Jacquie

Perryman in the soundtrack division, whom I'd had considerable interaction with during the *Airheads* campaign. But the nuclear core of Arista resided inside a narrow eleven-story building located at 6 West Fifty-seventh in midtown Manhattan.

During my first week, I received a crash course in big-label infrastructure, visiting the different departments and shooting the shit with dozens of the company's more than two hundred East Coast staffers. I mentioned the Bogmen to every person I met, most notably Tom Ennis, head of artist development. He had been at the Limelight show but left before we could meet. "The Bogmen!" he exclaimed as I pranced into this office.

"I feel like I already know you, Tom. Will you help me on this one? I'm not exactly sure what I'm doing."

He shook my hand and replied, "You're doing exactly what you should be doing, buddy. And I'm right there with you."

It came down to personality, something I'd always relied on to get me from point A to point B. The entire month of July, I ate, slept, and breathed the Bogmen. Those efforts culminated on August 2, when band and label reached an agreement. As synchronicity would have it, they were playing Irving Plaza that night, and I spent the entire day networking my New York Rolodex to get people out to the celebratory show. Clive and Roy stood behind me 100 percent, unprecedented behavior, I was told, since neither one had yet to see the band perform and rarely signed off on a two-LP, half-million-dollar deal before having the live experience.

The club was jammed to the rafters that night. Bogmen fans were loud, intoxicated, animated, knew every word to every song, and had no qualms about singing along with Billy whenever the urge hit. I was standing in the VIP balcony next to the soundboard. Clive arrived around the fifth song with Andy Schuon, head of programming for MTV. He told me they were having dinner together. This was an extraordinary show of faith. The band was on fire. Billy resembled an artist who'd toured the world five times, exuding a comfort and confidence onstage far beyond his pedigree. When the left-field resounding ballad "Dr. Jerome" came to its crashing end, Clive put his arm around me and yelled into my ear, "Lonn, I love them. I would have signed this band. Congratulations."

I felt like I'd just been knighted. "Thanks, boss," I said.

"Lonn, I'm going down to the pit. I want to experience them up close. I'll see you up here afterward." Clive Davis was heading for the pit at Irving Plaza to get down and dirty with the Bogmen faithful. You could have thrown a blanket over me.

A few songs later, an old friend appeared in the balcony. It was Michael Goldstone, the A&R visionary who'd signed Pearl Jam and introduced me to his brave new star, Eddie Vedder, a few short years before. "They're great, buddy," said Goldie. "Your front man is incredible. Good luck."

The Bogmen became a top priority at Arista. With the exception of a quirky novelty hit by a Canadian band called the Crash Test Dummies, the label had nothing going on in rock. No one expected me to sign a band so quickly, especially one this unique. Now that I had, however, there was no turning back. Clive and Arista wanted the Bogmen to hit, and hit fast, with their debut LP, an aggressive approach that could destroy the organic magic that helped cultivate the group's huge local following.

"The Luncheon" took place every Thursday at 1 P.M. in the executive conference room and usually lasted about four hours.

All label department heads gathered there to go over the progress of each and every record that Arista had out there in the marketplace. Attendance was mandatory, unless you were on the road or had been hit by a taxi walking to work.

Forty executives arrived with extensive memoranda and other pulp tonnage depicting what records were getting airplay, how much they were selling, who was getting press. You name it, if it involved the commercial aspect of a title, it was discussed. Statistics were everywhere. Clive sat at the head of the table like King Arthur as his knights spouted off one by one how well or poorly certain releases were doing. The topics ranged from video concepts to the minutiae of individual retail-outlet sales in certain markets.

This is where Clive stood apart from other music industry executives. He made the selling of music an exact science and drilled into his staff the philosophy that if you worked a record hard and long enough, it would have an impact. The sheer gravity of commitment to a project would ultimately result in success. That philosophy only worked, however, if the universe was also down with the plan. This was the conundrum faced by Arista with respect to rock music. It didn't adhere to formula. You could produce pop records according to a time-honored script and create inoffensive, saleable Top 40 hits and instant stars who were here today and gone later today.

Rock doesn't abide by those rules. It pays no mind to whether it ever crashes upon the shoreline of acceptance. It exists as a manifestation of expression, raw, wondrous, and if authentic, it will eventually find its audience. I was soon to discover, however, that my idealistic outlook on music flew directly in the face of how things got done on the inside. If certain swords aren't brandished and the right pockets aren't lined, no matter how great the act, they may never get a chance to rise above the underground.

"Let's all welcome Lonn Friend, our new vice president of A&R on the West Coast," said Clive. "Lonn has hit the ground running. Tell us about the Bogmen." I gave the captive, three-piece audience a Reader's Digest version of the campaign to date, thanking Tom Ennis for his support and outlining what was ahead. Though I wasn't quite sure what that was. When I showed a brief clip of the recently held *MTV Video Music Awards* where one of the presenters, Adam Sandler, was wearing a Bog-men cap—a favor to a friend—the room broke out in applause. Influence had its props, especially in here.

"You must put together a list of potential producers," urged Roy. I convened with Bogmen manager Steven Saporta, and we created a wish list of individuals that we thought would fit his outfit. Like most baby bands, they'd never worked in a profes-sional studio with a real producer. Now they had a major-label deal and a quarter of a million dollars to spend.

I offered up names from past relationships, like Mike Clink from GN'R and Michael Beinhorn, lauded for helming Sound-garden's *Superunknown*, released earlier that spring to critical and commercial acclaim. But the guy I had a good feeling about was relatively untested. His name was Eric Rosse, and he'd pro-duced only one major LP, Tori Amos's *Under the Pink*, a master-work of sound and creative vision. We'd become friends through chance encounters and a visit to the studio while Tori was mixing the disc in Los Angeles.

"What about Jerry Harrison?" asked Saporta. Harrison was a brilliant idea for a number of reasons. The former keyboardist for the Talking Heads had found great success behind the con-sole in the early '90s by shepherding the band Live to multiplatinum sales, most notably with 1994's *Throwing Copper*. "Clive will love Jerry," added Saporta. "He's a song guy, makes records for the radio. But it won't be easy. He's really hot right now."

On August 13, 1994, Clive sent me a memo in response to my producer hit list:

> We went over and studied your list of possible producers and went through all the background we also have on each of the suggestions. The two producers (apart from Eric Rosse) who should remain in contention are Jerry Harrison and Michael Beinhorn.

I'd already flown the band to L.A. to meet with Clink, but Campion didn't connect with his hard-rock résumé, and if the Captain didn't vibe, that was a problem. On August 3, the Grateful Dead were playing Giants Stadium with Traffic. Percussionist P. J. O'Connor was a tie-dyed Deadhead. The other guys loved Jerry Garcia's legendary traveling circus too. The Dead had been on Arista since 1977's *Terrapin Station* LP, so tickets were just an interoffice memo away.

I invited Eric Rosse to attend the concert with all six guys and me. I thought he and Campion would connect. While Traffic was whirling through their opening set, P. J. lit up a joint. We were all feeling groovy, anticipating the transcendental experience that was the Grateful Dead live. Campion then asked me if I wanted something to drink.

I said, "Yeah, get me a Coke."

He and Eric disappeared and returned in twenty minutes with my drink. "Here ya go, Lonnie," he said with a devilish grin.

A few minutes later, I started to feel really disoriented, far beyond the normal, recreational marijuana buzz. "P.J., what kind of pot was that?" I asked.

"Just some home grown. Nice stuff, huh?"

Campion was chuckling. "Lonnie, I gotta tell you something. We put a hit of acid in your Coke."

That's when I completely freaked out. "You what?" I yelled. "Oh, my God, Billy, I've never done acid in my life. Ever. Oh, God, this isn't good. I need to walk around." For the next imperceptible amount of time, I wandered about the stadium floor, bumping into the "spinners" (the stoned-out hippie girls who spun aimlessly to the music, creating sort of a loveable mosh pit). I'd been high before but not like this. I kept thinking about how much soda I'd drunk.

Finally, Eric grabbed me by the shoulder. "Lonn, come with me. The guys have something to tell you."

When we got back to our seats, their faces looked like distorted caricatures, straight out of *The Twilight Zone*. "Lonnie, we're fucking with you," laughed Campion. "We didn't put acid in the Coke. I swear. It's just P. J.'s homegrown and power of suggestion that's got you flying. Relax."

I will admit, "Sugar Magnolias" sounded exceptionally cosmic that night.

Campion loved Eric Rosse but Clive wouldn't hear of it. He didn't have the discography to warrant the big man's respect. Beinhorn loved the demos but had already committed to his next project. I had to deliver Jerry Harrison. Saporta called him at his home in Marin County, just north of San Francisco.

"I talked to him. He's really busy but mildly interested. Thinks the songs need a lot of work. I'm going to need your help to close him. This isn't going to be easy." Saporta set it up. Jerry and his wife, Carole, would meet us at our hotel downtown, and we'd take them to dinner at this fancy sushi place nearby. I wasn't nervous at all. I knew I had an ace in the hole. History. And one other thing—a T-shirt.

We emerged from the elevator and there they were in the lobby. Before we even shook hands, Carole screamed, "Oh, my God! Where did you get that T-shirt?" I was wearing a rare, original, slightly faded Talking Heads *"Psycho Killer, qu'est-ce que c'est?"* that I'd bought at Moby Disc Records back in 1977. "Oh, I love it! What a classic!"

Formal introductions were made, and right there, in the middle of the lobby, I ripped off the shirt and handed it to Carole. "Here, it's yours."

, Carole was glowing. "Are you serious?" Jerry was smiling ear to ear.

"I'd be honored. Gimme five minutes to go upstairs and change."

Dinner could not have been more enjoyable. I recounted my college tale, the outdoor show at UCLA, Patti Clark, and the Headhunters. Saporta did his thing, profiling the boys, the history and ethos of the Bogmen, their distinctive style, and the challenge of making the right record, for them and Arista. By dessert, the deal was struck. Sometimes, it's not the color of the chameleon's skin that makes the difference, but what he throws on top of it.

Clive called Jerry the next day and expressed his support and excitement. Arista believed in the Bogmen and felt they could hit right out of the box. It was up to Jerry Harrison to turn a ragtag bunch of street minstrels that had never seen the inside of a recording studio into a polished, major-label modern-rock band. There was no middle ground. I'd signed the bloody contract and so had the Bogmen. We would sink or swim together.

From December 1994 to March 1995, the band took up residence on a houseboat in the seaside burg of Sausalito, California, five minutes from the two recording studios where they
would birth their debut LP. Basic tracking was done at Studio D.
This is where Jerry Harrison and engineer Karl Derfler
schooled the boys (and their A&R guy) in the ways of record
production. Even though I'd had numerous glimpses of the
process, this was different. Now I was on the inside, a cog in the
creative machine, rather than a fly buzzing about the dials with
no attachment to the outcome.

I flew up almost every week to check on the progress, going
straight from the airport to the studio and then to a local restaurant where I'd run up my expense account keeping everyone
connected. Jerry loved the guys. They worked so hard on their
instrumental parts. Campion, on the other hand, was drinking
too much and chomping at the bit to track his vocals, but his
voice was in no shape to record. In late January, Jerry called me.
"Lonn, I think Billy needs some R and R. He's becoming a distraction. And his voice is shot."

The bandleader and key factor in the success or failure of the
Bogmen arrived at the small but comfortable Culver City enclave
of the Friends. *Artist and Repertoire* has a wide interpretation. It
means, "whatever it takes to get the job done," like giving your
lead singer the extra bedroom in the back. Joyce and I had closed
in December on a bigger house in the pastoral Cheviot Hills section of Los Angeles, but we wouldn't be moving in until March 1.

"Do you mind if Billy Campion stays with us for a couple
weeks?" I asked the empress of the house.

"Of course not. I love Billy. We'll fix him up." Joyce became
my A&R partner, fixing Billy healthy meals and special teas for
his throat. She washed his clothes and kept an eye on him when

I was at the office. I took him to my health club and we worked out together.

Billy was a big kid with an immense heart, and like so many gifted artists, he had demons, addictions that fueled his pen but brought harm to his person. I took him to a two-hundred-dollar-an-hour vocal coach who gave him exercises to strengthen his pipes and insights into how to deflect the trappings of stardom. He didn't drink a drop of alcohol the entire stay at our home and rejoined the band in Sausalito healthier, wiser, and in a great headspace to track his vocals.

Overdubs and mixing (helmed by Grammy-winning mix engineer Tom Lord-Alge) took place up the road at the Plant, where local residents Metallica had just financed the construction of a brand-new studio. As soon as we were finished, the quartet would begin sorting out their next LP, *Load*. "Don't let your Bogmen ruin our studio before we get there!" teased my old friend Lars Ulrich. "I'll be counting the fucking pencils!"

Life Begins at 40 Million was delivered in May 1995 to the raves of the company, including Clive. For the next two months, different departments began drafting their individual plans for how they would work the record into the marketplace. As Promotion, Artist Development, Publicity, and others weighed in with their thoughts and impressions, one thing was becoming clear: the record was so full of great songs, no one could figure out what the lead single should be. And I was just as confused as my diligent coworkers.

If there was a standout, "reactive" track on *40 Million*—a song that a programmer believes will solicit phone requests from listeners—it was "Suddenly." Clive and Roy wanted to put our best foot forward and release the core fan base's favorite ballad as the lead single. Arista wasn't about to invest hundreds of thousands of dollars in tour support to let the band build an organic following. If the Bogmen had signed a deal someplace else, that plan might have been an option. But when your company's success is based on slamming hits through the radio at Top 40, rock-'n'-roll patience doesn't figure well into the artist-development scheme.

At Arista the Bogmen were not going to get an armful of chances to break through. We had to lead with the song most likely to get airplay. But the band members thought differently, arguing that "Suddenly" was not typical of their sound. They pushed for "The Big Burn," the frantic, more rock-sounding opening track on the album.

We went with "The Big Burn" and quickly lived to regret the decision. Beyond their home station, WXRK-FM in New York, the song saw little airplay. In September 1995, when Clive asked me how I felt about the Bogmen's campaign so far, I had a meltdown in front of the entire Luncheon. "Why the fuck can't we get any airplay on 'Big Burn'? Maybe it's because we didn't make a video. What does that say to the industry? It says we're not committed! It says Arista still doesn't give a fuck about rock music!"

In the early '90s, the indie way of doing things was severely impacted by the advent of Broadcast Data Systems (BDS). BDS was the first company to monitor radio airplay by using computerized "fingerprint" technology, with songs being encoded. Computers placed throughout the country scanned the radio dial, "listening" to each song played and identifying it. Those airplay results were sent to eager record-company promotion and marketing reps, who used them to strategize their efforts.

Prior to BDS, radio stations would phone in weekly reports to industry trades like *Radio & Records*, which allowed for easy fabrication of airplay numbers and publication-chart manipulation. When BDS came on the scene, this chart game basically ended, as stations' actual airplay information was available for all BDS subscribers to see. All that being said, it was still an influence game to get the program director to spin the record in the first place.

The week after its August 29, 1995, release, *40 Million* sold 2,500 units, a respectable number for an unknown group. That was the biggest week the record ever had. After "The Big Burn" failed, we regrouped and threw our collective hands in the air. Harrison thought we missed by not leading with the infectious and unique "Raga," while my A&R compatriots Steve Ralbovsky and Kurt St. Thomas (former program director of the influential WFNX in Boston) thought "Yellar" was the right call. I was too close to the record to be objective. I thought every track was a hit.

The curse of having too good an album seemed to be hovering above our heads. Finally, we opted for the path of least resistance to radio acceptance—the most novel yet potentially reactive song in the band's catalog, "Suddenly." The decision was made as Clive brought a new major player into the company, as recently ousted MCA Records president Richard Palmese became Arista's new head of promotion.

A wheezy-voiced veteran member of the Illuminati of backroom-influence peddlers—who knew how to work the old-school strong-arm when it came to romancing programmers and breaking Top 40 records—Palmese quickly became the most important figure in the company with regard to the success or failure of a single. But MCA was as anemic a rock label as Arista, thanks in part to Palmese's inherent distaste for the genre. He also didn't get or care about the Bogmen. But Clive still did, so we lined up the ducks for "Suddenly."

Campion had befriended noted video director and avant-garde photographer Matt Mahurin, whose groundbreaking "The Unforgiven" clip helped set the dark, seductive tone for Metallica's earthshaking *Black* adventure. Mahurin had virtually stopped making rock clips, opting instead to concentrate on his still photography, where he would manipulate existing images into compelling presentations.

Mahurin was so taken by Campion and "Suddenly" that he agreed not only to shoot the video but also to do it for a fraction of his normal fee. The clip fit the song beautifully—a tongue-in-cheek vignette about a young man who "suddenly" discovers that his girlfriend prefers someone else. Just before the Video Music Awards (VMA) in September 1995, I screened the video at the weekly Luncheon, and the room was unanimously enthusiastic. "We can see here that Billy Campion is a star," proclaimed Clive. "And 'Suddenly' is a very reactive song."

I glared at Palmese, sitting to the King's left, who never lifted his head from the stack of BDS printouts sprawled out before him. He never tapped his toes. His mind was on TLC—the R&B trio he was hammering onto stations from Maine to San Diego. The only video images Palmese saw that day were "Waterfalls," the kind that pop princesses swim in and fledgling rock acts drown under.

Lewis Largent from MTV's programming department was schmoozing in the lobby—at the VMAs, this is where most music-industry folk can be found during the insufferably long and boring presentation. "I saw the Bogmen clip, Lonn. It's fucking awesome. You've got a shot, buddy. Go get some spins."

MTV only took risks on new bands if there was a radio story brewing commensurate to the excellence of the video.

At the lavish afterparty, I ran into Oedipus, program director for the powerful rock station WBCN in Boston. "Are you going to add 'Suddenly'?" I asked him point blank. "MTV loves the video."

He grabbed a couple carrots off the massive veggie platter, looked me right in the eye, and said, "Lonn, your label is a joke in rock music. You have no roster, no leverage. Everyone knows that. No programmer is going to step up and put his ass on the line for an Arista rock act. Not until they absolutely have to."

In my brief but enlightening tenure at the label, I'd seen Arista take some of the most pathetic, disposable, forgettable pop pabulum—bands like Ace of Base and the Real McCoy—and turn them into multiplatinum success stories. But this was rock, and Arista had failed in rock for so long, even the cocky rock journalist couldn't right the ship.

No matter how unique the Bogmen were, the commercial failure of *40 Million* was a foregone conclusion. The band toured sporadically, doing opening stints with Barenaked Ladies and drunken Irish poet Shane McGowan. Their agent, Mike Donovan of the Agency Group, worked his butt off but had a frustrating time finding them touring opportunities. The Bogmen were musical snobs and only wanted to play with other off-the-wall alternative acts.

In a different universe, they might have developed their career on the road—sans any appreciable radio support—à la Phish, Dave Matthews, Radiohead, and Tool. How ironic that Arista was the Grateful Dead's label, the godfathers of organic fandom that birthed the massive jam-band movement—but had lost complete connection to the ineffable magic of community that has always been the benchmark of long-term rock-'n'-roll success. In Clive's kingdom, bands lived or died on the radio.

By November 1995, the campaign was over. I went about my business, fielding tapes and heading out nightly to see mostly unmoving bands that didn't have one-tenth the Bogmen's energy or originality. The next two years were a struggle for me, both with the Bogmen, who by contract had a second LP to make and release, and with talent scouting in general. Everything I pitched was rejected, including a hardcore rap-rock hybrid from Florida called Limp Bizkut (later changed to Limp Bizkit). Arista still had no rock roster and no leverage to speak of.

If the Bogmen had hit, I may have had that A&R autonomy that Clive promised me when I came aboard. But they didn't, so what my friends in the business had foretold was ringing true. Nevertheless, a year into the gig, the Friends were living in a nice neighborhood, Joyce was opening her retail vintage-fabric children's clothing store, Baby Rose, and I was still looking for the next big rock thing.

In early November, I received a tape by messenger from a man named Carter with songs by an artist called E, who called his band Eels. The first song hit me the way "Raga" had—between the eyes, ears, and right down to the solar plexus. The track was called "Novocaine for the Soul." In both vocal tone and lyrical pathos, it evoked Peter Gabriel. I brought A&R reps Michelle Ozbourn and Jason Markey into my office and cranked it up.

"This is amazing!" exclaimed Jason and Michelle, almost in unison. I felt the same way. Then I played the other two demos on the tape and was further blown away. The second song was called "Susan's House," a bizarre, melancholy ballad laced with spoken-word samples and homegrown sound effects. The chorus was hypnotizing: "Going over to Susan's house, she's gonna make it right."

The third song on the tape was a passionate rocker called "Rags to Rags." We were speechless. I asked Michelle to get Carter on the phone immediately. "Okay, this Eels tape, uh, I'm in. What do I have to do?"

It was still early in the shopping season. Only one label had heard and passed on the band. "Move fast, get Clive into it, and you've got a great shot," said Carter, E's manager.

I started doing my homework. Mark Oliver Everett was a singer-songwriter who had grown up in Virginia and moved to L.A. in his midtwenties. He cited Neil Young's *After the Gold Rush* and the Beach Boys' *Pet Sounds* as the two records that inspired him to become a musician. He'd been around the industry block once before and was signed to Polydor Records, where he released 1992's *A Man Called E* and 1993's *Broken Toy Shop*. Both albums were commercial disappointments and he was dropped.

In 1995, E saw his musical persona transmuting from a lone balladeer to something more group-oriented, so he dropped the solo-letter moniker and formed Eels. He widened his instrumental repertoire to include a Wurlitzer electric piano played through a guitar amp and secured a rhythm section with Butch Norton on drums and Tommy Walters on bass.

The first time I saw Eels perform live was in the basement of the tiny Luna Park club in West Hollywood. They were mesmerizing. I went up to E after the show and introduced myself. It was the night ABC was premiering a big documentary on the Beatles. "I'd like to hang out more and talk, but I have to get home and watch the Beatles."

He stared me straight down and said, "That's tonight? I have to run too. I'll see you again, Lonn."

Connection made, I called Carter the next day and arranged for me to take E to dinner. "He liked you," said Carter.

I listened to the demo nonstop, at home, in my car. Megan, only five years old, had memorized the chorus to "Susan's House." After a Mexican dinner somewhere, I invited E to come back to my house so we could hang out and talk some more. When he saw my dad's one-hundred-year-old grand piano in the living room, he sat down and started twinkling the keys. Megan came downstairs and E did an impromptu performance of "Susan's House" for her as a bedtime lullaby.

Out back in the guesthouse—the private museum of my career where I listened to records, entertained visitors, and escaped when I needed to be alone—E and I got to know each other. "I come from a pretty dysfunctional family," he confessed. "My sister's a drug addict and my mom's a whore." I was surprised by his honesty. "I used to sit in front of the house where [failed filmmaker] Ed Wood committed suicide and write songs. I go into dark places but try to find sweet melodies." He reminded me artistically of Morrissey, a master of marrying the darkest lyrics with the most uplifting refrains.

We listened to *Pet Sounds* twice. I didn't hesitate to sing along with Brian when the urge called. "I guess I just wasn't made for these times." I asked E if he ever felt that way, because I certainly did, especially since leaving the media and taking a record-company job.

On December 7, the band performed again at the Alligator Lounge on Pico Boulevard, about fifteen minutes west of Cheviot Hills. There were A&R reps from other labels in the room. I was pressing Clive and Roy to spend time with the demos. The interest was rising on the band. I sent a memo to Clive and Roy on December 11, 1995, urging them to pay attention and show me some support. Clive wrote back that the songs were quirky and clever but they were hard to break. He was skeptical, but was bolstered by my enthusiasm and agreed to see them when he was next in L.A.

On January 11, 1996, I composed a fifteen-hundred-word memo titled "The Story of E," detailing the history of the artist, why Arista should sign Eels, and how we would break them. My stock had fallen with Clive due to the failed Bogmen campaign, and it was obvious that for me to shepherd another band into the building, I'd have to buckle down, talk the talk, and become one of them. Under the heading "How Do We Break It?" I wrote the following:

> There is a growing movement of quirky, ambient/pop artists happening at AA, Alternative, and Modern Rock radio. I've attached current soundscan figures on three acts from the genre, which I believe Eels fall into: Morphine (Rykodisc), Portishead (London), and the very hot Folk Implosion (London). I also submit to this category the new Eric Matthews release, *It's Heavy in Here* (Sub Pop), which is garnering raves from the industry and consumer critics alike. Radio and MTV are the key to breaking the Eels. The images in E's songs lend themselves to cutting-edge filmmaking that goes straight to Alternative Nation and beyond. I believe, however, that the Eels have great crossover potential, à la Crash Test Dummies, and that tracks like "Rags to Rags," "Your Lucky Day in Hell," and "Beautiful Freak" could very well, like "Novocaine," find comfort atop the Modern Rock charts. E is an artist who possesses a quiet,

subtle star quality that will be conveyed in press, video, and live performance.

I was dancing around like a court jester begging for attention. I used to write about rock 'n' roll for fans and musicians. I reported what I saw and felt. Now I was spending hours on memoranda begging aliens to take a look at life on Planet Rock through my eyes. I'd been reduced to a lobbyist, standing atop a soapbox, flailing my arms like a lunatic, shouting, "Please, please, O great and powerful Oz, look at me! Look at me! Listen to me! Trust me! And more than that, trust them. The artists. The ones who built your entire fucking gold-plated empire!"

Clive Davis's private Eels showcase was set for January 28, 1996, 6 P.M., at the Cox rehearsal studio in Hollywood. That afternoon I'd made a trip up to the bungalow at the Beverly Hills Hotel, where the boss was staying while in L.A. We'd moved to a new building a year before, but with the exception of one token appearance, the West Coast employees never saw Clive unless they were summoned up to the bungalow. He wasn't much for walking the halls, pressing the flesh with the rank and file, and rallying the troops. Beverly Hills was a vanity play, a satellite office, an afterthought.

"Michael Barackman doesn't share your enthusiasm for Eels." Clive's comment almost made me throw up. His journeyman tape-listener who had never signed an act since coming to Arista was passing judgment on my artist from the other side of the country, having never seen the act live. I didn't dignify Clive's comment with a reaction but rather shifted my energy to prepare for the evening's showcase. "I know I'm right about them," I said. "They're going to blow you away tonight."

Arista's head of business affairs was a skinny six-foot blonde with a no-bullshit personality named Carol Fenelon. And she was crazy about Eels. "I'll be at the showcase, Lonn. We're going to get this one, I can feel it." Carol wielded considerable influence with Roy, who would also be there. The ducks were lining up. The band was setting up when we arrived.

The six-song set was perfect. E was engaging, Butch slammed the kit, Tommy throttled the bass. Carol and I looked at each other when the music had stopped and smiled a giddy grin. I gave a muted thumbs-up to the band, Carter, and their attorney, Jonathan Haft. I'd assembled all the principals. If Clive's thumb went up too, I'd have closed my second deal.

We met in the hallway adjacent to the parking lot. I could barely contain myself. The boss didn't wait for me to speak first. "The songs are interesting but he's not a star. I can see 'Novocaine' getting modern-rock airplay and possibly 'Rags to Rags,' but the front man is not compelling. Arista signs stars, Lonn. I don't see it. I'm sorry; you'll have to pass. I have to get to a dinner."

I stopped him. "Wait one minute, please."

Carol spoke up. She believed Arista desperately needed to develop some hip baby bands to give the roster balance. I took her lead and pleaded the credibility case—we needed cool bands to seduce other bands to build a rock roster. The argument was flawed. Credibility to Clive was measured by the success quotient, how many platinum acts were delivered with the smallest number of overall releases. Cred comes when an influential program director like Oedipus or KROQ's Kevin Weatherly gives you a shot and adds your record to the playlist.

RIP running a feature gave a band cred. Lonn Friend pleading his case on a Hollywood sidewalk to the most stubborn icon the music industry's ever known didn't.

Clive zoomed away in his hired town car as I walked back into the studio and broke the news to the band. "You did your best, Lonn," said Carter.

"Yeah, man, don't stress it," added E. "You're a good guy. Some things aren't meant to be."

Yeah, like me in the record business, I lamented to myself.

The following week, I was playing golf with Interscope Records president Tom Whalley at the Riviera Country Club in Pacific Palisades. Walking up the ninth fairway, I asked him if he'd heard of Eels. "No," he said. "Who are they?" I told one of the most successful A&R men in the business my frustrating tale, pulled a copy of their demo out of my pocket, and handed it to him. "Here, bud. Enjoy."

Tom took the tape back to the office and played it for label founder Ted Field and CEO Jimmy Iovine, who both flipped out, called Carter, and began their quest for the man called E. In the interim, Mike Simpson—one half of the production team known as the Dust Brothers—had just landed an A&R gig at the brand-new record arm of DreamWorks, the entertainment conglomerate founded by Steven Spielberg, former Disney executive Jeffrey Katzenberg, and record mogul David Geffen. Simpson knew E from the Silver Lake/Echo Park artist community that included (what did Clive call him?) "novelty" artist Beck. DreamWorks Records, like Interscope, came to win, hiring a team of moguls to run the company that included former Warner Bros. titans Mo Ostin and Lenny Waronker as well as my old pal Michael Goldstone.

Over the next two weeks a bidding war ensued. David Geffen and Jimmy Iovine were courting the artist that I had to pass on. At the last Eels industry showcase, there were ten companies in the room salivating over E and his sad, whimsical, beautiful songs. I went down because I loved seeing the band perform, but the gesture was more masochistic than anything else.

Out of respect for my passionate pursuit of Eels, Clive wrote me a memo further explaining his decision to pass on the act. In the memo, dated February 6, 1996, he said he was concerned about E. Clive felt that he lacked staying power, and that he was not a tortured soul. He made a reference to E's quirkiness and said that he didn't feel it was star caliber. All of this sounded so judgmental to me, it discounted any validity the legendary music man had in my eyes with regard to evaluating the talent or integrity of the artist.

This was Clive Davis and his ilk—puppeteers of privilege who, because of their success and Donald Trump–sized boardrooms, had deluded themselves into believing that they could not only see inside the soul of another but calculate just how tortured that soul was. Clive's inflated sense of entitlement was representative of everything I'd come to despise about the record business. Ego, power, greed—Babylon's holy trinity. Thanks, but no thanks.

In the end, Eels became the first act to sign to the new DreamWorks Records. On February 16, 1996, I sent the following fax to Mo Ostin's and Lenny Waronker's office:

Dear Gentlemen:
I just wanted to drop a quick note congratulating you on signing Eels. The gentle, gifted man called E and his music have been a very special part of my life for the past four months. It was the most pleasant obsession of my career. E, Tommy, and Butch have found the perfect home for their remarkable songs. My envy is only superseded by my confidence in their future success and the delight you and

great people at DreamWorks are going to have making and breaking their records.

After I lost Eels, my desire for the job dissipated, though I and my staff kept up the search for new rock talent. Jason Markey brought in a hilarious, Santa Barbara–based three-piece called Nerf Herder, who had recorded a demo called "Van Halen" that sounded so instantly radio reactive, you needed lead gloves to hold on to it. I helped Jason ink the act, but Arista failed to get "Van Halen" or its brilliant novelty follow-up "Sorry" on the radio. For the latter track, I solicited the help of a golfing buddy, actor Miguel Ferrer, and his childhood pal Mark "Luke Skywalker" Hamill to do cameos for the video clip. The name Nerf Herder comes from a line uttered by Han Solo (my friend Ben's dad) in the original *Star Wars*. Miguel loved Nerf Herder. He thought lead singer Parry Gripp was a satirical genius.

The video for "Sorry" was awesome, but once again the label failed to get airplay, and Nerf Herder died an unceremonious death at Arista. Every time I hear that comical band Bowling for Soul, I think of Nerf Herder and what may have been. Then again, we're talking about the music business, an industry with a 90 percent failure rate. Sometimes just getting the shot is a miracle. Success, well, that's downright biblical.

I began to fall off Clive's radar like a UFO. With fifteen months left on my contract, I was content going through the motions, occasionally pitching acts that I knew would be rejected. Reality was that Clive gave all his A&R people the power to sign one act on their own. They called it a "put." You got one put, and if it hit, you were off to the races, had the man's respect, and the rope would loosen up a bit. If it didn't, you'd never get another act past Clive again unless they knocked his argyle socks off. I never saw the big man's bare feet again.

I saved whatever influence I had left at the roundtable for the Bogmen and their sophomore LP, *Closed Captioned Radio*. With far less money but equal passion, the band delivered a magnificent sophomore effort under the studio aegis of renowned producer Bill Laswell and SoHo studio character Godfrey Diamond, the man behind the dials for Lou Reed's ephemeral *Coney Island Baby*.

Radio hit the streets February 10, 1998, and was pronounced dead on arrival. It moved a paltry ten thousand units before the band was unceremoniously dropped from the still-lackluster Arista rock roster. As for their A&R guy, he'd turned in his last receipt for a plane ticket or restaurant on January 1, 1998. The new head of marketing, Jay Krugman—with whom I had history from his days at Columbia when *RIP* was heaping ink on acts like Dangerous Toys, Corrosion of Conformity, and Alice in Chains—had stepped up and kept the Friend family mortgage covered by securing me a six-month consulting extension (at a considerable drop in pay) on my original contract, which expired on July 1, 1997.

My three and a half years at the University of Clive taught me many things. There is no science to A&R. You do what your instincts tell you. Ultimately, I was not a record-company creature. I was a journalist, a music fan, who paid little mind to the industry's protocol or politics. I understood artists from an authentic place. I knew how to talk to them, on their level, without the invisible wall defined by the institution and suit. Hell, I didn't even own a suit.

Clive was a genius at hit making, but he no longer loved music. Based on my inside adventure, I could see that nothing mattered to him but the legacy of platinum success. "Novocaine" went to number one at modern rock, but Clive was unimpressed. Why? *Beautiful Freak* never sold a million copies, nor have any of the subsequent Eels releases, though the band developed a formidable following around the globe. They have a rock 'n' roll career—fans who love their music and come back again and again to see them perform.

In my opinion, E is a modern-day Brian Wilson, a gentle balladeer of exacting truth and melody. His musical legacy defines artistic credibility. Listen to Eels' 2005 somber masterpiece *Blinking Lights and Other Revelations*, the band's Vagrant Records debut and a *Pet Sounds* progeny if ever there was one. Dream-Works gave the group a solid decade of support, but they went through a consolidation in 2003, and I guess the bottom line is the bottom line.

In the weeks preceding my exit, I tasked Eric Greenspan to toss out some job feelers for me, but there was little interest in the former media player turned label failure. "Lonn, I think you better start thinking about a career change. The record business is about fitting round pegs in round holes. You're a square peg."

Really? I thought I was a chameleon.

11

Easy Riders on the Storm

"IF MY SPIRIT WERE ALWAYS WIDE AWAKE FROM
THIS MOMENT ON, WE WOULD SOON ARRIVE AT THE TRUTH,
WHICH PERHAPS EVEN NOW SURROUNDS US
WITH HER ANGELS WEEPING."

—*Arthur Rimbaud*

Well, I woke up this morning, and I got myself a beer!

A howl descends on the lobes of several thousand bikers. The man with the microphone summons their participation and repeats the verse, his volume upped in measure to the enthusiasm. "Well, I woke up this morning . . ." Vocal stops. Music stops. The verse soars to conclusion on the fuel-injected pipes of a crowd now fully, passionately engaged. "And I got myself a beer!" The collective croon can be heard a light-year away.

Harry and Beverly are clutching each other so close the emblems on their leather vests—tiny, intricate, shimmering miniplaques denoting the fifty states and million miles they've trekked together since tying the knot thirty-three years ago—touch, click, and almost spark. They are gray from stem to stern, and their taut, round bellies bounce in approval as the legendary strains suck them into a place where past has French-kissed present.

What's transpiring at the opening date of the Harley-Davidson Open Road Tour on the dusty floor of the California Speedway forty miles east of Los Angeles is utterly hypnotic. The Hog tribe is here, connected by a love for the road and rock 'n' roll.

If one was flying on earthen chemicals in some hallucinogenic Castaneda dream state and happened into this odd, amazing two-wheel tribal assembly by accident, the sight of the Cult's Ian Astbury wailing Jim Morrison would at least inspire a serious double-take. But on this warm Indian summer evening, it is he who sells sanctuary to those long awaiting the return of the Lizard King.

When the surviving members of the Doors reunited to perform at a biker festival in September 2002, no one was sure if it was the beginning of a new era for the seminal L.A. band or just some mad experiment. That day in Ontario, California, I watched an old friend realize a long-held dream while getting my first glimpse of a subculture that is absolutely devoted to the spirit of freedom.

I had last physically encountered the artist Astbury in December 2001. The Cult was opening for Aerosmith in Miami. Ian and his alter-ego sidekick, guitarist Billy Duffy, had buried a very rusty hatchet and started to make music again. They'd signed a fat new deal with Lava/Atlantic Records, reunited with Bob Rock, whose production guidance had taken them to multi-platinum a decade before with the LP *Sonic Temple*.

But as had often occurred in an industry of no guarantees, the new record failed to find its audience, and the Cult's revivification was put on permanent hold. Ian blamed the label, the industry, the earth, the moon, and the Milky Way. His vitriol was inconsistent with the enlightened traveler that a year previously had marched with the Tibetan Sherpas to base camp, where a near-death experience worked its cosmic magic to reveal the soul beneath the star.

My weekly Internet radio show on KNAC.com, *Breath of Fire*, debuted on the summer solstice 2000. From 8 to 10 P.M., PST, every Wednesday night, I went out live on the Web across the globe, playing and saying whatever I wanted to. I was given complete freedom to spin eclectic and rap uncensored.

As in the *Pirate Radio* days, I had guests in studio every week. Ian stopped by our Santa Monica studio one evening, and I devoted the entire two hours to him. We discussed the days of Guns N' Roses and the long rift between Axl and Slash. "You should mediate their reunion, Lonn," he said. "No, I'm serious. You're the perfect guy to do it. And if [Cult guitarist] Billy Duffy and I can get along again, anyone can. It's really all about ego." We went on to discuss his spiritual journey, more specifically the trip to the Himalayas, where he was stricken with severe frostbite and almost died. I identified with the changes he was going through.

I said good-bye to my listeners on June 21, 2001, and *Breath of Fire* morphed from sound to word, continuing as a semiregular missive that I'd distribute to my considerable e-mail list. Years before blogs, this was my online journal where I'd rant on the state of music, mankind, and anything else that happened to be passing through my fingers. Essays on everything from my blind goldfish to the Zen brilliance of L.A. Laker basketball coach Phil Jackson found their way into the virtual mailboxes of hundreds of friends and acquaintances from disparate parts of the globe. I'd receive responses ranging from complete adulation to "It might be time to seek professional help, Lonn."

Six weeks after September 11, I took a walk to Ground Zero with a group of dear New Yorkers. I reported the experience to my audience. On October 19, 2001, the subject of my mass mailing read "Something Wicked/Something Wonderful."

I am there, in the throes of catastrophe. I see the panic in the streets, the plumes of raging fire; chaos, destruction, hysteria. Hell in its first domestic manifestation; a three-dimensional Robert Williams painting of incomparable and disturbing detail. My mind's eye spies on the offices evaporated in a nuclear instant. How many saints were lost? How many scumbags? It doesn't matter now. The souls have all left the building.

Where we stand, here in this once bustling garden of commerce, creativity, greed, and goodness, swollen with grand New York gestalt, there is damage, sadness, and great loss. This site is now sacred land. Forever it will possess Holocaust importance, an eternal reminder to generations of *Homo sapiens* who venture forth from this spot, that it was here, on that day, that everything changed. Our descent and destruction, or ascent and salvation, depend on where we go from here.

Ian Astbury became one of *Breath of Fire*'s most loyal readers, as did unlikely rockers like Def Leppard's Joe Elliott, W.A.S.P.'s Blackie Lawless, and Mötley Crüe's Tommy Lee. They wrote back to me, often reflecting the same quandary with civilization as I. Most of my audience didn't respond, but I had a sense they were out there, listening and digesting. The twenty-four months between March 2000 and April 2002, when I sporadically composed and delivered *Breath of Fire*, represented a period of unprecedented truthful communication for me. Perhaps someday, I'll gather those essays into a book, a time capsule of a writer and a world at the brink.

But when I met up with the Cult singer after the Aerosmith gig in Miami, I found a different Ian Astbury. "This isn't you, man," I said. "The Cult comeback wasn't meant to be. Let it go. The record business is a falling kingdom. This is just a door closing. Another one will open." Ian was bottoming out on that fateful winter's night. So was I, for that matter. I hadn't worked in four months, and I had no clue where my next dime was coming from. The following morning, George Harrison died.

Then an e-mail arrived in August 2002 from a friend pointing me to a news item on the Web dropping hints that the Doors were preparing to tour again, but with a new vocalist. I saw Ian's name in the item and it took about ten seconds to process what I'd just read. *Fucking genius!* I said to myself. I sent Ian a note, asking for confirmation of the rumor, and he responded with humble brevity. "It's true, mate," he said. "I'm terrified."

When I found out that the big event was taking place at the speedway outside Fontana (birthplace of Sammy Hagar and occasional hang for skinheads and neo-Nazis—no correlation, of course), my first inclination was to complain about the venue and skip the gig. I was forty-six years old and my lower back wasn't what it used to be. And what did I know about the society of two-wheeled, motorized wanderlust? My only bike experience was the Schwinn ten-speed I owned as a teenager. I don't wear leather or eat much red meat. Come to think of it, in junior high, I had the classic Fonda/Hopper Hog poster from

Easy Rider on my bedroom wall (until my mother ripped it down).

I got to the concert site three hours before the first act of the day, local Latino legends Los Lobos, hit the stage. I took a seat on the grass near the entrance and watched the parade of fans. As they would all day, Morrison's lyrics floated about my brain. The people looked strange but I was the stranger. "We're all born to be wild for at least a few days," read a poster promoting the three-day event that would also see Billy Idol, Stone Temple Pilots, George Clinton, Journey, Nickelback, and Kid Rock perform.

They marched by me, two by two, mostly couples, men and women, many in their forties and fifties, hand in hand, having just parked their motorcycles in the special Hog lot, located closest to the front gate. The choppers were of all makes, models, colors, designs, and years, lined up domino-style across the asphalt.

Typically, these strident individuals are pigeonholed as hard, tough, and unwaveringly patriotic. But that's incomplete. I strolled the grounds all day, talked to these fascinating folks, and found they were freedom lovers, wanderers, thrill seekers, rolling across America on a red-white-and-blue carpet of confidence and conviction. Beneath their rugged carriages lay human engines that purred soft, smooth, and strong.

One woman with ass-length silver hair and a pair of painted arms that would have given Tommy Lee a run for his ink told me that she and her "old man" had come all the way from Austin. "I'm fifty-two years old and we stopped to make love every five hundred miles!" she said.

"What are you talking about, girl?" interrupted her rugged but less-illustrated partner. "I nailed you twice between Phoenix and Palm Springs! Ha-ha!"

A T-shirt stand was doing brisk business to my direct right. A classic Harley dude was massaging his cell phone, his long, silver hair pulled back into a ponytail, held taut by a red bandana. His faded Levi's toted a healthy chain of keys that jangled whenever his heavily tattooed arms rose in gesticulation. "I met this gal in San Diego yesterday," he blurted into the tiny receiver, his four-inch bearded chin supporting a wide, wicked smile. "She gave me her number. We're gonna hook up. Yeah. The *San Diego Street Scene* said that Steve Stills and Slash are playing . . ."

This man seemed to have no cares, no anxieties. I was in awe of how comfortable he was simply being himself. He didn't need to shape-shift to fit the moment or situation. He required no one's approval, and no matter how burned out he appeared, one thing was obvious: my man was getting his carnal chrome polished with great regularity. That theme would recur over and over again throughout the day. These folks enjoyed life. I envied their seemingly boundless liberation.

The distance from the box office to the exhibit area and main stage was at least that of five football fields. Laminated lads and lasses buzzed about in motorized golf carts while I hoofed it.

Two hours before the Doors' scheduled start time, I managed to get backstage, where I was greeted straightaway by Danny Sugerman, band manager and coauthor (with Jerry Hopkins) of the first rock 'n' roll book I ever read, *No One Here Gets Out Alive*, the original, quintessential biography of the Doors. I'd encountered Danny several times over the course of my twenty-year career.

In the mid '90s, during my Arista Records stint, Danny and Doors drummer John Densmore brought a singer-songwriter named John Coinman to my office for a meeting. Coinman was a very special, soft-spoken music man from Tucson, Arizona, whose songs harkened back to Tim Buckley and early Jackson Browne. But he was in his late forties; it didn't matter whether he had a "Doctor My Eyes" in his musical bag of tricks or not, Clive Davis would not have been interested. We were looking for hot, new talent, fresh, young meat to tenderize for mass consumption. John was like a fine wine, aged, full-bodied, poetic. His product was too hard to sell. This was but one of the umpteen reasons I loathed the modern record business.

"Hi, Danny," I said, offering my hand in reconnection. He appeared immediately fragile to me. We dispensed with superfluous pleasantries as he commenced to chronicle the last six years of his life—a period that included both addiction and cancer. Danny's story read like a prurient bestseller with two silver linings. First, his solid marriage to Iran-Contra poster boy Oliver North's former secretary, Fawn Hall, and second, the reason we were all gathered tonight, out here, at a bikerfest in the Inland Empire: the resurrection of the Doors.

"I've been working on this for ten years," he confessed to me. "For the first time, the presentation feels right. Ian is perfect. No one really knew what would happen until everyone got in a room and started playing. And they've only rehearsed seven times. But something's going on here."

I was out of the loop until I learned a few minutes later that John Densmore was missing the party due to a serious case of tinnitus, the maddening ear-ringing affliction that's haunted rock legends from Pete Townshend to Jeff Beck. But as the saying goes, "Out of adversity comes opportunity." Enter Police percussion patriarch Stewart Copeland to fill the seat in the back.

Danny is a year older than I am. We both grew up in Los Angeles. While I was typing my biology notes after a brain-freeze day at Grant High School—often to the vinyl vibrations of *The Soft Parade*, *Strange Days*, and *Morrison Hotel*—Danny was hanging out on Sunset Boulevard or in the canals of Venice with his mentor Morrison. He was there, in the company of the Lizard, as rock's Rimbaud slinked about the City of Angels in search of the devil.

Danny was the original, unwitting, rock-'n'-roll fly on the wall. He had the all-access pass to the five-year Season in Hell tour that ended abruptly on July 3, 1971, in Paris, France, when the incandescent star Jim Morrison suddenly burned out at age twenty-seven. French poet Arthur Rimbaud, the alienated genius with whom Morrison deeply identified, languished until he was thirty-six, though he'd written the bulk of his verses before his eighteenth birthday. Jim wanted to die in Paris, or so it's been said. Even Danny wasn't hangin' with him that dark day in the City of Lights. No one was.

My heart sank in Danny's presence. He was wearing the mask of suffering, something I recognized well after the past several maddening midlife spins of the globe. "Fawn and I want to have a baby," he confessed. His voice trailed off before constructing the next sentence. "We'll see what happens with the cancer." That was the last time I saw Danny Sugerman. He succumbed to the Big C on January 5, 2005, joining his shaman, hero, and friend on the other side of eternity.

"Hey, man, glad you could make it," uttered Ian, his short dark curly hair hanging down his brow, not unlike the way Jim used to wear it in the early days, before the bloat, the beard, and the bon voyage. The sexy Jim, you remember him? The Morrison that the young Eddie Vedder emulated with true emotional angst.

"I like the cut," I said. "The resemblance is a bit, uh, scary."

A reserved smile crept to the surface. "This is how my hair naturally looks," he replied, shyly. That day back in 1990 when Ian came to my house on my thirty-fourth birthday with Axl and Sebastian, his hair was jet black and practically scraped the floor. His girlfriend at the time told me that before gigs, she would iron it in the dressing room.

"I think this is amazing, Ian," I said. "I can hear you sing the songs in my head."

He pulled me close. "Lonn, I'm fucking scared shitless," he whispered. And for good reason. He'd idolized Morrison since he was toddler with a turntable back in Merseyside, England. What was transpiring on this mystical eve was no accident.

"Remember talking in Miami?" I said. "Talk about another door opening! 'God leads you to it; God leads you through it.' "

He smiled, twitched, and replied, "I think I'll just sing my ass off."

Ian Astbury was not always this self-effacing, gentle, respectful of a rock star. He and Billy Duffy locked horns over egotistical minutiae that would make even a five-star asshole retch with disgust. But he went through it; his career ebbed, flowed, and ebbed again. When he hit bottom in December of 2001, he was being tested. Like Job, he suffered. Like Job, he was about to rise again to heights unimagined. Like Job, he had been waiting for the sun, and it was about to shine in the desert darkness of California's smoggy Inland Empire.

"Lord, have mercy!" cried the evening's master of ceremonies, veteran L.A. disc jockey Jim Ladd. He approached the mike at the center of the stage with the same stoned-out swagger that had made him the grand high-exalted ruler of the airwaves for three decades. The crowd knew him and signaled their love with a resounding "Yeah!" I knew him because, like the Doors and Los Angeles, he was a part of where I came from. And it was Jim Ladd's smoky, soothing voice that came to me in my room that ebony night December 8, 1980—Morrison's birthday—and informed me of the news. The news that Lennon was dead and the music was over.

"Ladies and gentlemen, from Los Angeles, California, *the Doors!*"

It'd been almost thirty years to the day since that introduction landed on the ears of a concert audience. The Hollywood Bowl, an hour and ten down the road, September 10, 1972. Keyboardist Ray Manzarek and guitarist Robby Krieger, the instrumental alchemists who transmuted Morrison's poetry into song, stroked their familiar weapons of melody as Ian stood stoic and prepared to channel the most notorious and revered ghost in rock history. The instant the first line to "Roadhouse Blues" left his tongue, the fear was gone, the crowd was engaged, the clouds parted, and the ceremony had begun.

Well, I woke up this morning, and I got myself a beer!

I watched him carefully during the first song. He was gorgeous, powerful, sensitive, and clever, driven from note one by that inexplicable something that only an artist flying on the wings of expression can understand.

"Break on Through"—the metaphysical ballad that birthed a man, a band, a vibe, a cult, a city, a movement, and a myth—followed. The thematic foundation of the Doors' artistic mission was cemented in the embryonic grooves of the band's 1967 self-titled debut. At the height of Beatlemania, this was something entirely new. Ray Manzarek's keyboard, Robby Krieger's guitar, and John Densmore's drums, sans bass for the most part, this curious concoction bred aural textures that morphed from stripped-down bluesy garage to psychedelic symphony.

"When the Music's Over" floated by next. Almost every Doors LP with the exception of *Morrison Hotel* finished with an apocalyptic multilayered anthem. This was the ethereal masterpiece that closed out *Strange Days*, the Doors' second LP, released a scant ten months after their debut.

"Love Me Two Times" and "Alabama Song" were mischievous numbers that served as foreplay for the big bang. "I'm a backdoor man!" roared Ian, his vocal confidence now ascending exponentially. This was Morrison's homage to the "other guy," the sleazy fella from the across the tracks who knew the right moves and juicy words not just to find the little girl's emerald city, but how to get there through the dirty back road.

During "5 to 1," from 1968's *Waiting for the Sun*, Ian began to levitate. I mouthed the lyrics and glanced over at Danny, standing off to the left. I could see that he was pleased. How could he not be? What was taking place ten feet away from us was miraculous. At age sixty-three, the virtuoso Manzarek tweaked his ivory palette with youthful precision and grace. He addressed the crowd with a nod, a wink, a fist, and a flowing Hammond B3 knuckle-thumping noodle designed to humble the cocky kiddies who think their shit is lavender. Read 'em and weep. Jim and Ian were not the only ones reborn that night.

"Ghost Song," a fitting ode to the other side, followed "Strange Days." "Love Street" and celestial "Moonlight Drive" elevated the groovy vibe up to near freak-out levels. "Wild Child," "Summer's Almost Gone," and "L.A. Woman," the unsung hero of all Los Angeles rock gems, followed in perfect succession. Robby Krieger's guitar cruised through each verse and chorus of the locomotive "Woman" like a '71 Corvette racing up Pacific Coast Highway.

"Light My Fire" provided the kindling for the blaze that never seemed to ash. The band literally looked like they were floating, especially Ian, who bellowed the final verse of the land-mark hit with all he had to give: "Try to set the night on fire!" They had succeeded bravely in that quest. There was one more song in the set and that was "Riders on the Storm," the hypnotic lamenting finale off the last official Doors masterpiece, 1971's *L.A. Woman*. It was an apropos exclamation for the freakish faithful fanned out across the fairground.

The music was almost over, save a second time around for "Roadhouse Blues." I'd only seen a band perform the same song twice in one night on two occasions in the thirty years I'd trekked the concert circus. Duran Duran repeated "Girls on Film" at their debut L.A. show at the Roxy, and U2 reprised "I Will Follow" at their virgin L.A. performance at the Country Club in Reseda.

Ian, Ray, Robby, Stewart, and guest bassist Angelo Barbera took their bows and left the stage to a collective sense of gleeful accomplishment. Ian toweled off, grabbed a bottle of water, and waved me over. "This is just the beginning, man," I said. "You pulled it off."

That's when he put his arm around me. "I'm glad you were here to see it, mate," he said.

"Are you kidding?" I responded. "Soon as I've got some money again, I'm buying a Harley!"

12

The Screamin'
Prophet

"AND LET THERE BE NO PURPOSE IN FRIENDSHIP
SAVE THE DEEPENING OF THE SPIRIT."

—*Kahlil Gibran*

My first cover decision at *RIP* was Aerosmith. The shot featured
the legendary Boston rock group's lead singer, Steven Tyler,
with a slightly sinful, Jaggeresque smirk on his face, holding a
parrot. We were riding the historic rebirth of the band, ignited
the year before by producer Rick Rubin's groundbreaking "Walk
This Way" duet with Run-DMC and sent in full motion by the
band's smash LP, 1987's *Permanent Vacation.*

While I had no personal contact with the band members at
that time, it was reported to me by representatives inside their
label, Geffen Records, that everyone in the 'Smith camp loved
the issue, especially A&R executive John David Kalodner, a
highly eccentric, immensely gifted music-industry player known
for his Lennonesque white suits, burly beard, and frequent,
freaky guest appearances in Aerosmith videos.

The peculiar and powerful industry veteran's wedding-dress-clad cameo in the video for the hit single "Dude (Looks Like a Lady)" put him instantly at the top of my list of people I wanted to investigate in my new job. Little did I know that John wanted to meet me as well. "*RIP* is published by Larry Flynt, right?" he asked on that initial phone call. "That's great. Let's have lunch next week! Have you ever been to the Palm?"

For the next two years, I became Kalodner's favorite bi-weekly lunch partner. He introduced me to L.A.'s two most iconoclastic entertainment-biz eateries, the Palm on Santa Monica Boulevard and the Ivy on Robertson. The food was awesome but the conversation was better. Kalodner was a devout, unashamed devotee of erotic entertainment. He was fascinated by stories from my editorial days at *Hustler* and *Chic* magazines.

Before I was Lonn the metalhead or Lonn the grunge rocker, I was Lonn the porn guy. From 1983 to 1985, I wore the hat of X-rated film critic for the most influential sex magazine in America. Companies like VCA Pictures and Caballero Control Corporation were cranking out 35-mm big-screen erotica. A good review in *Hustler* could mean a million bucks in added revenue, which was nothing to sneeze at, since even the more ambitious films came in at under a hundred grand to produce.

"I loved how you wrote about porn," Kalodner remarked during one of our first meals together. "It was so honest. Like you were really a fan." He nailed it. I was a fan. And I had the keys to the kingdom. It was the era of VHS video and the titles were inundating my mailbox. I had so much masturbating material, it's a wonder I didn't go blind. I guess I can blame *Hustler* for my 20/300 eyesight. Kalodner was hip to my ribald résumé. He even pointed out what I considered my proudest journalistic achievement for Larry's flagship rag. "I really enjoyed the Shauna Grant article you wrote. It was fascinating."

That was her X-rated screen handle. Her real name was Colleen Applegate, and she was the subject of the last story I wrote for *Hustler* before jumping ship to *RIP* in July 1987. A sweet girl from a small town in Minnesota, she came to Hollywood, got mixed up in drugs and porn, and shot herself in the head on March 21, 1984, two months before her twenty-first birthday. Her last boyfriend—a forty-six-year-old coke dealer named Jake Ehrlich who resided in Palm Springs—sent a tape to the magazine of Colleen reading poetry she'd written. We bought the tapes from Ehrlich, and I made a road trip to the desert to interview him and see the house where the fallen angel had spent her last days.

I knew this was my swan song bit of adult reportage and wanted to go the extra mile and find out who this poor girl was and how things went wrong. I asked Ehrlich if I could spend the night at his place. We leafed through photo albums till all hours as he answered my questions about Colleen. When the tape stopped rolling, he showed me the plastered-over hole in the bedroom wall, six inches above the mattress. Three and half years after she'd blown her brains out, Ehrlich still hadn't painted over the mark.

Borrowing an old marketing idea from the British rock mags, I had the poetry tapes edited into a four-minute vinyl flexi disc with a sexy photo of "Shauna" on the front and bound directly into every copy of the December 1987 issue. My story was called "The Last Love of Colleen Applegate" and carried the footnote, "An editor for *Hustler* since April 1982, Lonn Friend has recently departed us to take on the editorial reins of *RIP* magazine, a rock-'n'-roll monthly. We wish him the best."

Every time Kalodner picked up the pricey tab for an afternoon's magical munch, I popped a package in the mail to his office loaded with the latest prurient pulp and video fare. It wasn't kissing ass so much as it was fostering a relationship by utilizing the resources I had at my disposal.

Throughout 1989, Kalodner kept me in the loop while Aerosmith tracked their next album, *Pump*, giving me early hints on song titles, release date schedules, and most important, clues to who these five musicians were, as both artists and people. "Steven is going to love you," he said to me.

Steven and Keith Garde, from Collins Management, soared into my office in August of that year for my first-ever interview with the "lips that launched a million tight hips." I was told I only had twenty minutes to do my thing, but I wasn't worried. The minute I shook his hand, I felt something, like a shock of electrostatic energy followed by a warm sensation of familiarity. Maybe Steven had this effect on everyone. My bet was he'd been briefed by Kalodner, just as I had been.

I shut my door but didn't roll tape straightaway. Instead, I sat him down on my floor in front of my VCR. "You wanna see something kinky?" I asked.

"Hell, yeah!" he replied as I cued up a scene from *Rain-woman*, featuring the geyserlike ejaculatory vaginal acrobatics of Fallon. We watched like two teenagers that had snuck into a Pussycat theater. After her initial watery burst, Steven jumped up and cried, "Oh, man! Show me that again!" Which, of course, I did. With five precious minutes now evaporated, I grabbed my tape recorder and vaulted into an effortless conversation about sex, drugs, and rock 'n' roll.

The interview began with, "Okay, you're recording an album and having a baby at the same time. Hectic?" Whereupon he responded, "Man, let me tell ya. We finished the *Permanent Vacation* tour in September. That month I bought a house. October, we had off. November first, I went in the studio with [guitarist] Joe Perry and started diddling, you know, every day, just fucking around. I sat behind the drums, and Joe and I came up with eighteen songs. In the meantime, I'm getting an addition put on my house, so I'm living over the garage with my wife, Teresa, and her twin sister, Lisa. It's crazy."

Pump hit the world's record stores on September 12, 1989—six days after Mötley Crüe released its deliciously vicious *Dr. Feelgood* LP—and rocketed up the charts on the back of ballbusting ballads like "Love in an Elevator," "F.I.N.E.," and "Young Lust." But while *Pump* sizzled with enough sexual imagery to incite another Boston Tea Party (the cover of the album featured two old trucks humping), a pair of serious ballads elevated the LP to critical and commercial acclaim.

"Janie's Got a Gun" depicted a young girl lost in a nightmare of sexual abuse. Director David Fincher (who went on to big-screen success with films like *The Game*, *Fight Club*, *Seven*, and *Panic Room*) created a powerful clip that lived on MTV for months.

Then there was "What It Takes," a passionate, heartfelt refrain that hearkened the band's signature effort, "Dream On" from their 1973 debut, in symphonic scope and emotional authenticity. The video was shot in Dallas at an old biker bar. I was invited to visit the set during filming. Kalodner and I made a cameo appearance as a pair of deranged-looking drinkers who're watching the band perform from behind a chicken-wire screen as redneck patrons pelt the stage with beer bottles. Our footage, sadly, wound up on the cutting-room floor, but the video soared to the top of the MTV playlist.

This was actually my second invitation to a *Pump* video shoot. "Love in an Elevator" was filmed about fifteen minutes from my house at a seaside Santa Monica high-rise hotel that boasted a showy outdoor glass elevator. Lots of downtime notoriously plagues video shoots. It's boring for the artist, but it worked out well for a magazine editor who was always in search of new and exclusive content.

"Lonn, I'm loving those videos," said Steven, walking me around the location grounds.

"I'm glad," I replied. "It's nice that those old porn connections are proving to be good for something."

I saw no harm in sharing the wanton wealth. Hell, I was passing porn all over the industry. I singlehandedly built Rick Rubin's and Goth crooner Glenn Danzig's erotic collections. Rick loved adult entertainment. The first time I met him, when I was still on staff at *Hustler*, he was dating a porn actress. All the metalheads were into it, so whenever the opportunity arose, I gave out gift packages. To me, who had been surrounded by T&A since I walked into the Flynt building in April 1982, it was harmless, hedonistic fun. Dirty mags and vids were expanding the comfort zone between Steven and myself, and the closer I got to Steven, the tighter I became with the entire 'Smith camp, and it was about to get way more—xxxciting.

"We want some special B-roll footage for the *Pump* home video," said Keith, Aerosmith's day-to-day management rep. "Do you think you can hook it up?" He went on to elaborate how Steven would dig a private performance by a pair of select adult-film stars. "He just wants to watch," assured Keith. "Nothing shady or illegal." We're talking 1990 here, several years before pornography magically shed its evil stigma to become a mainstay of the *Howard Stern Show*, HBO, and hotel room pay-per-view menus across the globe.

"No problem, Keith," I said. "It'll put it together."

A couple weeks later, I secured the *Hustler* photo studio in Culver City, where those infamous spreads were shot. Kalodner asked me if I could get the X-rated actress Viper to come down. Renowned in erotic circles for her body-length tattoo of a boa constrictor, she was a favorite of the eccentric record exec. Steven had requested a young starlet who went by the name Raquel, a waiflike creature with a diminutive ass and rocket-shaped silicone-enhanced breasts. Through the formidable influence of the Flynt talent coordinator, both girls were booked.

I decided to have some fun and make our little afternoon B-roll blackout a party by inviting a few fellow fans of erotica down to join the Prophet of *Pump* in his private peep show. By 3 P.M., the studio was buzzing with a three-man film crew hired by Keith, two naked female porn stars, Steven, Kalodner, and invited guest voyeurs Lars, Rick Rubin, Skid Row guitarist Dave "the Snake" Sabo, and Aerosmith tour photographer and *RIP* freelancer Gene Kirkland.

Steven pranced about the studio, peeking and grinning, while the rest of us muddled about rather clumsily. Truth be told, the whole scene was ludicrous and far from stimulating. But when it was over, Steven pulled me aside and thanked me for stepping up, going beyond the call of duty—for being a friend. As the town car was about to pull away, Kalodner rolled down the window and quipped, "Boy, that Viper is sleazy. This was great."

It was August 1990 and I was on assignment covering the Monsters of Rock festival at Castle Donington, four hours outside of London. The headlining act was Whitesnake, the big-hair, big-riff arena-rock phenom fronted by veteran crooner David Coverdale of onetime Deep Purple fame. Aerosmith was second on the bill, attesting to the 'Snake's immense commercial charm overseas. Like Aerosmith, Whitesnake fell under Kalodner's A&R watch.

The phone in my ninety-pound-a-night West End hotel room rang early. It was John. "You should come by and say hi to the guys before we leave for Donington," he said. "I have a surprise for you." I'd stopped questioning him some time ago. Once John invited me to the Ivy for lunch without telling me that David Geffen himself would join us during the meal.

I hopped out of my black cab in front of Aerosmith's upscale inn as the crew was loading up two giant tour buses. I said hello to the roadies, most of whom I knew by face, and waited. All of a sudden, three figures materialized from within the hotel's revolving door. It was Kalodner, Steven, and Joe Perry. "Lonn Friend!" cried Tyler, all smiles. Joe offered a similar though less vocal salutation. I hugged Kalodner good morning and had chit-chatted with the guys for a couple minutes when Tyler said, "So, Lonn, I hear you're riding with us."

This comment required a double take even though I was sure I heard him right the first time. "Uh, I'm riding with *you*?" I responded with giddy incredulity.

Kalodner had a poker face on. "Yeah," Steven fired back. "This bus is for you, me, John, Joe, and Jimmy." Before I had time to process that last sentence, the revolving door behind the guys spun, and out onto the cobblestone poured the one, the only, Jimmy "Fucking" Page.

Kalodner cracked the slightest smile. As the crew gently loaded Joe's and Jimmy's guitar cases into the belly of the bus, I inched next to John. "Nice surprise," I said, still shaking.

"He's going to jam with them tonight," said the man in white. "It's going to be historic." What a brilliant way to upstage the headliner.

"Get on the bus, Lonn!" shouted Tyler. "Or we'll leave you here with the rest of the press." Up the bus steps I marched, my stairway to heaven.

Virtually no tape rolled for the entire four-hour trip with the exception of an hour when Joe Perry and I moved to a quiet section of the cabin so I could knock out a one-on-one Q&A with the reclusive guitar hero. "Anger has been the inspiration of some of our best songs," Joe told me that day. How we got on the subject of anger I can't recall, because I'd never been happier in my life than during those four hypnotic hours between London and Donington.

They rapped like four musical historians at a mobile think tank. Jimmy brought up the blues—Robert Johnson, Muddy Waters, Leadbelly, and several artists I'd never heard of. These men all owed their musical legacies to the brave black men of sorrow and song who paved the way for every contemporary success story from Elvis to the Beatles, from Led Zeppelin to Aerosmith.

Jimmy Page is historically untouchable. He's the elite of the elite when it comes to slinging the axe with alien skill and abandon. The best evidence of this inarguable fact was the 5.1 surround-sound audio production of *How the West Was Won* and the DVD simply titled *Led Zeppelin*, which were released simultaneously on May 27, 2003. "While I was searching through the archives for visual and audio material for the Led Zeppelin DVD," wrote Jimmy on the inner sleeve, "I rediscovered these 1972 performances from the 25 June L.A. Forum and 27 June Long Beach Arena. This is Led Zeppelin at its best and an illustration of *How the West Was Won.*"

How the West Was Won is Jimmy Page's ultimate tour de force. It's like he has fourteen fingers. He is not human. No mortal creature given a Les Paul and a pick is supposed to be able to do this kind of shit. And just imagine, this was *live*, no overdubs, no Pro Tools, no soul-depleting hindrances of any sort. If you do not own this disc, you cannot fully comprehend the majesty of Jimmy and Zeppelin. In the rock library of live recordings, this one's on eternal checkout.

Robert Plant, Jimmy Page, John Paul Jones, and John "Bonzo" Bonham invented a form of rock 'n' roll that permitted no format and begged no acceptance. Their breakout single "Whole Lotta Love" is a filthy, spread-your-legs serenade with a deadly locomotive hook much like another smoldering FM staple burning up the charts at the time, the Rolling Stones' "Sympathy for the Devil." Plant's vocal did not just undress the ladies, it tore their undies to shreds and made no apologies.

The Immortal Ones are recognized by their catalog of great songs and a penchant for anthem composition. "Stairway to Heaven" is arguably *the* archetypal rock-'n'-roll anthem. John Paul Jones laid the perfect bottom and Bonzo Bonham crashed the kit with complete disregard for cadence or personal safety. He and Keith Moon were in a league of their own. To this day, they have yet to be surpassed as the purest rock drummers to ever wield a pair of sticks. But truth be told, Zeppelin marched to rock Mecca on the broad shoulders of the man sitting across from me on the bus.

About an hour from our destination, the cabin quieted down, and Steven looked over to me and said, "Lonn, don't you have any stories to tell? C'mon, man. You work for Larry Flynt, for

God's sake!" Jimmy, Joe, John, and Brian Goode, Jimmy's manager, all turned their heads in my direction. This was it; time for the fly to stop buzzin' and start talkin'.

"Well," I sighed, summoning the deepest breath of the trip so far, "I do have a story about Chuck Berry, but it's pretty gross." Four pairs of eyebrows rose in unison.

"Chuck Berry?" Joe said, his eyebrows slewing ever so slightly.

"Yes, Chuck Berry," I returned, my confidence suddenly boosted from the subtle yet positive reaction. Steven wiggled on the padded bench and shot me a reassuring glance.

I recounted the afternoon that two strange men with Southern accents walked into Larry Flynt Publications during my last editorial days at *Hustler* magazine. All the lunatics with scandalous wares to peddle for potential profit and publication were pointed directly to me. And so came the phone call to top them all.

The man on the line said he had tapes to show me allegedly depicting rock-'n'-roll legend Chuck Berry partaking in numerous questionable sex acts with various women. The footage, he claimed, was shot by Berry himself at Berry Park, the Missouri compound where he lived.

"How did you come to possess these tapes?" I asked.

"Well, let's just say I found them," he replied.

I didn't press the matter. I was curious. I wanted to see the stuff. So did *Hustler* senior editor Allan MacDonnell, whom I called in to help me evaluate the situation.

Later that same day, these two men show up, the guy I spoke to on the phone and his attorney. "Now, get ready, fellas," warns the man, popping the first of two VHS tapes into my office VCR. What followed knocked me and Allan off our asses. We'd both worked for *Hustler* for years and seen just about everything. We had never witnessed anything like this, though. It's Chuck Berry—one of the most well-known figures in the history of rock, identified by his signature muttonchop sideburns and a paisley long-sleeved collared shirt—draining his lizard on the face of a young blonde female squatting on a bare bathroom floor. "Take it, baby, love it," cries Johnny B. Bad. "You love the burn, don't you? You love the burn!"

The man with the tapes then pops in number two, and Allan and I take in the images of Sir Charles spanking his ding-a-ling, as well as girls changing their tampons as captured by a hidden camera allegedly planted there by our hedonistic hero. The man stops the tape. "Okay, fellas, prepare for the grand finale," he says. "You're not going to believe this."

The image shifts to another bathroom and another girl. It's a close-up of Chuck's face, his burns nearly filling the screen, but not quite. There is something else in the frame. A big, white rear end! "Oh, no!" Allan and I look at each other as Chuck Berry epoxies his gaping mouth to the poop shoot of our femme fatale, who commences to then drop her entire morning movement right down the gullet. Every last bran flake and peanut, gone, southbound down the throaty highway where once emanated the immortal chorus "Roll Over, Beethoven."

As I drop this final nugget, the bus explodes with laughter! Tyler is wheezing frantically, Perry's chuckling, Kalodner has an ear-to-ear grin, and Brian Goode's feeling really good. But beyond all that, the loudest and most animated response of the bunch is coming from Jimmy Page, who is literally doubled over in absolute hysterics.

"That's fucking fantastic!" he says. High fives and backslaps ensue. It took ten minutes for the laughter to completely dissipate and the bus to stop vibrating. As it turns out, *Hustler* never bought the videos, but a couple years later, they hit the black market. I saw them only once. That was enough.

A little while later we pulled into the massive backstage enclave at Donington and started to unload. Jimmy tapped me on the shoulder as I exited the bus and said, "Lonn, you wanna carry my guitar in? Chuck Berry! Fucking brilliant!" And there I was, toting the axe that birthed the modern rock riff in its vintage, beaten-up Hammer of the Gods leather case, two steps behind the man himself. When we hit the dressing room, Brian pulled me aside and said, "I've never seen Jimmy laugh like that, not ever. Well done, man."

Page and 'Smith shredded Donington that night. Jimmy and Joe's guitar give-and-take elevated "Walk This Way" and "Train Kept a-Rollin' " to new heights. I watched from the side of the stage seated atop a road case, the absolute best seat in the world. You could hear the Les Pauls screaming all the way back in Piccadilly. Everyone was in incredible spirits at the London afterparty much later that night. Aerosmith, the sober pirates, did not attend, nor did Jimmy.

In February of 1993, I had the honor of interviewing Jimmy Page for the June *RIP* cover story on the Coverdale/Page project. Only Kalodner could have pulled that pairing off. He brought me into the loop, long before the other magazines, while Jimmy was tracking at Criterion Studios in Miami. I had two gifts for Jimmy that day. One was from a musical colleague and passionate admirer; the other was from me.

I had recently befriended singer-songwriter Tori Amos after composing an editorial exalting her debut solo LP, *Little Earthquakes,* for *Hits* magazine. We got together for tea after her 1992 Roxy performance, and she gave me a special promotional EP for the song "Winter" that contained three inventive covers: Mick and Keith's "Angie," Nirvana's "Smells Like Teen Spirit," and Zeppelin's "Thank You." I told her that I knew Jimmy Page, and she asked that if I encountered him again, to give him the disc. "The first time I masturbated was to Led Zeppelin," she told me. "Jimmy Page is my greatest musical inspiration."

That afternoon in Miami, I passed on the love and admiration, explaining to Jimmy who this brave new female artist was. "I'll give it a listen," he said with a smile. "What else do you have there, Lonn?" I had found a copy of Chuck Berry's *Greatest Hits*, given it to my art department, and had them strip onto the cover a balloon above Chuck's head that read, "If these songs don't rock you, I'll eat shit!"

He apparently took some pleasure in the gift and returned the favor by sending me back the photo taken of us backstage at Donington with the inscription, "Lonn, Give my regards to Chuck! Jimmy Page." Kalodner also gave me a present, an early copy of the Coverdale/Page record. Upon receiving it, I called Tori, who was in L.A., and invited her to dinner and a private listening of her hero's latest work. After a sumptuous meal at the Palm, we headed back to my empty office, shared a couple shots of Wild Turkey (that was enough for two lightweights), and drifted away to riff land together.

The night of our formal interview for the *RIP* cover story at the Bel Age Hotel in West Hollywood, Jimmy bestowed on me a brand-new thirtieth-anniversary Gibson guitar signed, "Lonn . . . Rock On! Jimmy Page!" I was blown away and had to compose myself for the on-the-record exchange. I had courageously (or stupidly) prepared myself for my first question-and-answer session with the legend of legends by composing only *one* query. My gut told me that if I simply got the conversation off on a good note, everything would just flow from there. "So," I began nervously, "when Bonzo died, did you know that it was over?"

He paused, took a breath, and launched into an exquisite response. "If anybody questioned the decision to break up Zeppelin after Bonzo's death," he reflected, "all they have to do is listen to *The Song Remains the Same* and the studio albums and compare any one track. They'll hear how we were stretching the numbers and how we worked ourselves. We would just steer off at any given point, and everyone was together on it. I could just take it in a direction and John [Paul Jones] and Bonzo would click like that. We couldn't envision bringing in another drummer to do that, because there just wasn't anybody. There was never another Bonzo anyway—let's face it."

Later that year, I took part in the ceremony inducting Jimmy into the prestigious Hollywood RockWalk in front of the famed Guitar Center. With Eddie Van Halen, Steve Lukather, Dweezil Zappa, and other local axe prodigies looking on, DJ Jim Ladd introduced me to the podium, where I read a proclamation of love and respect to Jimmy written by Les Paul and then brought out the man himself. Forgive me, but the shit doesn't get any better than that.

One of Jimmy's proudest prodigies is Joe Perry. He and I finally bonded on the *Pump* tour during an uplifting interview I conducted for the *Hard N' Heavy* video magazine, the text of which I published in the October 1990 *RIP* under the head "Joe Perry: The Fine Art of Obsession." When you're an old fan of the artist you're questioning, it's fun to find out what was happening inside their heads when that good shit was being made. "Is it difficult for you to recall, with clarity, that drugged-out period when so many of those classic Aerosmith tracks were born? For example, where did 'Toys in the Attic' come from?" I asked.

"It's one of those flashes that I can remember the exact room I did it in," he said. "It's funny. We were doing preproduction for that LP with Jack Douglas, and I remember sitting on a Marshall cabinet. We wanted a fast song, and I just came up with the riff, like, really fast. Sometimes when I play, like, 'Back in the Saddle,' I close my eyes, and I'm right back where I was when I wrote it. I can smell the smells. 'Sweet Emotion,' I can remember the lead at the end of that song and every night I play it, I'm back at the Record Plant in New York City. I can tell you the color of the chairs in the studio and what I had to eat that day. Or the lead to 'Walk This Way,' I remember doing that at four in the morning with Jack and Steven standing right there. That's probably why I like playing those songs, because they take me back to a time that really made me feel good."

As for Steven, well, it wasn't long before I was popping more videos in the mail, mostly for shits and giggles. This time they were addressed to Little Mountain Studios in Vancouver, Canada, where the Toxic Twins (the nickname for Tyler and Perry from the '70s drug days) had taken up residence to continue work on the next LP. Production had started months before in Los Angeles under the guidance of the late, great Bruce Fairbairn but was netting less-than-satisfactory results. Once back on Fairbairn's familiar home turf, they would reclaim their balls-to-the-wall creative mojo, and the river of rock started flowing.

The guys broke media silence on September 26, 1992, when they made an on-air phone call to my *Pirate Radio Saturday Night* program.

"How's the record coming?" I asked.

"Well," fired Steven with a chuckle in his voice, "it's a damn sight better than those videos you've been sending!"

Whereupon Joe chimes in, "How do you expect us to write and perform important music when . . . Jesus, Lonn!"

The atmosphere was light and lively and I dug right in. "So I really wanna know if it's happening up there, if the vibe is cool, if you guys are angry," I said.

"We're pissed we spent so much money in L.A. and don't have anything to show for it," joked Joe.

"Yeah, angry!" laughed Steven.

"But the stuff is definitely feeling a lot different now," continued Joe. "People are saying it has a *Rocks* vibe to it."

As much as I was enjoying this, I only had a couple of minutes left. That's when I popped the big question. "So are you guys gonna tell me the name of the record?"

"I dunno," answered Joe. "We were debating that in the car this afternoon."

More teasing. But I knew it, so I played along. "Listen, guys, we're friends, right?" I asked. "We've shared a lot together, been in many intimate circumstances . . ."

"This is true," they responded in unison.

"What if we called the album *A Little to the Left*?" joked Steven. "What comes to mind immediately? See if you can guess."

Faux frustration settled in. "C'mon, fellas, who's gonna know?" I pleaded.

"Get a grip, will ya, Lonn, you're losing it!" said Steven.

"Get a grip?" I launched back. "Get a grip on what, Steven?"

"On your big ten-inch, Lonn!" he laughed.

"Whatever the record's called, you'll be the first to know," added Joe.

"That's right, because we come to play, baby," mused Steven.
"And play to come!" I responded.

"All right, enough of that," interrupted Joe.

We chitchatted for another few moments. Steven told me about a song called "Lizard Love" inspired by two tiny humping reptilians that entered the room while they were doing some tracking at Jeff Lynne's Studio F in L.A.

"I really appreciate this, guys. I know how intense it is right now," I said, wrapping up the conversation.

"Anything for you, Lonn," replied Steven.

The relationship that had been budding over the past four years was now netting me unprecedented content opportunities and much more. I got my second chance at a cameo when I was asked to be in the opening odd-face montage for the "Eat the Rich" video. This time, the shot wasn't left on the cutting-room floor. I was also invited down to the set to witness the filming of the black-and-white sequence for the LP's first single/video, "Livin' on the Edge."

The decision to lead with this track was a fearless one. Geffen's promotional machine was much more suited to working a straight-ahead sexy rocker or an in-the-pocket ballad than a six-minute anthem with deep sociopolitical overtones. But Steven wanted to make a statement with this new album that Aerosmith could stimulate more zones than the erogenous. Sure, the seductive love songs were there, and they would eventually blow the record through the roof, thanks in great part to director Marty Callner's videos for "Cryin'," "Crazy," and "Amazing," which introduced to the world teen heartthrob Alicia Silverstone. Regardless of the risk, however, Steven and Kalodner pushed and won for "Livin' on the Edge," and that leap of faith took Aero-

smith to the next level, twenty years into their remarkable rock-
'n'-roll journey.

The tour was as explosive as the record. Massive stage, state-
of-the-art lights, a set list brimming with two dozen songs per
night, ranging from the classics to roughly half of the new LP—
it was the concert circus of the year, and I had another laminate
with my picture on it.

On July 29, 1993, I spent my thirty-seventh birthday at the
America West Arena with 'Smith and Jackyl, another Kalodner
signing. The Southern outfit's lead singer, Jesse James Dupree,
coaxed twenty thousand fans into singing me "Happy Birthday."
After the show, none other than Mr. Tyler honored me with a
private performance of said song. When he was finished, he
kissed me on the cheek and told me that he loved me. Wanna see
a grown man cry? I've got the videotape.

Three months later, Joyce accompanied me to Brussels, Bel-
gium, where I cohosted a Westwood One satellite broadcast of
the band's Halloween Night concert from Forest National
Arena. Boston DJ Mark Parenteau did most of the on-air rap,
but I chimed in frequently with personal thoughts about the
guys and their music. We stayed at the Conrad Brussels Hotel
and had dinner with guitarist Brad Whitford and his wife. That
trip was the best rock-'n'-roll road trip Joyce and I ever had. Being around Steven and the energy of the road, having her in my
element, was an elixir for our love life. There were no groupie
distractions, and we didn't need to purchase any pay-per-view
porn.

These were the best of times for me personally and professionally. I was riding a synchronic wave of influence, creativity,
and purpose with one of the greatest rock bands the world had

ever seen, having fun, and making—as Jeff Spicoli would say— "righteous bucks." In a few short months, however, I would make the career decision that would lead to my eventual undoing. And the man—the band—I'd come to call "friend" would disappear for almost six years.

The final leg of the long *Nine Lives* tour stopped at the Hollywood Bowl in the spring of 1999. I had not seen Aerosmith since Brussels. My once-shoulder-length hair was gone, as was the beard, the mask I'd worn during those rip-roaring *RIP* days. Kalodner walked me backstage for my reunion with the guys. They were on a tight schedule, so it was a quick hallway hello or nothing.

Bassist Tom Hamilton came out first and gave me a hug, and so did Brad Whitford. Joey flipped me a quick, acknowledging "Hey, man." Then Joe Perry walked by. "Hi, Joe," I said.

"Oh, hey," and off he went. He didn't recognize me.

"Joe, it's Lonn!" I yelled.

He stopped and turned around. "Wow! Hey, man, I didn't know that was you. Good to see ya." And he was gone. I felt out of place. Then I saw him, about twenty feet away, surrounded, as usual, by a gaggle of onlookers praying for a touch of his hem or a kiss on the cheek.

He glanced up and politely completed the autograph he was signing before making his way toward the beardless former rock journalist. He embraced me, stared me down, and said, "Yeah, I can see it in your eyes. Grow your hair back. This isn't you. We'll meet again, my friend. I love you."

Nine Lives was the first Aerosmith LP to boast mystical imagery, from lyrics to packaging. "Hole in My Soul," "Fallen Angels," "Kiss Your Past Good-bye," these were pop psalms of awakened self-expression. The Mystic River does run through New England. Boston blood flows with immense heart and soul. The band was finally tapping into their rich, numinous heritage. Of course, "Falling in Love (Is Hard on the Knees)" was the obvious hit, vintage Aerosmith in groove and groin, designed to sell records, keep the train rollin'.

Serendipity brought me into a Detroit-suburb hotel on the evening of Bon Jovi's back-to-back sold-out shows in July 2001. Aerosmith was on their way out of town as Bon Jovi was coming in. And there I was, arriving a day early, sitting in the lobby, when the entire band appeared.

It was a far warmer reunion than the hallway of the Bowl. Tom Hamilton and I walked around the neighborhood that evening, talking about music and where I'd been personally and professionally for the past few years. We sat in the bar and drank tea until 2 A.M. The next morning, drummer Joey Kramer and I had a most transcendent conversation. He spoke of his near-psychological-death experience and how faith in the Hindu avatar Sai Baba brought him back from the brink. Like Townshend, a rocker saved by a Baba. Brad Whitford had his entire family on the road with him, homeschooling the kids, renting a bus—what an adventure. Joe Perry was Joe Perry. Quiet, cool, polite, short on small talk, but utterly kind.

They were hopping in their cars to leave for the airport when Tyler and I finally had a few moments to reconvene. "Steven, we gotta talk," I said as the driver gunned the town car's engine, signaling it was time to go. The rest of the group had departed already.

"Yeah, we do," he replied. What followed were twenty surreal minutes on a sidewalk forty miles outside of Motown. "Do
you know who Marianne Williamson is?" he asked.

"Of course I do," I responded. Williamson is a writer and
motivational speaker who based her career on *A Course in Miracles*, a New Age bible published in the early '70s.

"She's a very enlightened woman, Lonn," vibrated Tyler. He
got excited, pulled me closer, and started whispering in my ear.
"She was just in my hotel room, performing a private Sunday-
morning service for me. This woman has a direct line to God!
We laughed, cried, and sang hallelujah."

He positively glowed. I told him about my pain, confusion,
disgust with the egos of the industry, and desire to bring a revolutionary consciousness to rock journalism. I was venting, judg-
ing, making excuses for having lost my way. I had failed as
a record executive. My return to journalism at KNAC.com
had been short-lived. Now I was chasing the pipe dream of a
VH1 TV show. If you can't bitch to your friends, whom can you
bitch to?

Tour manager Jimmy Eyers, the accommodating British
gent who has guided the band in and out of trains, planes, and
automobiles since the mid '90s, loaded up the town cars and sent
them off to the airport while Steven and I continued our conversation on the sidewalk. The regiment never pulls out until the
sergeant is on board.

"You know, I wanted you to write the liner notes for *Get a
Grip*, but [former manager] Tim Collins nixed the idea."

That knocked me back onto the sidewalk. "Really, I never
knew that."

"There's a lot you don't know about that period." He smiled
sardonically. "I'm saving it for *my* book." Before departing,

Steven gave me his cell-phone number. "You use this anytime. No barricades. This is how you reach me. I'm serious." He held me close and told me to hang in there.

"I'm coming out on the road to see you," I said. "I don't know when, but when I do, we're gonna talk. Really talk."

He shook his head, grinned that Cheshire-cat Tyler grin, and disappeared into his chariot, the chains on his wrist jangling, the hair on my arms quivering.

T.C. and I arrived in San Diego a little after 6 P.M. on a chilly day in January 2002, early enough to ensure that there would be plenty of time to talk. She was the only one I could find to make a two-hour trip south at the last minute to see a rock concert. T.C. used to be married to David Gahan from Depeche Mode, so nothing much freaked her out. I'd met her in a yoga class led by Guru Singh, a Kundalini master whose teachings were helping to hold me together while everything around me seemed to crumble. I had no designs on T.C. The fly just wanted a butterfly along for the voyage this time.

Steven's dressing room felt sensuous, sweet, organic, and fantastically alive. I entered as the rock star was having his faux tattoos applied by the band's traveling makeup artist. The once multicolored, fuzzy-boa'd, fashion-flash-of-decadence past had given way to muted earth tones that evoked a tender Eastern serenity. Spacy New Age strains floated off a boom box as candles and incense burned.

"Is that your war or peace paint?" I asked.

"Both. And neither," he responded. The small talk that so long ago concentrated on pornography and professional agendas had completely changed. Five minutes in his lair, the discussion moved to Lebanese poet Kahlil Gibran and his 1923 master-piece, *The Prophet.*

"Someone told me a year ago to do this, and I did, and it was a spiritual experience," he began excitedly. "Find a place—a beach, a forest, a solitary spot where it's just you and Him—and read the book aloud. Every word. It will change your life. Trust me."

As he moved over to his dressing table, I replied without hesitation, "Oh, I'm going to do it. When the moment presents itself, I'll know."

That was when he hugged me, like he did every time I happened to fly announced or unannounced onto his radar. Not an obligatory embrace either, but the kind that implies you're reconnecting with someone who knows and cares about you. Steven wasn't aware that I was coming that night until I rang his cell phone outside the back gate when security failed to buy the argument that I was a friend of the band. In fact, at 3 P.M. that afternoon, 120 miles away at home in L.A., I didn't know that I was showing up. But something inside urged me on.

"I don't think I've ever shown you the preshow ritual, have I, Lonn?" he asked. The question was rhetorical. He was fucking with me and I loved it. "Come over here. I can't believe you've never witnessed this. Now pay close attention." On Steven's dressing table sat a tiny cauldron of viscous liquid. In the middle of the goo, there was something small sticking up from the bottom.

"When I was very young, at the beginning of my career, I met a soothsayer," he explained. "This seer instructed me to perform this ritual before I took the stage. He told me to do this every night and I would have all the success I could possibly imagine. The ritual was for me to fill a pot with honey and place

in the middle of the honey a rat's tail and, before every performance, remove the tail from the liquid and bite off the end of it.
Like this."

With that, he reached down into the liquid and pulled up the
curly twiglike substance, placed it in his mouth, bit off the end,
and swallowed. Then he replaced the remaining piece into the
honey. "And that's it. I've performed this rite before every show
for the past thirty years."

There was a deep, pregnant pause, after which I blurted out,
"That's bullshit!"

He looked me in the eye, raised his eyebrows an inch, and
responded, "Okay, it's gingerroot. But it's a great story, isn't
it?" Then he kissed T.C. on the lips and dashed out of the
room.

We sat right on the stage, like old times, two feet from the
ramp that Steven pranced upon like a cat the entire two-plus
hours Aerosmith destroyed the San Diego faithful. It was the
best I'd ever seen them. Joe Perry had found onstage Viagra, ex-
ploding out of a closet of cool into a cataclysmic tornado of confidence. He sang, danced, and did a six-string mambo far beyond
anything ever attempted before. Aerosmith was at the top of
their game, and the mythical man at center stage was positively
radiant.

I arrived home a little after 3 the next morning. It wasn't just
the concert that had my innards banging about like toys in the
attic. I crept silently into the library room and pulled *The Prophet*
off the shelf. "And the Orator said, 'Speak to us of freedom,'"
wrote Gibran. "You shall be free indeed when your days are not
without a care nor your nights without a want and a grief." Then
I lay down on the sofa, closed my eyes, and dreamed of a vacant
beach somewhere.

•   •   •

It was a damp, windy morning on the Telscombe Cliffs of Brighton, England. The skies were violent, dark. All was in motion today. The air crackled with sound and flutter. My only concern was the book, keeping it dry. I tucked *The Prophet* into the pocket of my twelve-year-old Anthrax "Bring the Noise" Stussy overcoat and headed out into the mystery.

Whether it was fate or destiny that brought me here, I cannot say. That is a matter of interpretation. I'd spent the past three years in therapy with Guru Singh, the shamanic Sikh, a bearded, musical, mystical sage whom Kalodner resembled in appearance and personal décor. They both wore white, but that's where the similarity ended. Even facing down and beating thyroid cancer didn't permit the jaded John a glimpse of the other side. Steven, on the other hand, had actually visited the guru, sat in that same tiny room in his Wilshire-district home, and received the same dose of Vedic wisdom and meditative instruction as I.

I took my place on the lone concrete bench that faced out over the choppy English Channel. There wasn't a soul in sight. The village people were either in their cottages, sipping tea, or at work. Only a fool would be out on a morning like this. I closed my eyes, took some deep breaths, and settled into absolute presence. When I opened them, I saw a cosmic crack in the sky, a sliver of light ripping through the blackness. The rain had stopped completely, though the wind continued to blow strong and firm. The Channel spread out in front of me like slippery gray satin.

Pete Townshend wrote, "Nothing is planned, by the sea and the sand." Here by the water, I reverently digested that immortal lyric as I completed my reading assignment. I had spoken with uncustomary clarity and purpose, for in that moment they were not words, but ethereal fireflies that buzzed from my lips en route to nothing, and everything. If I could talk this way, I mused to myself, perhaps I might learn to walk this way.

13

Ballad of
Jon and Richie

"IT IS ONLY WHEN WE HAVE THE COURAGE TO FACE
THINGS EXACTLY AS THEY ARE, WITHOUT ANY SORT OF
SELF-DECEPTION OR ILLUSION, THAT A LIGHT WILL
DEVELOP OUT OF EVENTS, BY WHICH THE PATH TO
SUCCESS MAY BE RECOGNIZED."

—*I Ching (Book of Changes)*

By 1990, *RIP* had taken up residence in the eye of a metal hurricane. Bands like GN'R, Metallica, Mötley Crüe, Whitesnake, Poison, Def Leppard, Warrant, L.A. Guns, Faster Pussycat, Ratt, Scorpions, AC/DC, Queensrÿche, Extreme, Van Halen, Ozzy Osbourne, White Lion, Great White, and Megadeth were ruling the charts. If they were loud and had hair, they were selling records and *RIP* was covering 'em. And that meant we were selling magazines.

No group, however, during these unprecedented days of metal prosperity was more monstrous than Bon Jovi. I'd gotten to know the band professionally in 1989 and personally when principal players Jon Bon Jovi and guitarist Richie Sambora visited my office in the fall of '88. The brief but pleasant encounter planted the seed for what would grow into one of the most enduring, fun-filled, chaotic, and educational relationships of my career.

I observed during that initial encounter what I'd previously only heard and read about: the dichotomy, the balance, the yin and yang of these two. Mick had Keith, Axl had Slash, Bono had the Edge, Tyler had Perry, Plant had Page, Eddie had Dave (and Sammy), and Jon had Richie. Through several astonishing adventures, I would come to know each of these men of music in a different way and, in the process, come to know myself a bit better as well. The first Bon Jovi escapade took me halfway around the world.

"Dawn Bridges from Mercury Records is on the phone, Lonn," shouted my assistant, Kristina. "She wants to talk to you about Bon Jovi!" Whispers from our peeps in the street said trouble had come to Jersey paradise.

"You've no doubt heard the rumors," said the fast-talking press princess. "I've talked to Jon and he wants you to do an exclusive feature dispelling the rumors. Fans think Bon Jovi is breaking up, and the band wants you to write a truthful, revealing cover story setting the record straight." I began to smile. This was big.

"We want you to go to Japan for a week," she explained, her voice rising. "You'll attend the New Year's Eve show at the Tokyo Dome and then the Yokohama gig two days later. Hang with the guys, total access, get the truth, and report it to your readership."

The truth, huh? I chewed on that for a moment before responding. "Are you sure, Dawn, that they will tell me the truth?" I asked frankly.

A pregnant pause ensued before Dawn responded. Record companies are very protective of their artists, forever spinning facts and figures to keep their stars shining in the brightest light. I was a trusted member of the press, yes, but we're still talking about celebrities here.

"They like you, Lonn," she replied. "You're a friend. They know you'll write a great story. And there are no constraints, none whatsoever."

I would have been a fool to think twice. Bon Jovi over New Year's in Japan? I'd been to Tokyo the previous November with White Lion and loved it. But they played the three-thousand-seat Sun Plaza Hall. This was the fifty-thousand-seat-capacity Dome, a different league altogether. The exclusive would be a huge coup for *RIP*, and I'd get to cross an ocean again on the company's dime and write another big-profile rock-'n'-roll road story. "Domo arigato, Dawn!" I said. "When do we leave?"

The *New Jersey* tour had culminated on February 17, 1990. The next ten months, the guys in the band barely saw one another, gathering but once in August for keyboardist Dave Bryan's wedding. They had a gig scheduled in Red Bank, New Jersey, on December 23, a warm-up for their return to Asia, where they had last rocked Tokyo into a New Year on December 31, 1988. But time apart causes band members to drift, get back to normal lives, explore solo creative ventures, disconnect from the whole. That's when the fragile threads that hold together a rock group—no matter the size—can fray.

Jon had released his first solo LP, modestly titled *Blaze of Glory: Songs Written and Performed by Jon Bon Jovi, Inspired by the Film Young Guns II*, on August 7, 1990. It was a big ballad effort that featured guest appearances by Elton John and Jeff Beck. The album peaked at number three on the Billboard Top 200 chart, and the single went to number one, giving the Jersey rocker his fifth number-one single in as many years: "You Give

Love a Bad Name" in '86, "Livin' on a Prayer" in '87, "Bad Medicine" in '88, and "I'll Be There for You" in '89. The glory was great, indeed, but Jon celebrated the achievement alone, without his bandmates.

During the final leg of the *New Jersey* jaunt, Richie dated Cher and began writing his solo record *Stranger in This Town*, escaping into frequent solitude. Drummer Tico Torres set up his easel and began to explore a new kind of artistic passion as a painter. Dave was recovering from a parasite that had eaten away a portion of his stomach and was tending to his new wife (or vice versa). Bassist Alec John Such broke his collarbone in a motorcycle accident.

Things were falling apart at the seams in Bon Jovi land. Richie wanted to go home from the *New Jersey* tour early. Jon vetoed it. The last date of the campaign was originally slated to be a headline performance at the Moscow Music Peace Festival in August—the rock extravaganza organized by Doc McGhee, as a plea bargain for his pot bust, that was also featuring Mötley Crüe, Scorpions, Skid Row (all managed by Doc), and Ozzy Osbourne—but *New Jersey* continued to climb the charts like a chimpanzee. The album spawned five top-ten hits, eclipsing its multiplatinum predecessor, *Slippery When Wet*. So the tour was expanded.

When the band hit Europe in December 1989, a five-date run quickly swelled to thirty. An extended Christmas break went out the window, and the tour continued. Richie spoke up for the guys, who were complaining of exhaustion, but Jon wasn't listening to anything but the roar of the fans and the sound of his wallet stretching. I was being invited to Japan during one of the most tumultuous times in any band's history.

I wanted, I needed to be there, feel it, cavort unencumbered through the backstage shadows, get down with the fans in the pit, break bread with the natives, and wallow in the excess and access that becomes fame and fortune.

In Tokyo, Richie opened up about the trappings of success and the speed bump he knew his relationship with Jon had hit. He was a bit sarcastic—maybe jealous is a better word—about *Young Guns II* and spoke to me of his *Stranger in This Town* solo project and how much it meant to him. As independent a musical creator as Richie was, he looked to Jon for affirmation. Why wouldn't he? Just check out what they'd built together.

Jon was preoccupied most of the time, either by the logistics of the shows or with entertaining his family. His mom and dad made the trip overseas, so he was being a good son. Our conversation time was limited. One afternoon in his hotel room, I tried to get inside his head, find out what was causing the friction between him and Richie. He said he was exhausted from touring but offered no revelations about his relationship with Richie, or the rest of the band for that matter.

Bon Jovi was such a close-knit bunch, when their leader was disconnecting, the fear of complete dissolution weighed over the organization like a thundercloud over Mount Fuji. I asked Jon if he enjoyed Japan (he'd been there six times by that point), the Eastern energy, the Zen gardens. He replied that the only view of the country he'd ever had was through the window of a tour bus.

Here I began to see a man suffering from burnout that no amount of success could soothe. Jon had no intention of connecting with me. What I learned in Japan from Jon Bon Jovi was perseverance and the power of performance. No matter where this man was at in his own head, when it came to getting onstage and doing his job, he delivered and would not leave the stage until both band and fan were completely exhausted.

Jon, Richie, Dave, Tico, and Alec rocked the Asian faithful and rang in 1991 with a volcanic blast that put a collective Buddha smile on every fan's face. The big anthem numbers like "Lay Your Hands on Me," "You Give Love a Bad Name," and "Livin' on a Prayer" brought fifty thousand Japanese fans to their feet.

Jon was in high sermon from the rock pulpit. He jumped, screamed, crooned, hurdled, boxed, kicked, and worked his ass off. While most of the eyes were on his blazing front-and-center eminence, I bounced my peepers back and forth to his sidekick, the soulful shredder, hitting the notes with prideful perfection, balancing the aura with his cool. You'd have never known that until a week before, they hadn't seen each other or jammed together for almost a year.

The offstage friction, however, was undermining the strength of the performance. The ride to Yokohama—the next date on the Japan excursion—was long and, for the most part, painful. Jon and Richie weren't talking. I didn't engage in substantive banter either, because I sensed no one really wanted to talk shop. Richie and I were both reverent fans of Peter Gabriel, and we started singing his songs. "Dreaming of Mercy Street, wear your insides out." Our harmonizing seemed to make Jon uncomfortable. He gazed out the van window, watching the gorgeous, emerald-green mural unfold, and acknowledged nothing but what was clanging around in his own noggin. He'd never tell me what was really up, so I just played along, getting most of my story from Richie. On the record for a feature or off the record to let off steam, that was the case for years to come as Richie and I remained great friends. When it came to coughing up the truth, Jon was a sound bite. Richie was a conversation.

As for Jon, I'm not sure I knew him that much better after a week on the road than I did before I landed in Tokyo. I had to chip away slowly and respectfully at the barrier that divided him from the rest of humanity.

Returning from Japan, I was drained. This trip exhausted me. It was a microcosm of what a band the size of Bon Jovi must endure on a world tour that goes for a year or more and doesn't stop until as many fans as humanly possible have been properly, personally, and profoundly rocked.

Band manager Doc McGhee parted ways with Bon Jovi in late '91. Jon and Doc no longer saw eye to eye on where the leader of his band was going. Richie, however, still felt close to Doc and trusted him for career guidance. He fought for a brief while to keep him on as his private personal manager, but Jon nixed the idea, feeling it was important that the band remain on the same path, in unison, as they cleaned house and started anew in the spring of '92.

The group was now "self" managed under the corporate moniker Bon Jovi Management. Richie's brilliant and deeply personal solo endeavor *Stranger in This Town* had come and gone without making much of a commercial splash. Jon also changed booking agencies to the mighty CAA (Creative Artists Agency) because his mind was now on acting and Hollywood, and he wanted a major player in his corner.

I got a call inviting me to visit Little Mountain Studios in Vancouver—home of Fairbairn and his protégé Bob Rock—to get an inside glimpse of the *Keep the Faith* recording sessions.

The invitation was flattering, but I didn't accept it immediately. My staff, the editors that kept me connected to the cool, were concerned about Jon's new high-fashion haircut and how it would play with the molten-minded don't-fuck-with-us *RIP* readership. "Lonn," they chimed in unison, "he looks like Julia Roberts." I digested their concerns and agreed to have lunch with Jon and Richie at a fancy Japanese restaurant on La Cienega Boulevard.

"We want to be on the cover with the release of *Keep the Faith*, Lonn," said Jon. "And we want you to write the story." I wanted to, but the girls were right—he did look like Julia Roberts. I said so, in a courteous, tongue-in-cheek way. Richie laughed. I suppose I was having some fun, fucking with the invincible Jon Bon Jovi. It was my turn to flex the ego.

I collapsed like a cheap suitcase before the green-tea ice cream arrived and committed to the cover story, with one provision: Bon Jovi had to play the sixth-anniversary *RIP* party in October.

"Done," he said.

"Cool," I replied, shaking his and Richie's hands. Jon's haircut may have been softer, but one of the smartest businessmen in rock 'n' roll wanted the endorsement of the heaviest magazine on the stands. And he'd just gotten it.

That August in Vancouver, Jon let a couple more layers of skin peel off during our conversations, but he still played closer to the chest than just about any artist I'd ever interviewed. When he opened up, it was always about reaching for more fame, more success.

That night, the Lollapalooza Tour was passing through Vancouver, so with the help of the sexy, tattooed studio assistant Rhian Gittins, I talked Jon and Richie into taking a break from the studio and heading out to see a couple bands that were changing the landscape of modern rock.

The rain started to pour down as Eddie Vedder swung from a cable above the muddy crowd, leading Pearl Jam through a set of perfectly orchestrated mayhem. When Chris Cornell hit the stage and unloaded his Herculean cries of existential despair on the drenched, enraptured throng, I glanced over at Richie, who was grinning from ear to ear. "This fucking band, what are they called? Soundgarden?" he asked excitedly. "They're nuts! I love this!"

As moved as Richie and I were by the grunge growl, Jon appeared completely disinterested. He was thinking about his thing, Bon Jovi, not some punks in dirty flannel shirts and worn-out Doc Martens. I don't believe he felt threatened by the new kids on the Northwest block. He was too confident in his own craft and really wasn't paying enough attention to draw a conclusion one way or another. Pearl Jam could have covered "You Give Love a Bad Name," and he still wouldn't have budged.

I returned home, penned the December 1992, sixth-anniversary *RIP* cover story, "Bon Jovi: Born Again," and hosted another incredible party at the four-thousand-seat-capacity Hollywood Palladium that, true to his word, Jon and the boys headlined, opening their set with the Beatles classic "With a Little Help from My Friends," which reminded me of sound check in Yokohama on that remarkable Japan journey when Jon and Richie sang the chorus "I get by with a little help from Lonn Friend," causing the visiting writer to blush a bit.

The *RIP* party was the pinnacle of a remarkable year, but when the band had left and the fans had all gone home, I remember sitting in my car, alone in the parking lot, wondering what to make of things. Bon Jovi had just played *my* party.

Should I have been patting myself on the back for negotiating the gig? Did I really know the superstar singing his ass off as a favor for a friend who had done a favor for him by writing a decent magazine article? Looking back, I wasn't sure of anything anymore except that I was caught up in the illusion that this shit actually meant something not just to the artist but to the fans. Jon was singing about faith, but did I have a clue what that meant? Did he?

When I went inside in '94, I lost almost all contact with Bon Jovi. The educational-experiment days as vice president of A&R at Arista Records ended in January 1998. I saw Jon only once during my tenure, but Richie phoned me several times, once from Frankfurt in the summer of 1996, giddy over the immense concert success the band was enjoying in Europe. While I was running about the country scouting for the next big thing that I never did find, the Bon Jovi beast had grown into a stadium-swallowing King Kong.

In the old country, no rock band could touch them when it came to attendance or fan loyalty. "We're doing three weeks of just German dates!" chimed Richie, forever pinching himself from the band's incredible longevity. I could hear the genuine excitement and humility in his voice. I asked how Jon was. "He's good. We're good. Everything's beautiful. How you doing, buddy?" I told Richie that the record business wasn't my cup of tea, and I wasn't sure where I would be when this gig was over. "Listen, man, you'll be okay. Just have faith." Faith.

In early 2000, a call from VH1 blew the boys from Jersey back into my life. "We're doing a *Behind the Music* on Bon Jovi," they said. "And everyone up here says, 'You have to talk to Lonn Friend.'" I felt honored and agreed to the sit-down, doing very little homework before my session. VH1 had resurrected my public persona the previous fall when they asked me to take part in the Metallica and Mötley Crüe episodes of *Behind the Music*. I'd been away from *RIP* and the heavy-metal life for five years, but when I sat in that chair and the producer asked the questions, I was instantly back in the day, offering anecdotes and insights on the rockers I'd traveled so far with.

The Bon Jovi Q&A was a lot of fun. I recalled with enhanced perspective the tumultuous Tokyo trip. VH1 even ran a copy of the "Bon Jovi: Dead or Alive?" *RIP* cover. I was very happy with how my sound bites played and, apparently, so was Jon, because on June 21, 2000, I was surprised by a special delivery at my office at the streaming hard-rock Web site KNAC.com, where I'd taken up editor-in-chief duties the previous December. It was an expensive bottle of champagne wrapped in a leather casing with a handwritten note from Jon that read,

> Dear Lonn,
> What a surprise it was to see your smiling face on *Behind the Music*. I wanted to drop you this quick note to thank you for your kind words. The *Sopranos* bit was priceless. Should I ever be able to repay the favor, don't hesitate to ask. *We're there.*
>
> With respect,
> Jon.

I was touched by the sentiment and the gesture. Rock stars don't usually go out of their way to thank the press. It wasn't entirely sincere, however. Jon could not have been surprised by my appearance. He handpicked most of the people he wanted VH1 to go after. Not only that, he negotiated for approval on the cut before it was aired, a mighty display of influence. Regardless, I showed the bottle of champagne to the people in the office. "Look what Jon Bon Jovi sent me." Synchronicity soon orchestrated a personal reunion with the band and a concert review that would lead to my most revealing Bon Jovi adventure of all.

It was November 2000, and I was in the Windy City doing a segment for KNAC.com, part of my streaming-video series for them. I'd just finished a rollicking hour-long interview with Sammy Hagar in his room at the Ritz Carlton and was regrouping on a sofa in the palatial lobby and who came waltzing down the hall toward me but Richie and Dave.

"Oh, my God, what the fuck is this?" they beamed. We hugged like old friends who hadn't seen each other in years. "What are you doing in Chicago?" they asked.

"Interviewing Sammy," I said. "I'm leaving in the morning."

They looked at each other and smiled. "Uh, no you're not, buddy," ordered Richie. "We're playing here tomorrow night, and you're coming! In fact, we're going to the House of Blues tonight to see blues guitarist Keb' Mo'. Snake [mutual old pal from Skid Row] is here! You best get ready to rock, my brother!"

Just like the *RIP* days, I was changing plans in a heartbeat. Jon quickly got wind of my presence and invited me to ride to the gig with him. He asked about my life, what I'd been up to, and showed me photos taken of a rally he'd performed at for Al Gore, who would soon lose the most controversial presidential election in American history.

"You seem to have calmed down a lot, Lonn," he observed.

"Yeah," I replied quietly. "I'm not the high-volume metal dude from *RIP* anymore. I'm not sure that I ever really was."

He reached over and gave me a pat on the shoulder. "I'm glad you're here, Lonn," he said.

The ride was good, but the next night's gig was great. Bon

Jovi played their hearts out, ignited the audience into a good old arena-rock frenzy. I'd caught many shows in the Windy City; they have the most enthusiastic fans in America. For a kid from affected Tinsel Town, where the crowds at times couldn't muster enough chaos at the end of a performance to seduce the band into an encore, the night hit on all cylinders.

In June 2001, I called in the favor promised in that post–*Behind the Music* note to ask Jon to help create a demo for a TV show that I had conceived called *Rock a Mile with Lonn Friend.* I needed a huge band for my reel, and he obliged, inviting me across the Atlantic to be the fly on the grandest, most successful touring wall in Europe. Just like the old days, I had an all-access laminate and the freedom to roll digital videotape wherever and whenever I wanted. The only difference between this jaunt and those I made for *RIP* was that this trip was on my dime. Call it a leap of faith.

First stop was Zurich, Switzerland, and the legendary Dolder Grand Hotel. I arrived the night before the show so I'd have time to catch up with the boys before the concert madness and videotaping began. I found out that evening that the relationship between Jon and Richie had scaled some serious hurdles in recent years. Richie wasn't complaining as much about being the axe in the shadow of the superstar. He'd released a second unsuccessful solo LP, *Undiscovered Soul,* but wasn't blaming the album's poor performance on anyone. Richie had cut a new publishing deal that gave him a much bigger piece of the Bon Jovi songwriting-royalty pie. He and his wife, actress Heather Locklear, had brought a little girl into the world. There was a resolve about my old buddy, a sense of peace with respect to his lot in the Bon Jovi life. I wondered if Jon had made the same transition.

I'd mapped out a ten-day trip that would include five stadium shows in exotic European locales I'd never been to. First night was Zurich; next night, Padova, Italy; then a day off before Vienna, Austria; and concluding in Munich, Germany. I was flying with the band on their private jet, older, wiser but just as curious about what this megarock thing really meant.

Zurich was a painful show for Jon, as was Padova. He was suffering from old knee problems and near exhaustion after four concerts without a break. But we had a day off, and Jon decided the caravan should make a slight detour and spend the night in Venice, the floating city of concrete. Richie and I spent four hours at a café in San Marco Square, talking about our lives while the pigeons lovingly accosted the tourists sprinkling seed on the cobblestone. "I feel great," he said, pausing to take a breath. "But you know, Lonn, after twenty years, it gets harder to keep yourself together."

Richie articulated in fervent detail the journey of his relationship with Jon, the balance they strike, the secret to their extraordinary success, which is really quite simple in construct. Jon is the fire that brings the moths to the flame; Richie makes those moths feel like butterflies.

The rest of the guys feed off the strength of their union. The true fan knows when it works, when the chemistry is authentic. That these five guys are going to take them to that higher place by, as Richie said, "doin' it until they fall down." I sat the digital video recorder on the table, and we just floated away into three hours of conversation.

A band dinner was planned at Robert De Niro's favorite Venice eatery, and I was hoping for some quality time with Jon, but that continued to be problematic. An audience with the pope seemed a far more doable Italian dream.

Over antipasti, Jon and I talked about the songs that resonated loudest with the Euro crowds. "I think 'Keep the Faith' has developed into something larger than life," I said. "That track has come a long way from Little Mountain. I remember when you played it for me up there, Jon." "Faith" in live performance had begun to beat with a stronger pulse and purpose that set it apart from almost any other Bon Jovi song. Driven by Hugh McDonald's urgent bass line and Tico's machine-gun drum beat, the boys ratcheted up the once-average rock song to anthemlike proportions. Jon's passionate delivery of the message and Richie's incendiary solo brought the sold-out stadiums to their frenetic feet.

With the bill paid and the band members dispersing, I found myself strolling through San Marco with Jon, on a mission to finally breach that sacred space between writer and rocker and get to the truth. We were walking back through the square to the hotel after dinner. It was very late and a lot of expensive Pinot Grigio had been imbibed.

"I've got a feeling, Jon," I muttered as we approached the front steps of our palatial resting spot, "that this trip is gonna be like William Miller in *Almost Famous*, desperately trying to get his interview with the big guy but not succeeding until the final scene in the film."

He laughed, flashing the smile that's broken a million hearts, and said, "Oh, yeah, wise guy? You got your camera?"

It was around my wrist, where it'd been virtually every moment since I landed in Switzerland. I witnessed the power of celebrity again as Jon snapped his fingers, and quicker than you could say "Volare," a boat was waiting for us at the dock, prepared to take us, in the dead of night, wherever the rock star wanted to go.

We cruised through the canals, the water splashing up the

sides of our aquataxi, our hair blowing in the midnight Venice breeze. "I know the place," Jon shouted to me over the drone of the engine. "The Cipriani Hotel. We had the *U-571* wrap party there. The bar is nice and open all night." Jon had worked hard copping roles on the indie film circuit, but *U-571* was his first gig in big-budget film. It was released in April of 2000, and Jon shared the screen with seasoned Hollywood heavies like Matthew McConaughey and Harvey Keitel. "I really loved doing that picture," he told me. "I learned a lot about acting. Everyone treated me so great." Jon died forty-five minutes into the film, but his performance was solid.

That hour with Jon yielded the most honest exchange we'd ever shared. He confessed to me his physical ailments on this tour. "My knees from the past surgeries felt like they were giving out," he confessed. Jon was literally running on life support in Zurich. At one point in the show, he actually felt like he was going to collapse during the playful ballad "Bad Medicine." In midverse, he handed the mike to Richie, who picked up the song without missing a beat. The crowd thought the brothers in arms were kidding around. "That never happened before," he said. "Richie saved me up there. I'm tired, Lonn. I'm really tired."

Jon revealed his ego when proclaiming how few acts in the history of music had sold more than ninety million records, as his did and, in the most telling moment, dropped his head to his chest, confessing that all his songs—no matter how they were interpreted—came from the heart. Here, for the first time in our long journey together, the hero with the Superman tattoo on his shoulder had turned back into Clark Kent.

This was a man of immense strength who was also acutely fragile. He loved the spotlight but longed for privacy. "They come from all over Europe, on trains, sometimes they travel for days to feel the music," he said. "I understand it but I don't get it."

That comment summed up how I felt about the whole metal culture since the *RIP* adventure began. Voracious fans devoted to furious, ofttimes dissonant musical styles. We covered every clique from glam to speed to thrash to death metal, where the vocalists sang in deep, garbled demonic baritones, spitting out indecipherable lyrics over earsplitting guitar strains. As the editor, I didn't have to "get" every scene or dig every band. I just had to make sure we covered them, because the readers got it, and that's what mattered.

The next day on the private-jet flight to Vienna, Jon was revitalized and so was the band. The atmosphere was fun and free. I rolled tape and joked about the freshly made cookies being served at thirty thousand feet to the passenger manifest of eight bodies. Life on the road at this level was still a blast. But the flight over was nothing compared to the incredible show that night in Austria.

There were times when I met *RIP* fans on the road and they fawned over my cool gig and great publication. "You have the dream life, Lonn," they would say. "You get to hang out with rock stars. You're famous!" But famous people get rich. Bon Jovi made more in T-shirt sales during that one Vienna show than I'd earned in the past ten years. For me, it wasn't about amassing wealth necessarily but rather about acquiring an abundance of moments that touched me, that moved me. The Vienna show was one of those moments, and another came three nights later in Munich, Germany, at the final show of a massively successful European tour at the renowned and notorious Olympic Stadium.

I sat in the dressing room with keyboardist Dave Bryan, my

Hebrew brother in the band, and we talked about what happened here in 1972 when the Israeli athletes were assassinated by Palestinian terrorists. Dave was warming up on his electric piano. There was a large bathroom attached to this room. "That's probably where they showered," he lamented. "On the day they died." Then he played some Mozart as I sat cross-legged on the floor.

"Something incredible is going to happen tonight, buddy," I whispered, closing my eyes. "I can feel it."

Two hours into the set, the seventy thousand fans had congealed into one magnificent entity, united by the music and band they loved above all others. The skies were threatening bad weather as the air began to mist and a strong wind started to blow out of the west. Jon and Richie strummed the opening chords to "Wanted Dead or Alive" over the thunderous roar of 140,000 quivering tonsils, and it was as if the collective vocal vibration uncorked a celestial water balloon.

I'm a cowboy, on a steel horse I ride
I'm wanted dead or alive.

The chorus leading into Richie's timeless solo literally cracked the heavens. "Come on, rain, you don't scare me none!" screamed Jon as his partner crept out from under the tent that was protecting him and his electric axe.

For me, the whole scene was nothing short of baptismal. I was sitting in the pit, on a lone folding chair—the masses behind me, the band above and in front of me—wearing a pair of shorts, a sleeveless T-shirt, and an Ernie Ball cap, soaked to the scrotum, and feeling nothing but high. A couple months later, my demo made the rounds at the music network, soliciting kudos from the production department but falling short of a green light from programming executives. I wasn't surprised. And I didn't really care. I was rejected and strapped, but I still carry the moments from that trip with me. And those will last me a lot longer than any paycheck could.

Bruce Springsteen's *The Rising* hit stores on my forty-sixth birthday, July 29, 2002. And I was in Mantoloking, New Jersey, on the shore—half an hour from Asbury Park, where the Boss had grown up—hanging out at a seaside mansion owned by my friends Melanie Meyer and Tom Whalley. I'd been to this special spot before and had written a couple *Breath of Fire* rants there. One visit, I sat on the back porch with Les Claypool from the funk-rock band Primus (whom Tom had signed at Interscope) and talked for hours about the deteriorating state of man. For the deteriorating state of Friend, Mantoloking served as both a sanctuary and an escape.

I called home and told Joyce and Megan I was having a good time; Melanie threw me a party and the house was alive with visiting well-wishers. It was a lie. I was completely confused—five minutes from checking myself into Bellevue Hospital's mental ward or a split second from revelation. I missed my daughter but was afraid to go home.

And then who do I run into while walking through the Plaza Hotel en route to my friend Neal's apartment on Manhattan's Central Park South, five minutes from the legendary manor where the fictional Eloise once lived? You guessed it, Bon Jovi, en masse, having dinner. A collective smile of recognition and a wave to come join them led to a pleasant reunion. I was out of the loop and had no idea they were in town mastering the new LP *Bounce* and performing a private show for the marketing and promotion people of Island/Def Jam Records, their label. Another campaign was about to begin.

Jon invited me to visit his suite the following night for a private unveiling. I arrived around midnight. He had a bottle of Pinot Grigio chilling and the speakers to his portable stereo set up on either side of the living-room sofa. After some small talk and a glass of wine, he let the disc whirl. Track after track played, and I offered benign comments like "Cameron will love that," after the song inspired by the line from *Jerry Maguire*, "You Had Me from Hello." When the big ballad "Misunderstood" blasted from the boom box, I felt some authentic body movement. "That's a great Bon Jovi song," I said.

"Thanks," he said softly.

I told him the title track sounded a bit narcissistic, like he was still pissed off at the critics for knocking him down, never giving him the props that his hero Springsteen always got. "No. *Bounce* is about America bouncing back after 9/11. About our strength as a nation, a people." That sound bite didn't resonate. Neither did the record. The world was bleeding and the artists were our only tourniquets. Rock 'n' roll in the light of 9/11 had to say something more than "I love you." It had to say, "We're a fucking mess but don't lose hope—we can get through this together." It had to say, "Keep the faith."

That's what Springsteen's *Rising* said with courage and conviction. Jon, however, was playing it safe, relying on the big-hooks formula that had made Bon Jovi so successful. There was a chink in my old friend's armor. The times they were a changin', but he wasn't. And I provided little comfort because I was completely falling apart inside and out. I left his room around 2 A.M. and wandered out onto Central Park South, feeling dead from the neck up, sad over the unfulfilling listening experience, and ashamed that I'd lacked the nerve to be as truthful with him as he'd been with me in Venice.

The next night, I was invited to dinner with the band.

My relationship with Jon and Richie had morphed. I realized that even though I was still welcome in their camp as "family," something had changed. I had changed. I didn't care about hanging out anymore. I had no assignment, no real purpose for being in New York or with the band. I was running away from home, from Joyce, who didn't get why her husband was lost in space and wasn't about to throw him a line as long as he was gallivanting around the globe without a job. The fly had smashed into the wall, and his guts were everywhere.

The next time I heard from Jon was in March 2003. The record was not resonating with the marketplace, and the Bon Jovi brain trust was spinning its wheels looking for new and original ways to put the spring back in *Bounce*. Jon said he had an idea for a marketing experiment and needed my involvement.

Jon's concept was to perform a concert in San Jose and during the performance sell, live and on-air, a specially produced *Bounce* DVD over the massively successful QVC cable TV network. "Dude, QVC?" I queried. "That's a shopping channel for women who watch soap operas and buy stuffed animals and designer dishes."

"I'm just looking for new ways to sell our music," he argued. This smelled more like "sell out," but again I didn't say those words, not then anyway.

He asked me to cohost the evening's broadcast, "keep it

real," while the fast-talking TV mannequins pummeled the product down the gullets of music-loving couch potatoes across the U.S. My heart told me that this was a train wreck waiting to happen.

I was in bad financial straits. I told Jon I was really uncomfortable with this whole concept, but if the gig paid well, I'd do it. "I'll make sure you're taken care of, Lonn. Trust me. I need you. You'll be great."

It was two hours before show time, April 12, 2003, and no one at the HP Pavilion in San Jose seemed to know what was going on. Tech people from QVC were meeting the principals from Bon Jovi. In the satellite van outside, the two lady hosts were viewing the DVD for the first time. This is the product being pushed to a million viewers in one hour, and they'd just started their homework. Lisa Robertson—the Katie Couric of QVC—and some other girl whose name I can't recall, who was brought in for her "exceptional high energy," introduced themselves to me. "So you're the rock expert!" they bubbled in unison. Lisa wouldn't know Bon Jovi from Bon Ami.

"I'm going to talk about the music," I said emphatically. "That's it. I will not sell anything." Heads nodded in agreement. I felt nauseated.

This network represented everything I despised about corporate America. Buy this now because you need it. Don't stop to grab a sandwich or take a dump, or you'll miss the next special deal coming up in thirty seconds! We came out of a segment on collectable flatware when the lights went green and the mouths on the Stepford ladies started moving so quickly that I thought time and space had sped up. I was asked to make a quick comment about "what Bon Jovi was all about" and coughed up something about the band, their music, their commitment to their fans, whatever I could squeeze into the fifteen seconds I was allotted.

Lisa's counterpart rattled off a light-speed pitch and threw to me, whereupon I responded, "Your enthusiasm is a bit intimidating." They both froze for a split second. That may have been the first moment of dead air in the history of the network. My job was done before the concert began. The experiment got more bogus when I discovered that the viewers weren't getting a complete concert but rather three or four brief partial-song break-ins during the course of the show.

Just before the band took the stage to play their official sold-out gig for the fans of San Jose, I walked into Jon's dressing room. I'd completed my task and was happy it was over. The inner voice of doom was screaming at me. *All those years of journalist cred—up in smoke after one fleeting appearance on QVC.* "Lonn, listen," said the immortal blue-eyed rock-star-turned-home-shopping sellout, "I just got off the phone with Dorthea [Jon's longtime wife]. She's my harshest critic and said that you saved my ass. 'You owe Lonn big time, she said.' "

Unfortunately, Dorthea wasn't in charge of the budget for this fiasco. I wanted to get paid, get back on the private jet, and get home. Flying back with us, NFL pro Doug Flutie was a guest passenger, counseling Jon on how to finesse his multimillion-dollar dream to buy an Arena Football team. Another experiment? I didn't care. I was huddled in the back of the plane with Richie and Heather, getting drunk and feeling sorry for myself. "Give me something for the pain!" I shouted, echoing the Bon Jovi song. I could hear the forced laughs from the guys. Tico came back and rubbed my shoulders as if to say, "It's okay, buddy. You done good and we appreciate it."

Bon Jovi grossed over $600,000 in DVD sales that night alone, and there were plans to rebroadcast the event in two months. I didn't know if that was good or bad. It was still a fiasco in my book. A week had passed since returning from San Jose and I hadn't been paid yet.

"I think you should be getting 5 percent of the gross," opined my mother, a fan of QVC but a bigger fan of mine.

"Well, I should be getting a check this week," I said.

She rolled her eyes. "You should have had a contract," she lectured. "Haven't you learned yet? These rock stars are not your friends. They've always taken advantage of you."

A week later, on April 19, 2003—the twenty-first anniversary of my hiring at Flynt Publications—Bon Jovi was doing a special concert for the Tiger Woods Foundation at Mandalay Bay in Las Vegas. I'd flown in with the band from Los Angeles for the show. I had not been paid yet. Actor (now California governor) Arnold Schwarzenegger and wife, NBC broadcaster Maria Shriver, were in the crowd, as was TV's Ray Romano, Latin singer Marc Anthony, and the golfing wunderkind host of the event himself. We were all hanging out upstairs in the Foundation Room of the House of Blues when Jon came up to me.

"Thanks again for the other night," he said warmly.

"You didn't need to do that QVC thing, Jon," I replied, feeling the time was right for honesty. "You're Bon Jovi. You rule the world. What the fuck were you thinking?"

He dipped his eyes south for a moment and responded, "I was just trying to find a new way to get the music to the people. Maybe it was a mistake. I don't know. You stepped up and took a bullet for us. And that meant a lot to me."

I pulled him close to me. "It's cool. I love you, man. Just pay me. I'm hurtin'."

He smiled and said that whatever amount QVC sent me, he would double it.

The check came three days later. I opened the envelope and stared in disbelief: $1,000.00. I thought at first a zero was missing, but no such luck. So this was the payment doubled by Jon Bon Jovi? I cursed myself and I cursed the band, the latter in an e-mail to every member, including the management team. Why couldn't they cut a struggling brother a break? What was a few grand to the Bon Jovi empire of gold? I guess I should have had a contract. That's the way professional businessmen do things. I didn't see myself as a businessman, another characteristic I inherited from my pop, who struggled with debt most of his life.

"Your embedded journalist has left the tour." That's how I ended the e-mail that no one responded to. In the time it took to say "Shot through the heart," Bon Jovi left the radar screen and I fell into deep depression. On October 15, 2003, I left my eternal home, Los Angeles, and relocated to Las Vegas, where I would face down my demons, confess to my wife, apologize to my daughter, and spend the next two years in deep personal deconstruction. A bedouin in self-induced exile, I sat in silence every night and tried to figure out what force had brought me to where I was and why.

With time came clarity and the realization that I'd left home to find myself. I had family in Las Vegas, most significantly my father. I knew I'd need family to help me survive the separation and divorce. Most of all, I needed to spiritually forgive my dad for leaving so Megan could forgive me. When I finally stopped bleeding and began to let go of the past and the pain and started to forgive myself—that's when the healing began.

Guru Singh would say, "Forgive but don't forget, because if you forget, you lose the lesson." I thought I'd been forgotten by the band with whom I'd roamed a good portion of Planet Rock until one night in April 2004, when the phone rang, interrupting the quiet desert night outside. It was Richie. He was wondering how I was, hadn't heard from me in a while. I filled him in on the past challenging year. He claimed to know nothing about the embarrassing payment and never saw the e-mail I sent. Amazingly, none of the guys brought it to his attention.

For two hours on the phone, we talked like old mates who'd seen and shared wonderful times together and realized that our relationship transcended writer and rocker. "You finish that book, man!" he wailed. "You tell the truth, write your life, because it's amazing. Your heart is immense. Write that book! Your karma is good, my brother. You are a very rich man in many ways."

Being a writer can be a lonely gig. Sometimes the only way you get by is with a little help from . . . right.

Oh, and I forgave Jon for the thousand bucks. Next time, it's five grand or I ain't leaving the house.

14

Rock Your
Children Well

"AND WE SHALL TEACH ROCK 'N' ROLL *TO THE WORLD!*"

—*Dewey Finn*, School of Rock

"Uncle Lonn, Linkin Park is coming to town in February," said my twelve-year-old nephew, Sam. "Do you think you could get us tickets?" It was obvious that this was not just another concert to him. This was an event. "They're playing with P.O.D.," he added. The younger of my brother's two sons did not have to twist my arm. I'd been laying the rock experience on these kids since before they were potty trained. "Sure, Sam," I said. "I'll take you and Aaron and fly Megan into town for the concert as well. We'll all go on a field trip in Uncle Lonn's school of rock!"

It was December 2003, a scant two months since I had left L.A. and relocated to Las Vegas, where not only my brother Rick, his wife Lynda, and their two boys lived, but also my dad, stepmom Sherry, baby sister Michelle, and her husband Travis. Family becomes life force when you're going through a divorce.

I missed my daughter, Megan, immensely. Spending time with Sam and Aaron was helping me survive the transition.

On October 22, 2003, I took my nephews to see a movie that had just opened called *School of Rock*, starring Jack Black, whom I'd previously loved in *High Fidelity*.

Every frame of *School of Rock* was perfect. With aching gut and watery eyes, I exited the theater feeling blessed for the two-hour respite from my personal tribulation. The film embodied the essence of rock 'n' roll: what it meant to love the riffs and the wail, and the importance of passing that passion on to the next generation. I'm not sure who dug the film more, the kids or me. It didn't matter because it was meant for all of us.

On the drive home from the cineplex, Aaron popped Linkin Park's *Meteora* disc in the deck and cranked it up. The car was throbbing and bouncing as we cruised through Summerlin on the west side of the Vegas valley. This was the new rock, the next generation of sound and fury. In 2000, while I was working at KNAC.com, we devoted much airplay to the Park's single "One Step Closer."

I had considerable history with the group supporting Linkin Park on their massive tour of America, P.O.D. In June 2000, nine months after the release of their major-label debut, *Fundamental Elements of Southtown*, I was in Germany with KNAC.com founder Rob Jones, on the assignment we called "Lonn and Rob's Excellent European Adventure," which took us to five countries in eighteen days as we gathered text and digital video content for the hard-rock Web community. I had conversations with Iron Maiden, Slayer, Rage Against the Machine, Korn, and Slipknot, to name a few.

P.O.D. was on the Continent opening for Korn on the European tour and hitting one-off festivals. It was in Berlin, two days after the three-day, fifty-band *Rock Im Park* extravaganza in Nuremberg, that I spent an entire afternoon with the metal/hip-hop hybrid from the Latin quarter of San Diego. I found the boys refreshingly humble, thankful for the opportunity to play their spirit-driven songs for the fans of a band they deeply ad-mired, Korn.

I saw P.O.D. a couple more times over the next three years, and they always greeted me with kindness. In light of the huge success of *Satellite*, which broke them worldwide with the mas-sive hit "Alive" and the even more gigantic anthem "Youth of the Nation," I half anticipated a customary increase in attitude. But at the Universal Amphitheatre in 2002, it was nothing but gen-uine respect. I walked into their dressing room with Slash, one of their heroes, and we took some photos together.

On November 4, 2003—when I was in L.A. gathering some personal items and meeting with divorce attorneys—I joined members of P.O.D., MxPx, Extreme vocalist Gary Cherone, and Dave Mustaine from Megadeth for a private screening of Mel Gibson's work in progress, *The Passion of the Christ*. The contro-versial film that went on to gross a half billion dollars worldwide didn't even have a distributor at the time. It was, to say the least, a surreal experience, watching an immensely painful motion pic-ture, while I was emotionally hemorrhaging, with a gathering of born-again rockers and the filmmaker himself.

Mel Gibson was there, seated directly to my right, taking feedback from the assembled panel. "I'm a Jew," I said, com-pelled to speak. "Am I wrong, but isn't the theme of this film forgiveness? And isn't that a spiritual rather than a religious con-cept?" It was a strange wall, and the fly wasn't exactly operating at full wing speed.

"Thank you," replied Gibson. "That is the message of the film and I hope it resonates with people of all faiths."

Back on the sands, I e-mailed P.O.D.'s manager, Tim Cook, requesting the hookup for the kids and me. Just before Thanksgiving, we headed out into the Vegas night, en route to the Thomas and Mack Center. I'd made mention to Tim in the note that I was writing a feature for *Las Vegas Weekly*, a story about the kids, their bands, meeting their heroes, and being able to do what I'd done for so long—talk to the artists about their music. We had four laminates waiting at the box office and none of us— including camp counselor Lonn "Dewey" Friend—knew just how far this field trip was going into the valley of rock.

We hit the backstage and were immediately ushered into P.O.D.'s dressing room, where privileged family and friends were drinking sodas, Red Stripes, and Coronas and taking hits of cherry tobacco off a giant exotic hookah. It was all legal. No contraband on this conscious bus. I caught an instant of déjà vu in the hallway outside the band's backstage enclave. I'd last walked these halls in 1993, when I spent the night with Metallica. Best I can recall, Lars Ulrich and I saw the sun rise at the Olympic Gardens gentlemen's club the next day. Another lifetime ago, it seemed.

Singer Sonny Sandoval and drummer Noah "Wuv" Bernardos greeted me, my daughter, and my nephews with hugs and bottles of water, welcoming us into the comfortable room covered with red sheets and posters of Bob Marley and Steel Pulse. Sam and Aaron were wide-eyed and beaming. Megan, my princess, who'd slinked into the inner sanctum with her old dad many times over the years, was excited but more reserved. I pulled out my fifty-dollar Sony tape recorder and handed it to Sam. "Okay, you're the rock journalist now," I said. "Ask Sonny some questions. Don't forget to hold the mike end up to your mouth when asking and up to his mouth when he responds. Go for it."

Sam froze for a second so I escorted him into the conversation. Sonny was easy to talk to; his disarming way settled the kid's belly in an instant. "So, Sonny, where did you find your drummer?" asked the virgin scribe, his brother and cousin looking on.

"He's my cousin!" the dreadlocked rocker responded with a grin. "We grew up together, me and Wuv. His mother and my mother are sisters. He's more like my brother."

Aaron made a comment about track six on the new P.O.D. record. "That's my favorite! 'Revolution'!"

"Yeah, man," replied the rock star to the rock student. "But you know, it's not a song about violence or uproar. We're talking about a peaceful revolution. It's not about politics or religion. I wore this shirt while we were recording, a Bob Marley T-shirt that says, 'It takes a revolution to make a solution.' So this is about an inner revolution, you know, like every day saying to yourself that this is going to be a good day, and I'm gonna spread some light and good and maybe make somebody smile, be nice to somebody."

Sonny was not patronizing the youth. He would have offered the same commentary to a writer from *Spin*, *Rolling Stone*, or *RIP*. Megan then asked, "Is Bob Marley the most influential artist in your life?" I was beaming with pride at that one.

"Oh, yes," he said, passionately. "But I also love Bono and Hendrix and Carlos Santana and Sting from his Police days."

We chatted with Wuv for about ten minutes, after which class broke for recess as the guys needed to do their preshow warm-ups. That's when Wuv blew my dedicated skin-bashing nephew's mind. "So, Sam, you'll sit with me tonight, next to my kit, onstage," he blurted matter-of-factly. "You okay with that?"

At thirteen, Sam already has a rock-star swagger and smile. "Are you kidding?" he vibrated. There's no messing around when you're behind the lines that few get to see. If this is not higher education, what is?

The world needs more conscious rock groups like P.O.D. Our kids are being bombarded in this moribund millennium by so much crap, it's a wonder they can see straight long enough to do their homework, play their sports, practice their instruments, and maintain healthy relationships at home and in the classroom. P.O.D. is loud, hard, powerful, reggae-tinged, hip-hop-grooved rock 'n' roll. Their music speaks to the youth of the nation. When they performed the song bearing that lyric, the audience became part of the play as twenty kids were brought onstage to sing the chorus in front of seventeen thousand of their peers.

Aaron Friend was part of the chaotic chorale. He roared, "We are, we are/the youth of the nation!" with pride and conviction as his little brother watched from the drum riser, fists and senses soaring. Megan stood at the side of the stage with her dad, proudly watching her cousins have their golden moment. She doesn't seek the spotlight. Her brilliance is acute, her courage immense, her strength far greater than mine. My daughter performed the miracle of pulling straight A's in her eighth-grade French private school the season her father left home. That rocked harder than anything in my career ever did.

Back in the hallway after P.O.D.'s stirring set, I gathered my students for phase two of the field trip, having reconnected with an old friend named Mike Amato, who just happened to be Linkin Park's tour manager. He was a veteran of the big-arena touring wars, and we'd known each other since the Mötley Crüe *Dr. Feelgood* tour of 1989–90. For the past several months, he'd been the man in charge of Linkin Park's triumphant traveling circus.

"At the tail end of the Linkin Park meet and greet, around 7:30, I'll come get ya by P.O.D.'s dressing room," instructed the affable Amato. "I'll make sure the kids get to spend a few minutes with the band." Thirty minutes later, we were hightailing it from one end of the backstage area to the other for our serendipitous encounter with the most successful contemporary rock band in America.

The room set aside for fans to meet the members of Linkin Park was now clearing out. The boys in the band sat behind a long table like they were at a press conference without microphones. The line was being monitored by an immense fellow (rock-security guys often resemble professional wrestlers), meticulously checking what each fan wanted to have signed. And one by one, the band that's been speaking the loudest in the world to *this* generation smiled, shook hands, and scribbled their John Hancocks. Rob, Joseph, Brad, Mike, Chester, and Phoenix, in street clothes or stage clothes, were approachable, human. Most of the room emptied and Megan, Sam, and Aaron waited to take their best shots.

"Guys," Amato announced to the band, "this is Lonn Friend, an old pal of mine. He used to run a magazine back in the day called . . ." before he could finish the sentence, guitarist Brad Delson chimed in gently, "*RIP* magazine. Hey, Lonn, I grew up on *RIP*. How's it going?"

I was speechless for a second, taken aback by the unscheduled recognition. In front of my flesh and blood, a solid prop from a hero of this day. We talked for a minute. "Where'd you grow up?" I asked. "My seventy-five-year-old father, the piano player, thinks you must be from Lincoln Park, Chicago, around the corner from where he was born."

"I went to Agoura High," he said.

"No way," I fired back. "That's five minutes from where my mom lives. I went to Grant High in the Valley." Out of the corner of my right ear, I could hear Sam engaging Chester, the high-octane co–lead singer with the most accomplished, ear-splitting banshee wail since Rob Halford.

"Chester, how do you do that with your voice?" asked Sam the amateur scribe.

"Well, Sam," replied Chester, "it's indescribable, really. Strictly modern science."

Sam smiled. His response was perfect. We chatted a while longer, then headed back toward the stage while the band prepared to go on.

As the clock approached 10 P.M., the arena throbbed in anticipation of show time. "Dad, I really love Linkin Park," yelled Megan over the drone of the PA blaring the last bars of intro music. "I listen to *Meteora* every day. I'm really excited to see them live. This is cool." As the lights went down, the arena erupted into a din as alive and authentic as any I'd ever witnessed.

"Meg!" I screamed. "Here we go!"

And so a thousand and one Chesters chanted through scratched tonsils, "Yeahhhhhh!!!!!" I saw their faces and knew what they were feeling: "Bring it on, make us move, make us mosh, make us surf, hit us between the eyes and ears, drive a stake through our rock-'n'-roll hearts." Okay, my words but their emotions. Here were six men—young, creative, awakened— and their musical machines embarking for ninety minutes on a futuristic starship of riff, lyric, and electro-scratch jump with absolutely no bullshit.

Meg was right. The kids were hip to all the songs and after tonight, so was I. "With You," "Runaway," "Papercut," "Points of Authority," "Don't Stay," "Somewhere I Belong." One dynamic dose of rhythm, rhyme, and tempo after another, and every one connecting. I observed the pierced tongues as they mouthed the words to the anthems. "Lying from You," "Nobody's Listening," "Breaking the Habit," "From the Inside." They stood so tall, so loud, yet unlike the heroes of my day, they built no wall between themselves and the audience. Robert Plant didn't talk to the crowd. Alice Cooper never left character. It was a different show then. They were not human to us, but aliens; their music made contact, but they never did.

Chester and DJ/MC Mike Shinoda stalked the stage and touched the children, the screamer and the rapper in breathtaking balance. The material was so strong, it resonated within the DNA of every fan, kicking them back into the cathartic electric chairs that'd been charged and juiced for their temporary salvation. "Faint," "Numb," "Crawling," "In the End," "My December," "Pushing Me Away," "A Place for My Head," "One Step Closer"—existential hymns for a population on the brink.

If *RIP* were still around, it'd be kicking some serious ass. Bands like Shadows Fall and Killswitch Engage are tapping into an aggressive, expressive youth brigade bent on "metal core," the modern hybrid of traditional heavy metal and hard core. The explosive and crafty Avenged Sevenfold, Aaron and Sam's new faves, bring back a bit of the GN'R/Mötley Crüe diesel-powered decadence. I've felt my own metal blood boiling again thanks to two imaginative European acts, Germany's Masterplan and Italy's Lacuna Coil. Brave new life sprouts aloud in molten homage to the metal gods of old. Rob Halford and Judas Priest and the immortal Iron Maiden—these legends continue to tour, deliver, and inspire. The next generation has found the crack in Planet Rock and shoved a stake in. You don't have to get it, but if you're a parent, it wouldn't hurt to at least try and understand it.

My g-g-generation created immortal rock 'n' roll. Crosby, Stills, Nash, and Young serenaded me with the prophetic ballad "Teach Your Children" from the stage of the L.A. Forum at the first concert I ever went to, in the summer of 1972. That night changed my life forever. My brother and I have tried to teach our children well. And now they are teaching us. No, they are saving us, because my generation has also brought the planet to the doorstep of Armageddon.

Okay, I better wrap it up. I've got some wiseasses waiting for me in detention. Don't worry. I've got today's punishment cued up and ready to rock: Avril Lavigne and Britney Spears, back to back. By sundown, they'll be begging for *Van Halen I*. Class dismissed.

Afterword

LIKE A ROLLING STONE

The moon was beyond full; it was swollen like a giant, celestial white-headed pimple about to burst. Kirk Hammett and I were standing beneath its glow outside the band's trailer behind San Francisco's SBC Park. Eric Burdon—lead singer of the '60s group the Animals—would have deemed this a "warm San Franciscan night," as it was unusually balmy for late fall. Metallica's lead guitarist and I were waxing spiritual, catching up on the past few years, translating the gentle winds of change off the Bay into words of recollection and connection.

"I've spent almost the entire past year the band has been off in Hawaii," he said. He told me that he'd become a student of Tibetan Buddhism and had been devoting considerable energy to surfing. I'd been watching Kirk's transformation for some time. At a 1999 rock festival in Copenhagen, I gave him an audiotape of author Ursula Le Guin reading the *Tao Te Ching*. "I still have that tape, Lonn," he smiled. When I asked him if he'd read *The Power of Now*, he looked at me with a grin and said,

"Rick Rubin told me about that book. He says it's amazing." I affirmed that sentiment and, trying not to be overly dramatic, told him that this book had kept me alive during my first year in the desert after I'd left Los Angeles.

Wholly embracing the present moment as the only authentic reality is what German author Eckhart Tolle's insightful volume professes. It's old-school Zen in a brilliantly coherent new context. And just as we were discussing the power and importance of the moment, feeling the moment, savoring the moment, the moment shifted and out of nowhere—as if he'd just materialized from thin air—appeared Mick Jagger, striding directly toward us. Before either of us could acknowledge what was happening, Mick had his hand extended toward the member of his opening act. "Have a great show, man," he said with a broad, disarming grin. And then he was gone.

"Dude!" I said to Hammett. "That was awesome." I'm not certain which one of us looked more like a deer in the headlights, but the feeling that we'd just experienced a sincere and transcendent moment was mutual. Kirk Hammett—the flame-fingered six-string hero of the near-hundred-million-selling-LP, global-touring-monster future Hall of Famers Metallica—had just been reduced to a spellbound kid, a fan. And right then it occurred to me that you can't be a hero, a rock star, or an icon unless you are, at the core, a fan.

The tale of Kirk's brief encounter with Mick made its way through the Metallica camp as the preshow festivities continued. But for me, this wasn't a party so much as a reunion, a chance to see old friends, an opportunity to give a hug to the drummer who'd stepped up so huge and delivered the words that open this book. And I had not seen or spoken to James Hetfield since the L.A. Coliseum show of August 2003. "I hear you've been through some changes," he said with a familiar grin. Having watched their courageous 2004 documentary, *Some Kind of Monster*, I knew the man I once dubbed the Mighty Hetfield on the cover of *RIP* so long ago didn't require a blow-by-blow account of my season in hell. He'd been there himself. Substance abuse, family problems, troubles with the band. If there's anybody who knows anything about tribulation, it's the Mighty H.

"I never got to tell you how brave that documentary was," I said. When James walked away from the band and the *St. Anger* recording sessions to face down his demons, he spent several months in a clandestine halfway house four blocks from where I lived on the west side of Los Angeles. I didn't find out he was there until long after he'd gone. On this evening in November 2005, all of that seemed like water under the Golden Gate Bridge. James had saved his band and his marriage. I had (mostly) finished this book and was breathing a bit easier after working hard to make things right with my ex-wife and daughter.

"We're an opening act again," laughed James. "It's fun. And we're right in our own backyard. Plus it's a nice kick in the ass to get us working again. Can't stay on vacation forever. Hee-hee. You look really good, Lonn—came through the storm okay." I'm not sure I fully realized how true that was until those words escaped his mouth. As curtain time approached, I hugged James and wished him a good show, but there was another reason for my being here, on the road, with no direction home, like a complete unknown.

The Rolling Stones came into my life via the radio. In grade school, they were as ubiquitous on the airwaves as the Beatles. Songs like "Satisfaction," "Ruby Tuesday," and "Jumpin' Jack Flash" made you bob your head and tap your feet. Even my mother liked the Stones, which was odd because most parents were terrified of them. Mick was out to screw the daughters, and Keith aimed to get the sons drunk and stoned. My mom was oblivious to the group's scandalous image. She liked the tunes, and I think the music helped her forget about my dad, the divorce, and how hard it was raising two boys on her own.

The instant the Beatles broke up, the Stones seemed to take over the world. Their creative recording output, commitment to touring, and professional and interpersonal longevity has been unprecedented. With every new release, they've taken it on the road and reconnected to the fans, an exponentially growing throng that has followed them anywhere and everywhere. As the years and decades passed and the greatest show on earth got bigger and more expensive to attend, the people kept coming because the band kept rocking.

In 1968, Mick and Keith composed the anthem "Sympathy for the Devil." Some have theorized that the song reflected the artist's classic Faustian moment where souls were exchanged for fame, fortune, and eternal life. How else can you explain men in their sixties still delivering the goods like troubadours half their age? I'm telling you now that this theory is poppycock, folklore, nothing more than the meanderings of the jaded and jealous purveyors of rock culture that do not possess a proper understanding of what's really been going on under the big top. How do I know the truth? The ringleader is a friend of mine.

The Kelly/Baruck Pebble Beach Golf Classic is a private and privileged tournament hosted annually by Grammy-winning songwriter Tom Kelly and veteran artist manager John Baruck. What started as a Labor Day gathering of two foursomes thirty years ago grew into the most iconoclastic links confab in the entertainment industry. When *RIP* was roaring in 1991, I got invited. During that debut week of golf and male bonding, I met many fascinating and successful "players," including the bearded Canadian concert promoter named Michael Cohl.

Michael was president of the BCL Group (Ballard Cohl Labatt). He'd made his reputation two years earlier by buying the concert, sponsorship, merchandising, radio, television, and film rights to the Rolling Stones' *Steel Wheels* tour, which was the most financially successful rock tour in history. That virgin trek at Pebble, I played a round with the man whose professional journey began in 1971 after seeing Genesis perform in a club of three hundred. Cohl was easy to talk to because he was a fan with a reverent love for rock 'n' roll.

When the *Voodoo Lounge* tour came through Los Angeles in 1994, Michael provided me and mine with killer seats and VIP laminates. Joyce was a Stones fan of the first order, so the no-holds-barred access made the experience even more enjoyable.

Later, in 1997, the *Bridges to Babylon* campaign was taking flight at Soldier Field in Chicago. I watched from the sound-board with my cousin J. J., one of many Windy City Friends. There was an elderly fellow standing in front of me wearing a scarf and leaning on a wooden cane. He had a look about him like he'd been around the block, seen some things, and survived with most of his faculties intact. When Michael came up to the board to visit his guests, I asked him who that man was. "That's Keith's father," he replied nonchalantly. "Or more importantly, Keith's best drinking buddy when Ronnie's on the wagon."

On May 10, 2005, the Stones announced their *Bigger Bang* tour. The world was once again both stunned and elated that entropy had not yet derailed the rock-'n'-roll circus. In September, they released the *A Bigger Bang* LP to rave reviews, and on November 6, 2005, I took my ex-wife and daughter to see them perform at the Hollywood Bowl. We had a wonderful, healing evening. Since the last time I'd seen the Stones live, my entire world had changed. I was divorced and lived in Vegas, though I was now a part-time resident in my hometown, working to mend the relationships damaged by my departure two years before. As it turns out, a Stones concert was the perfect medicine.

Having spent the past year pouring my life and career out onto the pages of this book, I didn't know where or how to wrap it up. Some days I felt like I'd seen too much for just a couple hundred pages—how can a single volume express the power and beauty of even one perfect moment, let alone a lifetime's and career's worth? And then, just days after seeing the Stones with my ex-wife and daughter, I found myself headed to San Francisco, a long and lonely drive from Los Angeles. I felt like the midnight rambler, rambling my way up desolate Highway 5 armed with a hallowed all-access pass to the most enduring and untouchable rock-'n'-roll circus of them all, on a mission of connection and closure—out to prove that sometimes you *can* always get what you want.

I made that drive on November 14, a week after seeing the Stones in L.A., a night after the first Stones/Metallica gig in San Francisco, and one day before I'd see the mythical double bill at SBC Park. I stayed with my childhood pal Mark Henteleff, who lives in San Francisco's Potrero Hill neighborhood, about three miles from where Barry Bonds has been making baseball history. "I heard the concert last night—from here!" he proclaimed. "They've had shows at the park before but this was unbelievable. So loud, I'll bet half of San Francisco heard it."

The next day, I met Michael Cohl at the Four Seasons on Market Street and rode with him to the venue. After catching up with Metallica, I remained Cohl's shadow for the evening, and we caught each other up on our respective lives. Talking to

Michael about the music, about his experiences, and about his relationships with the artists he works with never fails to remind me of why I love rock 'n' roll. And there's no other group on the planet that gets him as fired up as the Rolling Stones. He's not only the CEO of the circus, he's also one of their biggest and most sincere fans, and his love for the band makes you take your own deeper look at this crazy, amazing, seemingly immortal group.

Keith Richards' face resembles the floor of Death Valley. Every crack and crease illustrates a life lived and rocked with ineffable authenticity. Ronnie Wood has seen more rehabs than Robert Downey Jr. and Courtney Love combined, but he always bounces back and his sobriety on this tour makes him absolutely radiant. Charlie Watts battled cancer while Mick and Keith were holed up like old-school glimmer twins, tracking *A Bigger Bang.* On the stage in front of fifty thousand, the quiet and distinguished Mr. Watts keeps the syncopated beat behind every immortal song like a human metronome.

"Charlie said something to me on the last tour, and I'll never forget it because it defines the true greatness of the Stones," explained Michael. "He said, 'I can't believe that people still want to come and see us. But because they do, we have an obligation to those fans.' "

And there is no one with a more intense sense of commitment than Mick Jagger. Michael has known the legendary lead singer for almost twenty years, and he remains in absolute awe of his ability to dazzle and constantly raise the bar of his own performance. "Mick's got the groove this tour," he quipped. "Last tour, it was Keith. One before that, Charlie. But this one, this one is all about Mick. He's operating on a different plane."

I've seen front men half Jagger's age mail it in because they just weren't feeling it. Michael insists that after forty years at the top of the heap, what gets Mick going is what always got him going: the show and the fans who come to see it.

"He used to be uncomfortable with stardom and the lack of privacy but not anymore. He's been rich since the late sixties, seen everything, and been everywhere and has nothing left to prove. So why does he train so hard, stay so fit, work on his vocals, and refuse to give a half-assed performance?"

"He gets off on the rush," I ventured. "The crowd, the buzz when the connection is made—he still feels it. His mojo is mythical."

And Michael smiled, nodded his head, and said, "You got it! It's that simple. And if anyone thinks that we keep touring for the fame or fortune, well, fuck off. We do this because it's life force."

That same force unites the rock star, rock musician, and the rock fan. Whether you're Metallica, the Rolling Stones, the White Stripes, or that unsigned rockabilly outfit jamming on Friday nights at the local bar, you do what you do because you love it. The inexplicable high from a crowd in the throes of connection cannot be underestimated.

In knowing, befriending, and traveling with rockers as varied as Axl, Steven Tyler, the Mighty II, and Jon Bon Jovi, it's become crystal clear to me that the fans are as critical to the musicians as the musicians are to the fans. Axl could be crushed by a bad show or negative review. Tyler and Jagger deliver some of the most dynamic live performances because they get off on the energy of a full, happy, ecstatic crowd. James Hetfield and Lars Ulrich have had to work through countless obstacles, including changes in the lineup, drug and alcohol problems, and interpersonal issues because they can't see themselves doing anything other than what they've loved doing for the past twenty years. And you, you and me, writer and reader, we know it's only rock 'n' roll, but we like it, love it—yes, we do.

I've been a friend to rock and rocker, but ultimately I'm just a fan, and in the end, having the music in my head and in my heart means more to me than all the sex, drugs, fame, fortune, or any other trappings the devil can offer here on Planet Rock.

And for the moment, this moment, that's all I have to say. My loving cup runneth over.

Acknowledgments

There was time long ago in a land far away when the first thing I did when I got a new CD was turn to the liner notes and see if I was thanked. And I would say, "Wow, that's cool!" or "Hey, where's my name?" It's obvious that there's no way to get this right. With that being said, here goes, and please, if I forgot anyone, forgive me, Father, for I know not what I do.

Thanks to my literary agents Joelle Delbourgo and Jennifer "What's the Theme?" Repo (the first believer); to "Guru" Amy Hertz, thank you for seeing the spirit in the rock (and the *rocker*), for helping me transform a bunch of *fan*ecdotes into a memoir—next to the Dalai Lama, I am your biggest fan! Tremendous gratitude to Nate Brown, copy editor, confidant, closet president of my fan club, and relentless source of guidance and inspiration; ditto to Chicago's indefatigable Tony Kuzminski, my journalistic Jedi, fact checker, savant compendium of metal minutiae, and the most passionate music fan walking Planet Rock; and to Julie Miesionczek and everyone at Morgan Road, I am holding the miracle in my hands, so God bless you one and all.

To my yogi and shaman, Guru Singh at Yoga West, who

taught me the poses and *supposes*, tossed a rope down the whale's gullet, found me at the other end, and didn't stop pulling until I was out, my infinite blessings and gratitude. Sat Nam, music man!

Profound love to the Fantastic Friends, far and near: my dad, the piano man, finest musician and truest "friend" I've ever known, and his muse, Sherry; my courageous and brilliant mother, Queen of *Jeopardy!* and she who reflects that which is me like no other; my brother Rick, since birth we have rocked and till death we shall roll; my sister-in-law, Lynda, brave and delicate; my nephews Sam and Aaron (carry that torch!); my brother Michael, a blood fan of the highest order; my sister, Michelle, and her man of golden heart, Travis; Marsha, Howie, and Carolyn and all the cousins of Chi Town (home of the world-champion White Sox—yes, miracles abound!); my divine Aunt Esther; cousin Marc—the world's greatest Yankee fan—brother Bruce and sister Jill Russell, and Chrissie and all those who hold even the slightest strand of similar DNA, I love you one and all.

Infinite appreciation to the Fellowship: to my longest-running mate, archetype Deadhead and balladeer extraordinaire, Mark Henteleff (the year of the Deer is here!); Mike Ross, my Kabbalah brotha and L.A. landlord; to eternal soul mates Peter Weiss, Neal Zamil, and Jeff Gelb (and his divine other, Terry Gladstone), thanks for never being too far away; to Nick Ippolito (the real King of Las Vegas); the life-affirming Les "Garman" Garland; Rob "Andy Dufresne" Hill (you gave me *Tropic of Cancer*, it's all your fault!); "Rabbi" Rex Carpenter (you have carried my cross and our friendship is *rock* solid); "Godfather" Bruce Patron, Chef Ben Ford, Danny Zelisko, Tom, and John and the entire Kelly/Baruck Pebble Beach fraternity (help me make this book a hit so I can actually afford to play in the tourney again!); Jason Flom and Doc McGhee for their longstanding support and stipend when I hit the deep end. To Dr. Joan Mardell, thank you for the push into the place of least comfort. And to Ron Meyers, *goo goo ga joob*, wherever you are, my friend.

My deep appreciation to Larry Flynt, the man who set my foot on journalistic turf with no strings attached; to Jim Kohls, Tom Candy, and, above all, the staff, writers, and photographers of *RIP* magazine, without whom this book would have been considerably thinner—most notably Richard Lange, Kristina Estlund, Stella, Janiss Garza, Katherine Turman, Craig "Purple Reign" Jones, Peter Soikeilli, Del James, Steffan Chirazi, Judy Weider, Laurel Fishman, Don Kaye, Adrianne Stone, Mike Gitter, Jon Sutherland, Bruce Duff, Mick Wall, Mark Putterford, Glen LaFerman, Ross Halfin, Neil Zlozower, Robert John, Gene Kirkland, Mark Leialoha, Neal Preston, Annamaria DiSanto, Lisa Johnson, Marty Temme, Gene Ambo, Joe Giron, Eddie Malluk, Alex Solca, and the rest of the humanary stew that helped make hard-rock publishing history "back in the day."

Thanks to my radio mentors, Norm Pattiz, Thom Ferro, Marcia Hrichison, and Jamie Osborn (I want the airwaves again!), and to the most brilliant high-tech headbanger, Rob Jones, along with Long Paul, Bill Hein, Michael Abrams, and Bob "From Hero to Brother" Ezrin, and all the characters who made the Enigma Digital experience so rewarding.

Heartfelt props to those who've stayed human in the often inhuman music biz: Michele Anthony, John Kalodner, Jay Krugman, Roy Lott, Tom Ennis, Richard Sanders, Steve Ralbovksy, Kurt St. Thomas, Mark DaDia, Bob Chiappardi, Janie Hoffman, Kathy Acquaviva, Kevin Lyman, Tom Whalley, and Melanie Meyer. To Rod Smallwood and Merck Mercuriadis, thank you for giving me Sanctuary when I needed it. To the only attorneys I've ever called friend—Peter Paterno, Eric Greenspan, Ron Wilcox, Larry Blenden, and Henry Root—the Bard never met you beautiful cats or he wouldn't have asked for your heads. And to Professor Clive "Faust" Davis, your class kicked my ass, but the lesson shall live till the end of my days.

Massive shout-outs to Jeff Ressner, my "Christian brother" Mark Joseph, Big Ed Bunker, Todd Singerman, Peter Baron, Doug Goldstein, Forrest Reda, Doug Khoblauch, Miguel Ferrer, Ingrid Earle, Steve Hochman, Biff Malibu, Shep Gordon, Toby Mamis, Brian Nelson. And to the rockers who still picked up the phone when I lost my juice, Steve Lukather, Les Claypool, Nuno Bettencourt, Rex Brown, "Snake" Sabo, Derek "Fish" Dick, Lemmy Kilmister, Scott Ian, Charlie Benante, Joe Elliot, Rick Savage, and damn there might be one or two others, thanks for remaining down-to-earth blokes and true friends.

To the tribal troubadours Andy Ward and Warren Cann—the first stickmen I ever called "friend"—your beats remain in heart and mind. And to the mighty man on the kit who delivered those humbling words in the front of this book—Lars, dude, your foreword knocked me backward. It's no coincidence that you and Henry Miller share the same birthday.

Exaltations to Jack Black for incarnating Danny Z in celluloid as Dewey Finn, and Richard Linklater for *School of Rock* and the other film that spoke to my insides at a most essential time, *Waking Life;* Tim Burton for catching the *Big Fish* when I was starving in the desert. To Harry Shearer, Howard Stern, Joe Frank, Jim Ladd, Terry Gross, NPR, Lee Abrams, and XM Radio (fuck, yeah!), Art Bell, George Noory, and *Coast to Coast AM*—we *got* the airwaves back, Joey, rest in peace and be thankful you got out before the Illuminati got us. Or *thought* they did.

Hearty recognition to the unheralded queen of QPrime, Sue Tropio; Captain Dave Adelson, Roy Trakin, Jaclyn Matfus,

Nancy McDonald, Denise Korycki, Dave Weiderman, Scott Kamins, Jessica and Deb (the courageous Metalli-sisters of Havasu), Joe Romersa, Rachael Snyder, Isle Baca, Frank Meyer, David Konow, Mike Schnapp, Michelle Ozbourn, Jason Markey, Suzanne Chancellor, Steve Woolard, Record Surplus, Alana Sweetwater, and the great Harvey Kubernik; Mario, Michael, Tony, and the Rainbow Bar and Grill, keeping my table reserved even in absentia; and all my friends at VH1 who kept my profile alive whilst I was splashing in the belly; yo, Dime Bag, what's it like jammin' with Jimi?

Thanks to Billy Campion, Bill Ryan, Brendon Ryan, P. J. O'Connor, Clive Tucker, and Mark Wike, collectively known at one time as the Bogmen and still the greatest band no one ever heard; and huge respect to the crew guys from across the globe, one and all, you are the muscle behind the hustle and without you there is NO rock 'n' roll . . . period.

Thank you, Ray Bradbury, around the corner for ten years but an eternity in my writer's soul; Henry Miller, I shall not give up your ghost, not ever! Eckhart Tolle, you saved me from jumping in Spalding's river—how can I ever repay you? Aldous Huxley, Carlos Castaneda, Wayne Dyer, M. Scott Peck, John Grisham (my hero of fiction), Dan Millman, Krishnamurti, Joseph Campbell, Rumi, the miraculous mantras of Thomas Ashley Farand, poets and seers past, present, and future, I hail you all! Hey, Cameron—my greatest literary inspiration of all—I did it! Better late than never, eh, brother? Hailing!

Thank you, desert compatriots: Judy Alberti; Mike Love Jr.; Kurt Lambeth; Leah Burlington; the Las Vegas media folks who helped pay my rent and child support—Jack Sheehan, Phil Hagen, Pat Kelly, Valery Behr, and Scott Dickensheets. Thank you, Matthew Hanson, for the "readings," and Dr. Randall Robirds for your prog-rock alien psychic healing, muscle testing, magic, and friendship; and to all the brave souls struggling to find the spirit in Sin City, stay the course for the shift IS on! God Bless Red Rock Canyon, my personal Sinai and antediluvian meditation room. And to my hometown, the City of Angels, lonely as I am, together we cry . . . forever we're one.

To Joyce, who rocked the cradle while I rocked the planet, what Gibran and Sting said was true: If you love someone, set them free. Thank you for our remarkable daughter and eighteen excellent years. And to Chris, Matt, Phil, and the entire amazing Blue Man Group organization, thank you for nurturing the angel Carrie Ann, the biggest heart in a five-foot frame Creation ever fashioned and the life force that showed me how astounding life could be when it wasn't forced. Thank you, *beautiful*, for scraping me up off the sand and making me believe I could not just walk, but fly again. And to Megan Rose, who never ceases blooming nor escapes my thoughts for a moment. I am honored to be—as John Mayer sang—"the God and the weight of your world."

And to whoever, whatever, or whyever YOU are up there, out there, in there, around there, making me crazy, lazy, hazy, and dazy . . . I PRAISE thee from the bottom of my worn-out wandering sandals to the top of my kundalini crown. Fade to black and grab my things, they've come to take me home.

About the Author

LONN FRIEND is a music journalist and multimedia personality who lives in his hometown, Los Angeles. He was executive editor of the iconoclastic hard-rock magazine *RIP*, and hosted his own spot, "Friend at Large," on MTV's *Headbangers Ball*, as well as the weekly syndicated Westwood One radio program *Pirate Radio Saturday Night*. He composed the liner notes for Mötley Crüe's *Decade of Decadence*, Bon Jovi's *One Wild Night*, Dio's *Stand Up and Shout: The Dio Anthology*, and Iron Maiden's *The Essential Iron Maiden*. He is a frequent contributor to VH1, having appeared in several *Behind the Music* episodes, including "Metallica," "Bon Jovi," "The Year 1987," "Red Hot Chili Peppers (Ultimate Albums: *Blood Sugar Sex Magik*)," "Mötley Crüe," "Anthrax," and "When Metal Ruled the World." He is a veteran insider and confidant to artists and executives alike. He and his teenage daughter, Megan, have watched *Almost Famous* and *School of Rock* at least a dozen times . . . apiece. *Life on Planet Rock* is his first book.

Visit Lonn Friend at www.lonnfriend.com.